All That Remains

All That Remains

Varieties of Indigenous Expression

Arnold Krupat

UNIVERSITY OF NEBRASKA PRESS   LINCOLN

Acknowledgment for the use of previously
published material appear on pages 163–65,
which constitutes an extension of the copyright page.

© 2009 by the Board of Regents
of the University of Nebraska
All rights reserved
Manufactured in the United States of America

Library of Congress Cataloging-in-Publication Data
Krupat, Arnold.
All that remains : varieties of indigenous expression /
Arnold Krupat.
p. cm.
Includes bibliographical references and index.
ISBN 978-0-8032-1890-1 (pbk. : alk. paper)
1. American literature—Indian authors—History
and criticism. I. Title.
PS153.I2K78 2009
810.9897—dc22
2008040241

A long look back:
the sun is sloughing
its salmon skin
along the northernmost
horizon, a line so thin
that it steps through the dark
like a seal slips through water.
And what remains? dissolving
touch,
echo of whispers
begun long ago
but kept into summer
remaining to melt
                smaller and
                smaller into
                the sea.

"Alaskan Fragments"—Wendy Rose

"The more you know, the less you know for sure, but the richer what you know becomes."

Kathryn Shanley

Contents

Preface . . ix

1 Trickster Tales Revisited . . 1
2 Representing Indians in American Literature, 1820–1870 . . 27
3 Resisting Racism: William Apess as Public Intellectual . . 73
4 Representing Cherokee Dispossession . . 103
5 *Atanarjuat, the Fast Runner* and Its Audiences . . 131

Acknowledgments . . 163
Notes . . 167
Bibliography . . 203
Index . . 219

Preface

The year 2006 saw the publication of two very different books of criticism in Native American literary studies, *American Indian Literary Nationalism*, by Jace Weaver, Craig Womack, and Robert Warrior; and David Treuer's *Native American Fiction: A User's Manual*. These represent, on the one hand, a twenty-first century overview of and case for the most important trend—nationalism—in the criticism of Native American literature in the latter twentieth century, and, on the other, a strong reaction against this trend. Both of these books can usefully be placed in relation to Louis Owens's *Other Destinies: Understanding the American Indian Novel* published in 1992, in which Owens surveyed the field of Native American fiction of the preceding two decades, dating roughly from the publication of N. Scott Momaday's Pulitzer Prize–winning novel, *House Made of Dawn* (1968).

Reviewing what was already a rich body of work—important novels by Leslie Marmon Silko, James Welch, and Gerald Vizenor, among many others—Owens claimed that for Native American writers, "the novel represents a process of reconstruction, of self-discovery, and cultural recovery" (1992, 5). And yet, he added, because "the Native American novelist works in a medium for which no close Indian prototype exists" (10), the novel form itself poses difficulties for "the very questions of identity and authenticity the new literature attempts to resolve" (11). Considering the five-hundred-year-long historical trauma for American Indians that the date of Owens's book marks (1492–1992), the near-genocidal, extended colonial assault on indigenous peoples by the Europeans who would become Americans, it is easy to see why it seemed necessary for those who had not "vanished" but instead survived to consider just exactly what it meant to be culturally and individually Indian in the second half of the twentieth century.

But culture had been treated rather differently by other critics of Native American fiction. As early as 1981, Simon Ortiz had published "Towards a National Indian Literature: Cultural Authenticity in Nationalism," and as his title makes clear, Ortiz sought to foreground the political dimension of "cultural authenticity" in literature, as conveyed by the word *nationalism*. In 1985 Elizabeth Cook-Lynn, with Roger Buffalohead, Beatrice Medicine, and William Willard, founded and for many years edited the *Wicazo Ša Review*. Cook-Lynn relentlessly urged Native novelists and their critics to focus on the historical and present-day importance of Native *sovereignty*. In 1998 Gerald Vizenor, in his *Fugitive Poses: Native American Indian Scenes of Absence and Presence*, made a strong case for Native sovereignty as grounded in an ongoing tradition of Native storytelling both oral and written. He, along with others, argued that Native cultural integrity, based upon the values Vizenor termed *continuance* and *survivance*, was the strongest underpinning for American Indian claims to sovereignty.

In 1995 Robert Warrior had issued an impassioned call for "intellectual sovereignty" in his *Tribal Secrets: Recovering American Indian Intellectual Traditions*, and Jace Weaver, in his suggestively titled, *That the People Might Live: Native American Literatures and Native American Community* (1997), coined the term "communitism" to suggest the ways in which critical practice needed to be responsible both to Native communities and to Native activism. These critical moves were extended and elaborated by Craig Womack in his *Red on Red: Native American Literary Separatism* (1999), which, among other things, urged that criticism be "tribally centered," while Scott Richard Lyons, in an essay published in 2000, made a case for what he termed "rhetorical sovereignty." In this nationalist line as well is Daniel Heath Justice's recent study, *Our Fire Survives the Storm: A Cherokee Literary History*, also published in 2006. All of this work saw literary criticism as culturally contributing to an ongoing resistance to the internal colonialism or domestic imperialism still experienced by Native people in the United States.

David Treuer would have us read Native American fiction very differently. Considering novels of the decades following Momaday's Pulitzer, in addition to some that appeared in the nineties, after the publication of Owens's book, Treuer explicitly rejects readings for culture that relate it to questions of authenticity and identity, and he also seems to reject—or at least simply ignores—the nationalist use of culture. He has nothing whatever to say about the possible sociopolitical *functions* of culture in minority literature, insisting upon an *esthetic* orientation to the novel, attentive foremost—indeed, exclusively—to *language* and to *style*. He laments the fact that Native American fiction "has not been studied as literature as much as it should be" (*Native American Fiction*, 2006, 3), and asserts that "ultimately the study of Native American fiction should be the study of style" (4).

Although most of the studies in this book were initially conceived well before 2006, I cite these recent developments because they can be seen—in retrospect, to be sure—as providing the critical context for them. Native American novels, like any novels, need to be read as literature, and literary readings must certainly be attentive to questions of style at the level of the sentence or paragraph, and also to form and structure at the level of the chapter, part, or section, and, indeed, of the novel as a whole. But it is perverse and foolish not to consider what the style or form of a novel—of any work of art—*imply* and the way in which those implications relate to and work in the world. There are very few today—probably not even David Treuer—who would say that because something presents itself as literature its esthetic function must be so narrowly conceived as to allow for nothing other than the production of beauty.

All but one of the five studies in this book is concerned thematically with *both* the expressive beauty *and* the social function of Native oral stories, writing, and film.[1] Moreover, as I try to show, *both/and* modalities of thought predominate in traditional, oral, Native communities, persist in Native writing, and, as I hope to show, are operative as well in Native film of the twenty-first century. What I am calling *both/and* modes of thought are very different from the Aristotelean, analytic, *either/or* modes of thought that have for more than two thousand years been dominant in the West. I explain my understanding of that difference in detail in chapter 1, and attention to it is a thread that runs through the chapters of this book.

Another unifying thread is my concern for the ideological implications of narrative structures. Hayden White many years ago showed the ways in which narrative plot structures, "emplotments," as he called them, are not merely esthetic choices but carry within themselves sociopolitical preferences.[2] White taught us to appreciate not only the formal beauty of the four Western narrative structures—tragedy, comedy, romance, and irony—but the ways in which they implicitly envisioned and projected a social world. This was one more way in which culture, whether historical writing or fiction, performed powerful ideological work. I consider throughout this book the various ways in which Native American and U.S. American writing—whether in expository prose, literary prose and poetry, or even cinema—provide thematic and structural resistance to an ongoing internal colonialism.[3] So much—or little—about some central concerns of this book and where it stands in relation to current critical debates.

Now a few words about the book's organization. The first and the last chapters of this book, chapters 1 and 5, on oral trickster narratives and on the film *Atanarjuat*, examine attempts to dramatize aspects of a traditional worldview through modalities other than writing, for example, oral performance and digital cinematography. I mean these chapters to provide a frame for the three chapters that come between. Those chapters treat issues of representation and resistance. Chapter 2 for the most part considers non-Indian representations of Indians and Indian-white relations in the nineteenth century, whereas chapter 3, the middle chapter of this group, examines two texts by William Apess, the most powerful writer of resistance to colonialism in the nineteenth century. I offer close readings of his rhetorical—stylistic—strategies and the ideological functions of those rhetorical strategies. Chapter 4 considers strategies for the representation of Cherokee Removal and the experience of the Trail of Tears.

Thus, chapter 1, "Trickster Tales Revisited," takes up the subject of trickster figures in traditional oral narrative. Criticism of oral trickster tales has a long history, and tricksters have received a great deal of critical attention lately because of their virtual ubiquity in contemporary Native American literature, painting, and other visual and performing arts. I argue that the postmodern trickster appearing in these contemporary works is, in fact, only partly consistent with the trickster found in the oral tales. Although trickster in the traditional narratives most certainly is a boundary-breaker, he is also a boundary-maker; the oral trickster, to be sure, regularly transgresses cultural norms, but the consequence of his doing so is to affirm cultural norms. This is something the contemporary trickster's transgressions do not, and, for historical reasons, cannot, do. The social function of traditional oral trickster tales thus differs from the social function of tricksters in modern or postmodern written narratives, though both types are productive of esthetic pleasure in their audiences.

Chapter 2, "Representing Indians in American Literature, 1820–1870," takes the unglamorous form of the literary survey. It examines the ways in which Native Americans are portrayed in American literature of that particular half century, with major attention to the ideological implications of these narratives' structures. The chapter ends with a list of as many works as I could discover by or about Native people in this fifty-year period.

Chapter 3, "Resisting Racism: William Apess as Public Intellectual," considers the work of the Reverend William Apess, a Pequot, as "public intellectual." The visibility and importance of Apess's work have grown substantially since Barry O'Connell's edition of his collected works in 1992, and this chapter foregrounds my strong sense of Apess as a writer of resistance to colonialism. I place him not only in relation to some of his contemporaries, the public intellectuals Ralph Waldo Emerson, David Walker, Frederick Douglass, and Elias Boudinot, but also in relation to such twentieth-century oppositional public intellectuals as Antonio Gramsci, Jean-Paul Sartre, and Edward Said. The force of Apess's work, as I have said, is clearly a function of its rhetorical strategies—its *style*—which I consider in detail.

Although Apess wrote and worked from the Northeast, he was intensely aware of the threat to the sovereignty of the Cherokees of Georgia in the Southeast. The removal of the Cherokees is surely among the greatest American disasters of the nineteenth century before the Civil War. Chapter 4 is called "Representing Cherokee Dispossession." I focus predominantly upon the attempts of four twentieth-century Cherokee authors—Robert Conley, Diane Glancy, Glenn Twist, and Wilma Mankiller—along with one pretended Cherokee (Forrest Carter), and one part-Choctaw poet, William Jay Smith, to represent in writing the crime of Cherokee removal. My consideration of Glancy's *Pushing the Bear* remarks on its *both/and* logic and also on the ideological implications of its emplotment in the comic mode.

Chapter 5, the last chapter of this book, moves us north, above the Arctic Circle, to eastern Canada's semi-independent Inuit territory, Nunavut, to film, and to the present. It offers a detailed account of the prize-winning Inuit film *Atanarjuat, the Fast Runner* (2001), and its various audiences. I try to show the ways in which this work's great visual beauty, like much of Native American expression, is intimately tied to its social functionality. The chapter is followed by a brief section on the relation between *Atanarjuat* and an earlier film about "Eskimos," Robert Flaherty's 1922 documentary, *Nanook of the North*.

The book ends with an "Acknowledgments" section, to thank the many who have helped with this book and also to offer, for what interest it may have, a history of its chapters. I have been conducting my education in Native American literatures in public for more than two decades, and, while I think I know a bit more now than when I first set a tentative toe into these waters, I nonetheless felt it more appropriate to offer thanks rather than a conclusion. I take very seriously Kate Shanley's words, which I've used as the second of the epigraphs to this book. That is to say, I am acutely aware of the fact that the more I know, the less I know for sure, while I can only hope that what I know may perhaps be somewhat richer than it was before.

All That Remains

Trickster Tales Revisited

i.

The Native American stories Western critics have called "trickster tales" are set a long, long time ago, when the earth was new and still soft, not yet hardened into its present shapes and forms, neither physically nor culturally the way we find it now. It is in the age of myth that trickster appears to transform the world into something like its present state or condition. Thinking about a world without fire, oral storytellers told stories about how trickster obtained fire for mankind. Thinking about a world without death, they told stories in which trickster accidentally or intentionally brought it about that we all must die. It was also trickster who fixed the number of fingers we would have on our hands, and determined the appropriate relations between hunters and the animals they would hunt, between fishermen and the fish they would take, as he also established taboos against incest.

Stories about the trickster, called Wakjankaga by the Hochank or Winnebago, were classed among the *waikan*, what-is-sacred, for Wakjankaga is not only the "Foolish One," but Kunuga, first son of Ma'una, the Earthmaker, sent to earth by his Father to chastise or destroy monsters who would threaten the human beings soon to people the earth. A tale from the northwest coast published by Melville Jacobs has the title "Coyote Made Everything Good"—not the sort of thing trickster Coyote usually does, but something he certainly has the power to do.[1] Two contemporary Micmac storytellers remark that "God is called Gitji Manitou (the Great Spirit)

... and Glous'gap [an Eastern Algonquian trickster] is the embodiment of his power" (Running Wolf and Smith 2000, 9). Indeed, trickster is so powerful that stories about him, for most Native peoples, are to be told only in the winter, when the earth is asleep, and snakes are not above ground.

But trickster is also the violator of every known cultural convention, in a great many tales doing exactly what every good Navajo or Lakota or Hopi person should not do, and, further, erring in outrageously bawdy and excessive fashion. As his name indicates, trickster is one who dupes others in order to engage in obscene and taboo behaviors, copulating, for example, with his daughter, daughter-in-law, or mother-in-law.[2] Although he is able to change his sex, we see him, in one well-known set of Winnebago stories published by Paul Radin, fabricating female sexual organs in order to "marry" the son of a chief. In other stories, he sends his enormous penis (on occasion he carries it in a box) swimming across rivers in search of sexual adventure. He may excrete and ask his shit for advice, or he may decide to perform oral sex on himself. Some stories have him setting fire to his anus as a punishment for not obeying his instructions to guard his food while he sleeps. Although Iktomi, the Sioux trickster, according to some of Dr. James Walker's consultants (Walker served as physician at the Pine Ridge Agency from 1896 to 1914) may have been "the first thing made in the West that matured," and the one who "invented language" (1983, 106), named the animals, and "discovered colors" (107), he was also the "Imp of Mischief" (1980, 39). As Julian Rice notes, he was "always a smart-ass, even when naming things" (personal communication, March 6, 2004).[3] Although trickster is selfish, subversive, and often destructive, he usually emerges more or less unscathed by his actions, and his actions usually provoke laughter on the part of those who hear about them.

It has again and again been said in print that the term *trickster* first appeared in Daniel G. Brinton's *Myths of the New World* published in 1868. But Lewis Hyde, in an important study of the trickster, states that he has not been able to find the word in any one of the three editions of Brinton's book! Hyde suggests that it is in Franz Boas's introduction to James Teit's *Traditions of the Thompson River Indians* (1898) that the term first appears in English (Hyde 1998, 355). In any case, since the late nineteenth century, the term *trickster* has been used to describe a character who, as I have noted, is a wandering, bawdy, and gluttonous figure, typically male but able to alter his sex at will. Hyde notes that "all the canonical tricksters operate in patriarchal mythologies" (80) and that in Native America, the few female tricksters to be found appear primarily among the Hopi and Tewa people of the Southwest who are matrilineal and matrilocal. But even there, as Hyde acknowledges with reference to a detailed study of the matter by Franchot Ballinger, most of the tricksters are male.[4] It is possible, of course, that a body of narratives with female tricksters existed, but if so, it has disappeared with hardly a trace.

Of course, trickster figures of one kind or another are by no means unknown to the West. An image on a wall of a cave among the Trois Frères in France is believed by contemporary scholarship to represent a shaman or a trickster (it is unlikely we will ever know for sure) and to date back some sixteen or eighteen thousand years. More recently in Europe, although still from centuries ago, the French characters Gargantua and Pantagruel behaved in ways we call *Rabelaisian*, after the great author who wrote down some of their ribald adventures; Renard the Fox is another French trickster. It's been suggested that, among the Italians, some of the folk originals of the Pinocchio figure resemble trickster figures, while the Germans have Reineke Fuchs and Till Eulenspiegel. In Spain there is Gil Blas and Lazarillo de Tormes, and among Scandinavian peoples, Loki. Hermes, for the ancient Greeks, was a god, yet also something of a clown; in his youth he was a thief, as other tricksters have been. Trickster has been documented as well throughout Africa, where he is frequently figured as Anansi, the spider, or known as Eshu-Elegba; in China, where he is often the Monkey or Monkey King; in the Hawaiian islands, where he is Maui-of-a-thousand-tricks; and also in Tibet, Turkey, South Asia, and Polynesia. If not quite universal, trickster figures most definitely are widespread throughout the world.

Indeed, the Cherokee legal scholar and theologian, Jace Weaver, has suggested biblical parallels to trickster. "The biblical figure that most closely resembles the Native tricksters," Weaver writes, "is Jacob," and he cites Genesis 25:19–37 as "a trickster cycle" (2001, 248). Weaver goes on to claim that "there are aspects of trickster evident in Jesus himself," this time citing Luke 2:41–51 as not only illustrating "Jesus' messianic mission from an early age," but also as "a trickster story" (253). Weaver's intention is to show that another of Lewis Hyde's assertions, his claim that "trickster only comes to life in the complex terrain of polytheism" (Hyde 1998, 9–10, in Weaver 2001, 255) is an unnecessarily restrictive judgment. Weaver may be right, and yet the overwhelming majority of trickster figures *do* appear in polytheistic contexts. Reading strictly as a literary scholar, I don't find Jacob and the chapters of Genesis suggested by Weaver presenting a figure or behaviors that easily conform to those of the trickster, nor does paradoxical behavior on the part of Christ seem to me trickster-like. Jesus has godlike powers, to be sure, and he most certainly can work against the prevailing social order, but he does not—nor does Jacob, for that matter—change shape or sex, or in any regard engage in bawdy business or other sorts of what Hyde calls the "dirt work" (1998, 151) typical of tricksters.

Here it should be noted that the trickster, as he is generally called, has no such generic name among the various tribal nations themselves. Rather, all these peoples have very specific and concrete names for trickster. In California, Oregon, the inland plateau, the Great Basin, the southern plains, and the Southwest, the trickster figure is most commonly called Coyote. In the Southeast, trickster is Rabbit or Hare; Raven or Crow in the Arctic and subArctic; Jay or Wolverine in parts of Canada. Among the Lakota of the plains, whose people we call the Sioux, the trickster, as noted, is Iktomi or Ikto, a word translated as "spider." The Kiowa trickster is Sende or Saynday. Among the Hochank or Winnebago, as also noted, the trickster is named Wakjankaga, although Wacdjungega, Hare, is also a Hochank trickster. For the Anishinaabe, or Chippewa, the trickster is Nenabos or Manabozho, in a number of variant pronunciations and spellings, and also Hare. For the Gros Ventre of Montana, Nixant is the trickster's name, as it is Veeho for the Cheyenne, Sitconski for the Assiniboine, Istinike for the Ponca, and Napi for the Blackfeet. In the northeast we find a trickster I have mentioned above, known as Kluskap, Glous'gap or Gluskabe. Among the Cree peoples of Canada, the trickster is known as Wesucechak or Wisahketchahk, anglicized to "Whiskey Jack." Among the Modoc of California, there is someone called Tusasas or Joker. Northern neighbors of the Modoc, the Klamath people tell tales in which Skunk sometimes acts the role of the trickster, but there are also stories told of Mink and his younger brother Weasel in which they also behave in trickster-like fashion. And there are yet other names for Native American tricksters. New England Algonquian-speaking nations have Lox, who seems to combine characteristics of the beaver, the badger, and the wolverine, along with a figure known as Ableegumooch, who appears to be Rabbit under another name.

The fact that trickster, for Native American peoples, is at one and the same time a boundary-breaker but also an important boundary-maker; a destroyer of order and an institutor of order has long been noted by Western commentators.[5] Paul Radin, one of the earliest and most diligent Western students of the trickster noted that the "twofold function of benefactor and buffoon . . . is the outstanding characteristic of the overwhelming majority of trickster heroes wherever they are encountered in aboriginal America" (1956, 124). For Radin, as for some few commentators before him, and a great many after him, this "twofold function" was baffling, constituting a puzzle and a problem to be solved.

If Daniel Brinton was not the first to name the trickster, he may have been the first to offer a solution to the apparent problem of how trickster could be at one and the same time taboo-maker and taboo-breaker, benefactor and buffoon alike. Brinton concluded that trickster was a degenerated version of a much earlier culture hero of myth, not a single figure with the double nature I have described but, rather, the odd sum of two figures, an earlier and a later.[6] Franz Boas, generally considered the founder of American scientific, university-based, professional anthropology, near the close of the nineteenth century weighed in with a different solution to the double nature of the trickster. Boas, in effect, simply explained away trickster's transformative powers, claiming that "in most tales of the transformer or of the culture hero, the prime motive is . . . a purely egotistical one, and . . . the changes which actually benefit mankind are only incidentally beneficial. They are primarily designed by the transformer to reach his own selfish ends."[7] Boas continues, "With this conception of the so-called culture hero the difficulty disappears of uniting in one person the benevolent being and the trickster" (in Hultkrantz 1997, 6).

Radin's contribution to this discussion initially offered a reversal of Brinton's degeneration theory, contending that the mischievous trickster was not at all a relatively new version of an older and different mythic figure. To the contrary, as Radin wrote in his important volume, *The Trickster: A Study in American Indian Mythology* (1956), trickster is the "oldest of all figures in American Indian mythology, probably in all mythologies." In regard to the apparently disturbing conjunction in trickster of bawdy misbehavior and godlike powers, Radin again reversed Brinton's view, asserting that "trickster's divinity is always secondary and . . . it is largely a construction of the priest-thinker, of a remodeller" of older material (1956, 164).[8]

Although Radin's trickster stories were collected during fieldwork around 1912, and, although, as we have seen, Radin soon speculated on the historical development of the trickster figure, by the time he published the collected materials that came to be known as *The Trickster: A Study in American Indian Mythology*, he was also ready to affirm, in his "Prefatory Note" to the book, that, because the "amazing figure" of trickster must almost surely be "a *speculum mentis* wherein is depicted man's struggle with himself and with a world into which he had been thrust without his volition and consent, . . . our problem [in understanding trickster] is thus basically a *psychological* one" (1956, xxiv, my emphasis). Perhaps this is why Radin solicited for his book a concluding essay from Carl Jung, "On the Psychology of the Trickster Figure." Radin's deeply Western, Judeo-Christian sense of trickster stories as concerning the predicament of man "thrust" into the world "without his volition and consent" has not worn well, nor has Jung's sense that "considering the crude primitivity of the trickster cycle, it would not be surprising if one saw in this myth simply the reflection of an earlier, rudimentary stage of consciousness, *which is what the trickster obviously seems to be*" (201, my emphasis).

Jung is well aware that such an explanation "would certainly not meet with the approval of the Winnebagos" (Radin 1956, 200), but that is of no concern. For, Jung notes, "Radin's trickster cycle . . . points back to a very much earlier stage of consciousness which existed before the birth of the myth, when the Indian was still groping about in a similar mental darkness!" (202).[9] This utter dismissal of "the point of view of the Native" in regard to her own culture appears, today, not only ethically repugnant, but epistemologically disastrous.[10]

A psychological perspective of a Freudian rather than a Jungian sort was employed by another of Boas's students, Melville Jacobs, in an attempt to explain the double nature of the trickster figure among the Clackamas Chinook of the Northwest Coast. Commenting on a story called "Badger and Coyote Were Neighbors," which he published in *The Content and Style of an Oral Literature* (1959), Jacobs remarks that "the Coyote of this myth is to a degree consistent with the familiar Columbia River Valley composite of a *more or less entertaining narcissist* . . . and *an adult, mature, and deity-like* man" (30, my emphasis). Jacobs continues, "The structuring of such a personality in a plot which also has two parts—*the first Id-dominated, the second reality-oriented*—connects with the native conceptualization of genetic developments in the personality of a man" (my emphasis). He further comments that whenever Coyote "responds to a wholly internal stimulus or need, he is a bungler. When something entirely outside himself challenges, something much more important than himself, his responses are powerful, adult, even deity-like" (32).

Here, as just above, there is no explanation for why "the native conceptualization of genetic developments in the personality of a man" would make mature manhood include "deity-like" responses. But there is a proffered explanation of how the two aspects of trickster—persistently troubling to these researchers—can coexist. "When Coyote fails," Jacobs writes near the end of his account of this particular narrative, "it is as if he suddenly matures—in a manner which northwest Indians point up by his transition to a godlike enunciator of the future" (1959, 35). That Northwest Indians, like Native peoples elsewhere, see Coyote as both a selfish bungler and as godlike seems certain; that this is explained by a "*transition*" from the one to the other, from more nearly the child to more nearly the superhuman, seems far less certain.[11]

A few years earlier, in the 1950s, the world-renowned French anthropologist, Claude Lévi-Strauss, also took on the trickster. In an essay called "The Structural Study of Myth" (1955), Lévi-Strauss first claims that, contrary to popular belief, myth and poetry are not similar, but entirely different. This is because, while poetry is always in some measure untranslatable—something always gets lost in translation—myth, says Lévi-Strauss, is always fully translatable. No matter what culture it comes from, no matter what sort of story it tells, "the mythical value of the myth," Lévi-Strauss writes, "remains preserved, even through the worst translation"

(174). This is because the "mythical value of the myth," for Lévi-Strauss, is never in the culture-specific details themselves (and Lévi-Strauss seems to have had no interest at all in the actual performance dimension of oral stories, or even the specific words or details recorded). Rather, the mythical value of the myth resides in an abstraction from the details, one that arranged terms and/or thematic elements to show that myth "always works from the awareness of oppositions towards their progressive mediation . . . two opposite terms with no intermediary always tend to be replaced by two equivalent terms which allow a third one as mediator."[12]

Posing the question, "Why is it that throughout North America [the part of trickster] is assigned practically everywhere to either coyote or raven?" (1955, 188), Lévi-Strauss answers that it is because both are carrion-eating animals, and carrion-eating animals can be classified as mediators between prey animals and herbivorous animals. Like the first, they eat animal food, but like the second, they do not kill what they eat. From this perspective, trickster isn't so much a character in a story as a step in a logical analysis, albeit an unconscious analysis, as far as the storyteller and the audience are concerned.

Of course, there are many more trickster figures than Coyote and Raven, and, too, Coyote, in empirical fact (as well as in the stories) is not usually a carrion-eater. But Michael Carroll asserts that the error makes no difference! It is Carroll's view that Lévi-Strauss is nonetheless correct to insist that myths function to express a logical dilemma in such a way "as to provide some sort of cognitive model that allows the individual to lose sight of the inherent contradiction that the dilemma entails" (1981, 307).

Agreeing with Lévi-Strauss that myth mediates oppositions, Carroll also explains away the apparently contradictory double nature of trickster by turning him into one who mediates—or at least causes us "to lose sight of"—the contradictions or oppositions his behavior manifests.[13]

Although it is not my intention to offer anything like a history of trickster criticism to date—there is a great deal of it—I do need briefly to mention an influential paper by Lawrence Sullivan, "Multiple Levels of Religious Meanings in Culture: A New Look at Winnebago Sacred Texts" (1982).[14] Toward the end of his study, Sullivan joins the ranks of Western critics treating trickster's double nature as a problem; his solution is to refer the contraries or oppositions in trickster's character to the Western trope of irony. "Irony," Sullivan writes,

> binds widely separated opposites into a single figure so that contraries appear to belong together. In Trickster chaos and order, sacred and profane, farce and meaning, silence and song, food and waste, word and event, pretended ignorance and pretended cunning . . . [etc.] compose not only an ironic symbol but a symbol of irony.
>
> Trickster's character and exploits embody the process of ironic imagination. . . . In him the double-sidedness of reality reveals itself. (238)

This invocation of the ironic has a long history of Western rhetorical thought behind it; it also seems to offer a cogent solution to the problem of trickster's dichotomous nature, and, moreover, it probably felt "right" for its poststructuralist moment in much the same way as Lévi-Strauss's solution must have felt "right" for its structuralist moment.[15] Certainly most contemporary writers and thinkers have accepted the trickster as ironic, a matter to which I will return.

In Western discursive practice, irony is, as Sullivan notes, the rhetorical figure that deals with contraries—things that don't or shouldn't go together—and it does so in such a way as to make them "*appear to belong together*" (1982, 238, my emphasis). Trickster surely does represent ("reveal" conveys Sullivan's feeling about this representation) "the double-sidedness of reality," and it is, thus, entirely understandable that Sullivan (and, again, a great many others of late) would want to read trickster under the sign of the ironic.[16] There can be little doubt, after all, as to the ironic qualities of the contemporary, postmodern trickster in literature and in the visual arts. Yet one must be wary of reading traditional, oral, trickster tales back through the lens of this contemporary "trickster shift," to cite the title of Allan Ryan's influential book. I will be arguing that traditional oral storytellers and their audiences do *not* take trickster's double-sidedness as ironic (nor do they take any representation of "the double-sidedness of reality" as a revelation).[17] In what follows, I go against the grain of the scholarship I've cited and try to show that in traditional, oral narrative trickster's double nature—his actions, as I have said, establishing and affirming cultural convention and his actions transgressing and subverting cultural convention—does not constitute a paradox or a problem in need of solution by historical, analytical, or rhetorical means.[18] It is the poor fit between Western and Native American philosophy—by "philosophy" I mean simply the panhuman search for knowledge and understanding—that has led to a long Western tradition of misreading traditional trickster tales. Some clear recognition of the nature of that bad fit, as I have called it, is necessary in order to clear a space in which we may better understand the very particular cultural and social function of the double-natured trickster. In these regards, I want to repeat my contention that while the trickster figure who appears frequently in contemporary Native American writing, painting, and staged performance most certainly *is* ironic, transgressive, and subversive in nature and function, the claim that the contemporary trickster is consistent and continuous with the trickster of traditional oral narrative is a back projection of postmodern onto pre-modern or traditional thought. It is one that itself "solves" the problem of the dual nature of trickster by occluding his positive nature as one who articulates and establishes cultural boundaries as well as blurs them.[19]

The contemporary, postmodern, transgressive, ironic trickster is a powerful imaginative dramatization or visualization on the part of Native artists of what life beyond the constraints of colonialism might be like. But the trickster of traditional oral narrative was and continues to be *both* subversive *and* normative, "representational in the currently devalued sense," as Andrew Wiget has written, providing "symbolizations with a range of references restricted by historical, cultural, and social knowledge, and interpretable as dramatizations of *accessible truths about beliefs and values*" (1991, 478, my emphasis).[20]

To understand trickster's function in traditional societies requires that we recognize, acknowledge, and confront his doubleness—even, as I will suggest, that we embrace and celebrate it. A few recent critics of trickster tales have begun to do just that, and they have, thus, aligned themselves with the small but growing, and absolutely indispensable, accounts of trickster offered by traditional narrators themselves. It is toward the comments of these narrators that this historical and theoretical overview of the subject is headed.

ii.

I intend to offer some generalizations about the differences between Native American and Western philosophical thought. These categories—"Native American thought," "Western thought"—are themselves problematic, to be sure, and there are a great many particulars that my generalizations do not engage. Nonetheless, I think they can help us better understand why the double nature of traditional Native tricksters has been so bothersome to Euramerican critics, and can smooth the ground, as it were, for issues that will arise in the following chapters.

Individuals and cultures make sense of their personal and social worlds by differentiation and distinction, and this sense-making proceeds in important measure by means of the positing of categorical dualities or pairs that can be seen as simply *different* from one another or as *opposite* to one another. While my body/mother's body, like earth/sky are pairs that represent a universal distinction or difference, in the West such pairs as light/dark, and present/absent are taken to represent not merely differences but oppositions, and the Western way of doing philosophy has, historically, involved reasoning by means of an abstract logic that analytically constructs perceived differences and dualities as *oppositions*. This logic developed and, indeed, became fixed in Western thought as the internalization of the habits of alphabetic literacy slowly gained sway. (I will say more about that below.) But the traditional philosophy of an oral culture constructs its pairings not in *oppositional* but, rather, in *conjunctural* or *complementary* fashion, and it conducts its philosophical and pedagogical work of thinking through difference and duality not by means of an abstract, analytical discourse but, rather, by means of highly concrete narratives.

Daniel Justice has recently taken up this matter in the context of "theoriz[ing] Cherokee Nationhood." For all that Cherokee traditions speak of such things as an "Upper World of order" and a "Lower World of chaos," such apparent oppositions, Justice argues, are mediated by "the concept of balance" (2006, 28). "To acknowledge these dualistic pairings," Justice writes, "is not to presume an antagonistic relationship of supremacy between them. The emphasis, rather, is balance and complementarity." With reference to the work of Mary Churchill, Justice affirms that to understand "Cherokee dualism is to understand its necessary *complementarity*; [its] . . . dynamic and relational perspective" (my emphasis).

In much the same way, in an essay on Native American philosophy, Peter Whiteley writes that "dual forms of social and conceptual organization are common [among Native peoples], from the Red-White social binaries of the Creek confederacy to paired masks of the Kwakiutl and Salish, the Winter-Summer Tewa moieties, diametric town plans of the Winnebago and oppositive species in Keresan emergence myths" (1998, 668).

But Whiteley immediately cites Alfonso Ortiz to the effect that the "supposed insolubility" of the "pervasive dualism in Tewa culture" (and perhaps in other Native cultures) is more apparent than real. This is because these dualities are *not* constituted as oppositions; rather, it seems to be the case that "a major logical process in Native thought systems is autogenously dialectical."[21] This would mean, Whiteley notes, that "while of great heuristic value, Lévi-Strauss' semiotic reductions result in an abstract logical and aesthetic formalism, where the endless interplay of binary oppositions becomes a hall of mirrors" (Whiteley 1998, 668).

Lévi-Straussian binary oppositions can, indeed, be "of great heuristic value," I would agree—and all the more so if the brain is indeed "hard-wired" in such a way that it must always work in terms of 1's and 0's like computers, A's and non-A's. My layman's opinion is that the jury is still out on this. Meanwhile, the Western determination to see *oppositions* wherever there are strong *differences*—the determination always to interpret difference as opposition—is not conducive to understanding the trickster narratives that appear in cultures whose modes of thinking are more nearly dialectical.

Because difference rather than opposition is central to traditional Native American thought, so, too, is concrete narrative rather than abstract logic the privileged discursive mode of traditional Native American thought. Storytelling is the primary means of gaining and conveying knowledge, or of doing philosophy, as I have put it. Father Walter Ong tells the story of the Russian cognitive researcher, S. I. Luria, who worked with a group of illiterate rural people in Uzbekistan and Kyrgyzstan in the 1930s. One of the questions Luria asked was, "In the following set of terms, tell me which one doesn't belong: axe, hatchet, log, saw?" No reader of these words, indeed no *reader*, can fail to know the answer. But Luria's consultants insisted that all four terms belonged together, that there was no one of them that didn't fit. When Luria explained why the term "log" was the one that didn't go with the others, the rural people had no trouble understanding the explanation—but they nonetheless claimed it was absurd to think about things in that way. What way? In a way that processes the world according to an abstract logic, which, as I have said, in the West, appears to have developed from the internalization of the habits of alphabetic literacy.

Asked a question about an axe, a hatchet, a log, and a saw, Luria's unlettered consultants very likely tried to answer it by consciously or unconsciously constructing a narrative about these familiar things. And in just about any story one might imagine, axes, hatchets, logs, and saws all fit perfectly well together, no one of them out of place. As Ong comments, "If you are a workman with tools and see a log, you think of applying the tool to it, not of keeping the tool away from what it was made for—in some weird intellectual game" (1982, 51). That "weird intellectual game" is, of course, just exactly what Western literates have been playing for some two thousand years. We need not posit some great "divide"[22] between orality and literacy to accept Ong's well-known contention that "writing is a technology that alters thought." In the West, those who wrote, and, of course, read, came to think about the world in ways that were different from—although not necessarily *opposed* to—the ways in which those who continued to acquire, transmit, and preserve knowledge by oral means thought about the world. (This should certainly urge us to speculate further about the ways in which thought will be altered now that the technology of pointing and clicking has begun to replace writing.)

Although Socrates did not, himself, write, as Eric Havelock makes clear, his philosophical work "depended upon a growing written vocabulary" (1986, 112), and the method he innovated, the so-called Socratic method[23] of questioning traditionally transmitted truths, put an end to Greek oral tradition as an authoritative source of knowledge. For this, Socrates' community rewarded him with a hearty cup of hemlock. It was Plato who wrote Socrates—constructed, or represented him on the page in letters; and at least since Aristotle, Plato's literate student, Western philosophical thought in writing has proceeded by means of a dualistic logic that is oppositional, hierarchical, and exclusionary.[24] Something is A or not-A; a 1 is not a 0, nor is a 0 a 1. In the same way, a Greek is not a barbarian or *ethnic* person, nor is an ethnic person a Greek.[25] Women, as feminist scholarship has abundantly shown, are, in these schema, not merely different from men, but not-men; *logically*, they are an absence, a lack, a negative.[26] (Freud would, thus, have remarked that most of us had been thinking about male and female genitalia in Aristotelean terms.) Such logic, to cite Havelock once more, is *theoria*, theory—and *theorein* means to *look at* something, something like a text, for example, not to listen to or to hear something like a story.

Factoring in the Hebraic dimension of these matters, at least since the time the Ten Commandments were transcribed, we have known that *thou shalt* or *thou shalt not*: there are no two ways about it. Certain texts became canonical; others were adjudged apocryphal. You can read the apocryphal texts—but not in your Bible. The curious amalgam of Hebraic and Hellenistic materials that are considered to be the foundation of Western thought has been persistently a matter of either/or rather than both/and. It has been a matter of theoretically looking, and abstracting, and classifying logically.[27] In the beginning was the Word, which, *it is written*, was made flesh. But, as Havelock (1986) notes, one can only theorize the word once one has become used to writing and looking at it rather than listening to it.[28]

It should come as no surprise, therefore, that confronted with a figure who was *both* godlike *and* scurrilously indecent, *both* a benevolent shaper of the world *and* a rapacious seducer, the first gesture of Western critical thought would be to take this as a problem and attempt to solve the problem by finding a way to turn this both/and character into *either* one thing *or* the other. Thus, as we have seen, the major Western commentators from Brinton, Boas, and Radin, on to Melville Jacobs, Claude Lévi-Strauss, and Lawrence

Sullivan, work with great ingenuity to resolve what to them is an extremely troubling contradiction. But this is not at all the way traditional Native people have understood trickster.[29] As I have noted, at least some Western criticism has understood this.

iii.

In an important essay published in 1975, Barbara Babcock offered a thorough and detailed overview of scholarship on the traditional trickster of oral narrative in an account that holds up quite well, today, more than thirty years later.[30] Babcock compiled a list of six "propositions" that might elucidate the meaning and function of trickster narratives. The fifth of these, what she called "the reflective-creative function" of these narratives, is the one she nominates as "perhaps the most important." To elucidate the "reflective-creative function" of trickster narratives, Babcock references Victor Turner's accounts of what he called the liminal "Betwixt and Between," William James's description of what he referred to as the "law of dissociation," and, most importantly, Arthur Koestler's 1964 discussion of what he termed the "bisociation of two matrixes," as Babcock glosses it, "a pattern fundamental to the act of creation" (1975, 180).

Koestler himself tells us that "bisociation" refers to the "*perceiving of a situation or idea . . . in two self-consistent but habitually incompatible frames of reference*" (1964, 35). He coined the term "bisociation," Koestler explains, "in order to make a distinction between the routine skills of thinking on a single 'plane,' as it were, and the creative act which . . . always operates on more than one plane. The former may be called single-minded, the latter . . . double-minded" (35–36).

"In contrast to routine thinking," Koestler continues, "the creative act of thought is always 'double-minded,' i.e., a transitory state of unstable equilibrium where the balance of both thought and emotion is disturbed" (1964, 36). This disturbance of routine or ordinary thinking can provoke creative flexibility in individual understanding as it develops, something like what the psychologists David Abrams and Brian Sutton-Smith, discussing nonsense elements in children's play, called "adaptive potentiation" (1977, 46). Abrams and Sutton-Smith suggest that something similar—phenomena that increase possibilities for change and adaptation—may operate at the socio-cultural (not only the psychological) level. Human societies, this is to say, may benefit from exploring, at least imaginatively in narrative, possibilities beyond what current social conventions allow. Indeed, Lewis Hyde has insightfully articulated the "paradox . . . that the origins, liveliness, and durability of cultures require that there be space for figures whose function is to uncover and disrupt the very things that cultures are based on" (1998, 9).

Thinking of trickster, Hyde contends that "social life can depend on treating antisocial characters as part of the sacred" (1998, 9). This, he notes, contemporary American society finds it difficult, almost impossible, to do.

Of course, when social groups do explore these possibilities through narrative, they may experience, as Babcock writes, "an exhilarated sense of freedom from form in general" (1975, 181). In traditional societies (indeed, in any society), this exhilaration can most certainly pose a threat to all conventional forms—"form in general." But it can also provide exactly the sort of stimulus social and cultural conventions require if they are not to become lifeless and oppressive. Hyde may once more be cited as highlighting the fact that although all cultures require their conventional boundaries to be respected, cultural "*liveliness* depends on having those boundaries regularly disturbed" (1998, 13, my emphasis). As we shall see below, these ideas accord quite well with what narrators of traditional trickster tales have had to say about them.

iv.

And yet, the fact of the matter is that narrators of traditional trickster tales have had *little* to say about them.[31] In some measure this may be because the earliest recorders of Native American oral narratives transcribed the stories primarily as repositories of linguistic data and did not trouble to ask traditional storytellers about their understandings of trickster stories or any other stories they told.[32] But even if they had asked, it is not clear what sorts of responses might have been forthcoming. As Anthony Mattina has noted, "The lay members of these communities do not normally verbalize their abstractions of their literatures" (1985, 4–5). Thus, as Kathleen Danker states, "Few of the thousands of printed words explicating the various Native American trickster figures can be attributed directly to traditional storytellers" (1993, 505). Nonetheless, there is a small but important (and perhaps even growing) body of commentary from traditional storytellers that is absolutely indispensable for any understanding of the narratives from an indigenous point of view. Indeed, it is this commentary that has led me to argue against the persistent Euramerican belief that trickster is a contradiction in terms, a problem to be solved. I'll cite just a few more-recent—and, as I think, more sensitive—Western students of these matters before turning to the oral storytellers themselves.

The folklorist Barre Toelken articulates well the ways in which our generic term *trickster* may itself be an obstacle to understanding the stories about this figure in local circumstances. "When we look at [trickster] in each specific instance," Toelken writes, "we see that his character is constructed somewhat differently in every tribal tradition" (Wasson and Toelken 2001, 192). Mattina comments that when we talk about "Coyote stories of the Colville Indians, myths of the Kwakiutl, Wishram legends, etc., . . . we take for granted that these narratives mean essentially the same thing to all the members of the particular community" (1985, 5).

Meanwhile, to recognize that all community members may *not* take the stories as meaning "essentially the same thing" is not to deny the fact that community members nonetheless recognize and understand details of the stories in generally accepted, culturally specific ways. While no auditor of an oral story is constrained by anything remotely like an official or authorized interpretation—because that requires texts—it is not the case that anything goes. Toelken makes the point that when a story refers to a particular kind of tree or bird, translating that particularity into the abstract class "tree" or "bird," in the manner of Lévi-Strauss or certain folklorists, leads to no more than skimming "along the surface of a hypothetically conceived story, focusing on clearly identifiable motifs . . . [which] conveniently overlooks the more complex issues or relationships, ritual and social obligations, moral behaviors and responsibilities, issues that are the crux of Native American stories and that vary considerably in their organization and meaning from tribe to tribe (Wasson and Toelken 2001, 191).[33]

The finer points of this organization and meaning can be learned only from those who tell—sometimes, too, from those who listen to—the actual tales themselves—so far as these people are willing "to verbalize . . . the abstractions of their literatures" (Mattina 1985, 5).

Let me turn, at last, to the comments of some of the Native storytellers themselves. I'll cite Hugh Yellowman, a Navajo; and George Wasson, of the Coquelle people, both of whom worked with Barre Toelken. I'll also refer to Felix White, Sr., a Hochank or Winnebago teller of trickster tales who worked with Kathleen Danker; Louis Bird, a Swampy Cree narrator who worked with Paul DePasquale; Harry Robinson, an Okanagan elder who worked with Wendy Wickwire; Tommy McGinty, a Northern Tutchone person who worked with Dominique Legros; and a few other storytellers. Their words make clear that a commitment to telling stories about Wakjankaga, Coyote, or Nanabush is, for the narrators, a commitment both to doing philosophy and also, and importantly, to teaching the young and the not-so-young. I am suggesting that their stories are dramatizations based upon both/and rather than either/or perspectives of matters important to their communities. Indeed, their ongoing fascination with these stories implies a strong commitment to the continued "liveliness" (Hyde 1998) and "survivance" (Vizenor 1994) of their communities' cultures.

v.

Beginning in the 1970s, Felix White, Sr., narrated a series of Winnebago trickster tales to Kathleen Danker concerning that same Wakjankaga who appeared in the cycle earlier published by Paul Radin. Danker tape-recorded, transcribed, and, with Mr. White's help, translated his narratives, and she also asked him questions about the stories. Speaking of trickster, Mr. White told Danker, "The story character, he does so many unthought of things in there that it causes the listener to start thinking, 'Why does he do that?' It's a process of making somebody exercise his mind to think" (Danker 1993, 522). "The oral story," Louis Bird observed, "was the only way [the elders] pass on the knowledge to the next generation" (2005, 248). Sometimes "the teenagers question about many things," Mr. Bird noted. "So the *Wiissaakechaahk* [trickster] there is showing them what can happen. The old people don't speak to the teenagers. They let the *Wiissaakechaahk* show their youngsters" (251).

Describing Tommy McGinty's recollections of the stories he heard and how they affected him, Dominique Legros usefully recalls Walter Benjamin's classic essay "The Storyteller," in which Benjamin notes that "it is half the art of storytelling to keep a story free from explanation as one reproduces it" (in Legros 1999, 38–39). Like Louis Bird, Vi Hilbert, a Lushootseed storyteller and educator, recalls this aspect of the art of oral storytelling. Hilbert says, "While the stories were told to me in great detail . . . the moral was never ever explained to me. I had to figure that out for myself. . . . It is my belief that most of our story tellers followed this practice" (in Ryan 1999, 6). As a troubled and difficult youth, Tommy McGinty was put in the care of an accomplished and respected older man named Copper Joe. As Legros describes it, "Old Copper Joe had answers in the form of stories for nearly every question the young Tommy asked and *he told unasked stories to make the eager little boy think and raise more questions*" (1999, 253, my emphasis).

In the case of certain nightlong storytelling sessions, as Anthony

Mattina learned from his work with the Colville storyteller Peter Seymour, youngsters might even, after listening for some time, fall asleep "while they still don't comprehend fully that the stories told by their elders contain principle by principle the secrets of how to be Colville—*what it means to have been preceded in life by Coyote*, by the other animals of their land, and by the birds of their sky, and by the fishes of their water (1985, 16, my emphasis).

As an elderly man, Harry Robinson recalled how, in his youth, his infirm and partially blind grandmother would call to him, "Come here!" He continued, "And I sit here while she hold me. And she'd tell me stories, kinda slow. She wanted me to understand good. For all that time until I got to be big, she tell me stories" (1989, 12). Other elders also passed on their stories. "I got enough people to tell me. That's why I know," Mr. Robinson said (12). Louis Bird knows, he says, because he had the chance to listen to his grandmother's brother, David Sutherland, who told him the story "Wiissaakechaahk and the Foolish Women" on three different occasions, when he was about eight, then when he was twelve, and, later, when he was about twenty-two (Bird 2005, 253). Paul DePasquale notes that Mr. Bird "talks about Sutherland with the utmost respect and admiration; he remembers that the elder was always telling fascinating and interesting stories, always in Cree" (253). Listening close, half-listening, questioning, or maybe even falling asleep, young and old alike find that the stories make you exercise your mind to think.

Certainly, trickster, Felix White observes, "was a person that had a mind of his own, and you might say that he could be disobedient" (Danker 1993, 526). But that is no reason not to tell the stories to children. To be sure, Hilbert's comment quoted just above had the qualifier that "the stories were told to me in great detail, *allowing for my delicate ears*" (in Ryan 1999, 6, my emphasis), and Louis Bird says of the bawdy trickster story he tells that "nothing is dirty. [The story] is much easier to say in Cree; it is not harsh, not dirty." Indeed, teenagers' interest in sex is very much addressed by these stories. Bird explains, "[The] elders know the young people. So they created the legends which will explain things about life to the young people" (in Bird 2005, 251). Indeed, these stories form the basis of the child's education. As Hugh Yellowman replied in answer to Toelken's question "Why does he tell Coyote stories to children?": "'If my children hear [the stories], they will grow up to be good people; if they don't hear them, they will turn out to be bad.'" Hearing the stories is part of the traditional education system.[34] As for why one would tell the stories to adults, for one thing, we know that adults find them entertaining, and even adults occasionally need to be reminded of how one should behave in order to be a good member of the community. And, as Mr. Yellowman added, "Through the stories everything is made possible.... If [Coyote] did not do all those things, then those things would not be possible in the world" (Toelken and Scott 1981, 80).

And why does Wakjankaga, the Foolish One, do some of the things he does? A good deal of the time he does them because his nature—a combination, maybe, of human, animal, and divine nature, at a time when these distinctions were not so clear as they appear to be today—makes doing them possible.[35] To paraphrase Mr. Yellowman, the children will grow up to be good people by learning that a great many of Coyote's behaviors violate Navajo norms; good people—good Navajos, that is to say—know not to violate these cultural and societal norms. Thus Coyote's behavior teaches by negative example. And yet Coyote's complex nature—human, animal, and divine, as I have guessed—has the potential to go well beyond what culture and society allow. However culturally and socially good we should be, we are the sorts of creatures who want to know what is "possible," not merely allowable, in the world. As Mr. White told Danker, Wakjankaga "goes through everything—everything a human can do or has potential to do" (1993, 526).[36]

This is surely true, but because it is put so modestly, we may miss how much it really encompasses. On the basis of decades of work with oral storytellers, Barre Toelken concludes that the stories provide "culturally enjoyable correlatives to a body of thought so complicated and profound that vicarious experience in it through entertainment is one of the only access points available to most people" (Wasson and Toelken 2001, 110).[37]

Gary Witherspoon has called some of these "community-based American Indian intellectuals" the "Aristotles, Freuds, Webers, and Darwins" of their communities (in Molina and Evers, 9), but one doesn't quite have to put it as he has to acknowledge that these storytellers are gifted and extremely important philosophers and teachers in their communities.

Native American narratives, Karl Kroeber has wisely written, "offer . . . unique insights into the sources of unfamiliar modes of human imagining" (1998, 248n7)—unfamiliar, of course, in Euramerican narrative. One thing that has clearly been unfamiliar to Western critics is the complementary, conjunctural, or dialectical—the both/and—mode of trickster stories, which simply do not operate according to the oppositional logic that has characterized the thought of the modern, literate West. As Franchot Ballinger has noted, "In fact, it may be that the dramatization of the equivocal and paradoxical is a distinguishing trait of American Indian mythologies" (2004, 112), and not exclusively in trickster tales, for all that trickster tales most intensely dramatize "the equivocal and paradoxical."

Barre Toelken, in his work with the Coquelle storyteller, George Wasson, catches this dimension of trickster narratives well when he notes that these stories insist that "good and evil, sacred and secular, smart and dumb, are not mutually exclusive qualities, but are overlapping, interdependent aspects of each other" (2001, 193).[38] This is consistent with Lewis Hyde's observation that trickster "embodies and enacts that large portion of our experience where good and evil are hopelessly intertwined" (1998, 10).

If tribal storytellers who specialize in telling tales of the culture hero might, perhaps, be especially interested in the extraordinary and heroic potentialities of human agency; if those who specialize in the telling of cosmological stories are interested in aspects of what the West divides up into theology, metaphysics, teleology, and eschatology; then storytellers who specialize in trickster tales would likely be people especially interested in exploring and representing, as I have several times said, both/and rather than either/or modes of thinking and acting, engaging a complicated and profound body of material by modes of human imagining that are still unfamiliar to Western critics. The very particular both/and of trickster stories contributes to the vitality of the culture the stories might seem to threaten.[39]

As James Ruppert has remarked, "Native students [in his classes] never seem to find any contradiction in the trickster characteristics of Raven. That's just the way Raven is" (personal communication, May, 12, 2002). Of course, Western critics and scholars, as I have noted, might have learned this from Hegelian or Marxian dialectic, and, more recently, from the poststructuralist, specifically Derridaean critique of logocentrism. But the long-prevailing mode of thought in the West is either/or, yes/no, us/them, and so on; encountering "the double-sidedness of reality" (Sullivan 1982, 238), and what Whiteley has called an "autogenously dialectical" (1998, 668) mode of thought, a commitment to complementarity and multiple meanings, still can strike the Western critic as a problem.

There is no such problem for Felix White, Hugh Yellowman, George Wasson, Louis Bird, and other of the traditional storytellers I have cited. How can something be both good and bad? How can it not? So, of course, trickster is a benefactor and a buffoon; of course, he establishes the taboos and breaks every one of them. There is nothing ironic in that. Thinking about the full range of his actions teaches us that while we must submit to convention to live social lives, we have to know (if only through the stories) of possibilities beyond what the conventions allow. The more we meditate on trickster's actions, the more we find not puzzling oppositions but complementarities of an "autogenously dialectical" (Whiteley 1998, 668) nature that force our minds to think creatively. One learns these things in traditional oral societies by listening to the expert storytellers—listening first when we are children, with full attention or not, asking questions that are responded to with further stories, exercising our intellects; and listening later, as adults, when, perhaps, experience has given us further perspectives to bring to the stories.

For those of us, Native and non-Native, who have not had the opportunity to learn from the stories in the traditional way, there is still some hope, for we can listen to—more likely, now, we can read—stories told by those who have learned that way. Learning from the elders without hearing the sound of their voices is bound to be difficult; we won't, as William Bevis (1987) said, get Native American literature and philosophy as cheaply as we got Manhattan. But the effort may well be worth it. To recall a more felicitous formulation of Lévi-Strauss's than any I've cited thus far, trickster may be good for us to think.

2

Representing Indians in American Literature, 1820–1870

For Nina Baym

> For many critics, no matter how historically oriented they are or how sensitive they are to issues of race and class, Indianness is *still* taken to be only a naively constructed trope that is usually employed by bad novelists; as soon as Indians appear in a text, that text ceases to be ideologically interesting and complex and starts to become embarrassing....
>
> ... Indians still seem to embarrass most of us, or bore us, or make us feel quite uncritically pious. And these reactions do not translate well into the rhetoric of our critical discourse.
>
> Lucy Maddox 175, 178

i. Introduction

From roughly the 1830s to the 1850s, American thought about Indians was dominated by—to borrow a phrase from Reginald Horsman—the discourse of "scientific racism." In the sketchiest of summaries, we may note that this discourse, pretending to an empirical and scientific status it never could quite establish,[1] divided humanity into distinct "races" and then ranked those "races" in relation to their achievement of or capacity for "civilization."[2] The quotation marks are, of course, meant to signal the problematic nature of the terms they enclose. This "civilization" was assumed to be "universal," but as a very great many scholars have demonstrated, this putative "universal" was hardly that but more nearly the elevation and projection of western European and Euramerican preferences for Christianity, capitalism, and male domination by the "white" or "Caucasian" "race" onto the world. As Roy Harvey Pearce documented the matter in 1953, more than half a century before the time I now write, the white, "civilized," American man defined himself against an invented, ideologically constructed Other denominated the "savage." The singular is important to note, for it served to obscure or deny national and cultural differences among the indigenous peoples of the United States; there is only "*the* Indian" and "*the* savage." But, to state the obvious, although Native Americans, persons indigenous to the Americas, had existed for millennia, there were no "Indians" or "savages" until Europeans created them.

The rhetoric of savagism and of scientific racism, positing the white, male, Christian capitalist as the crown of creation, possessor of a civilization—I will, for the most part, drop the quotation marks for the rest of this chapter—that could not be pluralized (civilization*s*; later, culture*s*) operated according to an evolutionary logic even before Darwin's publications (from 1856 to 1871). This is not to say that some few writers did not resist the logic of racialism, continuing to believe (as, indeed, most thinkers in the eighteenth century had) that the Indians' sad condition in the nineteenth century was the result not of racial or, as we would say, genetically inherited traits, but, rather, of a variety of external factors—geographical, historical, cultural—that might be improved, thus bringing Indians to civilization in time.[3] They were nonetheless pessimistic about the chances of this happening, recognizing for the most part clearly that not fate (in the form of the will of God, the laws of Nature, or cultural evolution) but, rather, the violence of their fellow citizens would in a short time overwhelm Indian peoples. But many more writers in the nineteenth century believed that Indians were a savage race that simply could not rise to civilization, and so a race that would inevitably have to vanish. This belief, as Horsman notes, is a convenient "intellectual rationale for the realities of power" (1975, 153).

A considerable number of poems, plays, sermons, government

publications, narrative fictions, indeed texts of every historically available genre, again and again employed the rhetoric of vanishment either metaphorically (as the dew vanishes in the rising sun; as the night yields to day; as the primeval forest gives way to the cultivated field, etc.), or by an appeal to presumptively empirical science (their brains are small; their languages have only nouns; their religions are crude superstitions, etc.). Whereas in the seventeenth and at least part of the eighteenth century, writers who believed Indians would have to vanish typically assigned their sad fate to the will of God, in the nineteenth century it was for the most part assigned to the laws of nature—laws that no act of man could alter or impede. As I have noted just above, on those occasions when some few nineteenth-century writers managed to recognize that there were indeed living, breathing, intelligent, and quite able Native persons before them, they nonetheless spoke of them as odd relics or remnants of a once proud race whose fate, however sad, was simply to vanish. And, indeed, as we shall see, a virtual cottage industry arose in the representation of Indians who had indeed been vanished, in particular those who had succumbed to the Puritans in the Pequot War of 1637, and in King Philip's War of 1675.

Just as the condition of "civilization" was defined in opposition to that of "savagism," so, too, was the story of civilization's progress narrated in relation to the story of savagism's decline. Thus, the narrative of the U.S. Americans was emplotted as *comedy* while the narrative of America's indigenous peoples was emplotted as *tragedy*. Comic plots—whether in Shakespeare, Jane Austen, or in Puritan writers like William Bradford or John Cotton—are stories that have "happy" endings. A happy ending finds the protagonist—in the instances we are considering, a collective protagonist (e.g., a race, a nation, a people) as often as an individual protagonist—overcoming coarse, brutish, or evil obstacles to achieve ends that the audience understands to be good, right, and just. By contrast, tragic plots—whether in Sophocles, Shakespeare, or the many nineteenth-century American authors I will soon examine—are stories that have "unhappy" endings. These unhappy endings come about because individuals—or, again, races, nations, peoples—have some basic and (in the view of "scientific racists," irremediable) flaw or defect, leading to their downfall or demise, a downfall or demise that, for all its sadness, is nonetheless felt to be just.

Comic structures are integrative, cheerfully reconciling and reuniting their characters; tragic structures are dispersive, fearfully casting out and severing their characters from the places and persons they would be near. Both structures, however—let me emphasize this point once more—strongly imply the *justice* of their outcomes.[4] Tragedy's insistence on the inevitability of the status quo makes it profoundly conservative from an ideological perspective; tragedy tells us that "the way things are," however painful they are, is right and just. Comedy, to the contrary, tends to be ideologically progressive, or at least reformist; it allows for the rightness and justice of at least some modest change in "the way things are."

When comic or tragic narratives are used nationally, they have, as Edward Said noted, "the capacity to authorize and embody certain sequences of cause and effect, while at the same time preventing the emergence of counter-narratives" (1988, 58). Thus, to narrate American progress or Native decline in something other than the comic and tragic mode would require, as the historian Francis Jennings writes, "painful revision of the pleasant myths we all learned in grade school" about the "winning of the west." Jennings is referring to America's national mythology or "master narrative," the comic story of decent folk "bravely setting out with their families to conquer the wilderness and create civilization.... [T]hese sturdy, God-fearing folk endure all the hazards and toil of their mission, standing constantly at arms to fend off attacks by savage denizens of the wilderness," and, "almost as a matter of course, they create democracy" (1993, 312). Jennings minces no words; for him, "the myth is nationalist and racist propaganda to justify conquest of *persons* who happen to be Indians, and their dispossession" (1993, 312). So far as this is accurate—and I believe it is—the parallel tragic myth of Indian disappearance or vanishment is itself "nationalist and racist propaganda." Both myths need correction by the instantiation of an ironic narrative that makes clear that it is American might that has made right by means of violence and a near-genocide that is hardly consistent with justice. A narrative of the relation between whites and Indians in the ironic mode for the first time makes a powerful appearance in the nineteenth century in the work of the Pequot William Apess, whom I will consider in the following chapter.[5]

This chapter offers an overview of the representation of Indians in the work of some of the major and a few of the minor Euramerican literary authors of the period roughly from 1820 to 1870.[6] At least two questions may occur to the reader: Why these dates? And, what about the Native authors of this period? Other fifty-year periods may well be said to be more important in the history of Indian-white relations, 1838–1887, for example, the first date marking the Cherokees' forced march on the Trail of Tears from their Georgia and North Carolina homes to Indian Territory, present-day Oklahoma, and the second marking the passage of the Dawes Allotment Act seeking to break up the tribally held land base and to wrest more land from Indian nations. But 1820 is the year when James Eastburn and Robert Sands published their poem, *Yamoyden*, which ushered in a very great deal of attention on the part of American writers to Metacomet or King Philip, and it is close to 1821, the year in which Sequoyah is said to have completed work on the Cherokee syllabary. Only a little ingenuity might supply other justifications for the 1820 date and as well for the rough cutoff date of 1870. There is, however, another reason for these dates that I should acknowledge. I began work on what eventually became this chapter for a project on "American history through literature, 1820–1870." I never did discover exactly why that half century was chosen, but it seemed reasonable enough, if somewhat arbitrary. The second question (What about the Native authors of this period?) is an important one. Indeed, it is so important that I won't try to answer it here in a few sentences but will take it up in the last section of this chapter, where I respond as fully as I can.

The bulk of what follows does indeed examine the representation of Native peoples in the literature of the dominant society, and I'll try to note aspects of the language used to speak of Native people, and the type of narrative, the kind of story—almost exclusively, as I have said, a tragic tale—told about them. These representations should serve to illustrate the generalizations offered just above—which generalizations, it must be admitted, derive from these representations, a sort of hermeneutic circularity that is unavoidable in studies of this type. My account of the representation of Indians in American literature from roughly 1820 to 1870 makes no claim to be comprehensive or to provide full coverage; it is, although lengthy, only a sketch. In addition to what intrinsic interest it may have, this chapter means specifically to provide a context for the extraordinary work of the Reverend William Apess, as I have said, in the chapter to follow.

One last prefatory note. Because it limits its focus to the representation of Native people, this chapter inevitably flattens out, or treats in a somewhat reductive manner, a number of texts that in other regards are extraordinarily rich. If *The Scarlet Letter*, for example, were to be judged solely on the basis of its representation of Native American people, it would be a thin, unappealing, perhaps even repugnant book. This is not to say that in acknowledging its rich and complex appeal one should pass over or dismiss its unfortunate treatment of Indians; not at all, for that, too, is part of Hawthorne's book. But the specific focus on the representation of Indians must inevitably leave out a good deal. With that warning, I will proceed.

ii. Indians and the Canonical Writers

The writers we presently consider to be the major literary authors of the nineteenth century included Indians in their writing for the most part only marginally, usually assimilating them into the mythic national master narrative of the comedy of civilization's inevitable advance and the tragedy of savage decline. As I have said, even those sympathetic to Native peoples could not quite manage to believe that Indians were not destined, doomed, or fated to "vanish," at least as Indians—culturally and nationally, as one might put it today—if not physically.

Fifteen years before his reputation as a major American author was confirmed by the publication of *The Scarlet Letter* (1850), Nathaniel Hawthorne published a sketch called "Our Evening Party among the Mountains" (1835). This contains what Renée Bergland—who has combed Hawthorne's work for its references to Indians—calls his "best-known pronouncement on Indians," in particular, the phrase, "I do abhor an Indian story" (2000, 145). Yet this phrase, as Bergland notes, "is embedded within a passage so strikingly self-contradictory that it can be called self-deconstructing" (145–46). Short of repeating Bergland's analysis, I will say only that in the passage in question, Hawthorne acknowledges the potential appeal of Indian places, traditions, and history to the Euramerican writer, in addition to his awareness of a call for American authors to accept the challenge to center their work on Indians.[7] Hawthorne even acknowledges a desire to respond to that challenge, admitting, however, that he cannot do it.

In 1837—I take this example from Bergland also—Hawthorne wrote, "Our Indian races [the plural is unusual] having reared no monuments . . . when they disappear from the earth their history will appear a fable, and they misty phantoms" (in Bergland 2000, 147). Lucy Maddox has further observed that when Hawthorne wrote "about Indians in *The Whole History of Grandfather's Chair*, his history book for children, his assumption seems to be that they are already as good as extinct" (Maddox 1991, 113).

In *The Scarlet Letter* (1850), Hawthorne's greatest book, Indians are infrequently mentioned, and when they are mentioned, there is some suggestion that they are in league with the devil. Native expertise in the use of medicinal herbs is useful to the malevolent Chillingworth, who may also have learned the pleasures of revenge from the Indians with whom he has resided for some unspecified time. Near the climax of the story, when there seems yet a possibility that Hester Prynne and the Reverend Arthur Dimmesdale, the father of her child, may go off together, leaving the constraints of Puritanism in seventeenth-century New England, Chillingworth, her lawful husband, is seen with some Indians, "wild . . . painted barbarians," and also with some who are even wilder, "swarthy-cheeked sailors" whom Hawthorne calls "the wild men of the ocean, as the Indians were of the land" (in Maddox 1991, 122). Maddox points out that the sailors' eyes have an "animal ferocity," while the Indians have "snake-like black eyes" (122). Clearly, for Hester to set sail with this company is to give herself once again to sin and possible damnation.

Herman Melville, in his epic novel, *Moby Dick; or, The Whale* (1851), names the whaling ship the *Pequod*. "*Pequod*," the narrator, Ishmael says, "you will no doubt remember, *was* the name of a celebrated tribe of Massachusetts Indians, now extinct as the ancient Medes" (1967, 67, my emphasis). It is true that the tribe's numbers had declined considerably by the time Melville wrote, but the Pequots were by no means "extinct." Indeed, Melville might possibly have known of the Pequot William Apess, whose last publication appeared in 1836, hardly the time of "the ancient Medes."[8]

Why might Melville have chosen to compare the Pequots to "the ancient *Medes*" rather than, for example, to the ancient Greeks, a better known people who are also "extinct"? Perhaps because the ancient Greeks are *our* "racial" ancestors, founders of classical "civilization"? Even in regard to the matter of "extinction," this is to say, Pequots were not so much like Greeks as like "the ancient Medes"—Persians, of who knows what "race," certainly not "ours."

Even living, breathing Indians before Ishmael's eyes are seen as relics of the past. Ishmael introduces "Tashtego, an unmixed Indian [i.e., pure-blood] from Gay Head, the most westerly promontory of Martha's Vineyard, where there still exists the last remnant of a village of red men" (Melville 1971, 107). Tashtego is described strikingly: "Tashtego's long, lean, sable hair, his high cheek bones and black rounding eyes—for an Indian, Oriental in their largeness, but Antarctic in their glittering expression— all this sufficiently proclaimed him an inheritor of the unvitiated blood of those proud warrior hunters, who, in quest of the great New England moose, had scoured, bow in hand, the aboriginal forests of the main" (107).

The passage continues, but I want, for the moment, to stop here. It is obvious that Melville has made the Gay Head Indians a "last remnant," soon, perhaps, to be as "extinct" as the Pequots.

Yet Melville's description of Tashtego seems uneasy. Tashtego's hair, for example, may be long and black, but it can't be "lean." Only his frame or physique can be "lean." Next, Melville guesses accurately the origins of Indian peoples at a time when many still believed them to be descendants of the ten lost tribes of Israel. Although some Native writers today strongly disagree,[9] it remains likely that Indian peoples came from the east, through the Arctic regions, crossing, perhaps some fifteen thousand years ago, over what then existed as a land bridge across the Bering Strait to the North American continent. Tashtego, "an unmixed Indian," has inherited the "unvitiated blood of . . . proud warrior hunters" (107).

Ishmael's description of Tashtego continues, "To look at the tawny brawn of his lithe snaky limbs, you would almost have credited the superstitions of some of the earlier Puritans, and half believed this wild Indian to be a son of the Prince of the Powers of the Air" (107), that is to say, a son of the devil. Looking at Tashtego's "tawny brawn," Ishmael is perhaps tempted by Tashtego, as Eve was tempted by the snake. Although Puritan beliefs that Indians were sons of the devil are called "superstitions," Ishmael apparently needs to call them up in order to warn himself that Tashtego's erotically alluring "tawny brawn" includes "snaky limbs," and that both the snake and the son of the devil are to be resisted.[10] This is where the description ends. Having racialized Tashtego—references to his "blood" and his "tawny" color—Ishmael may perhaps take comfort in believing that this descendant of "proud warrior hunters" is, nonetheless, part of a last remnant. However glorious he may appear, his fate is to disappear.

It would be unjust to Melville, however, to leave this brief account without acknowledging the degree to which, again and again in *Moby Dick* (and in other work), he relativizes or calls into question the matter of savagery and civilization. In *Moby Dick*, Captain Ahab and the whale hunters, for example, are referred to as the real savages of the day, and Queequeg, the South Sea islander, descendant of cannibal royalty, Ishmael's friend, is again and again celebrated for his civility. It is curious to note that Melville may have taken the admirable Queequeg's name from a Narragansett Indian mentioned in accounts of "King Philip's War," Queequegununt.

Melville's novel, *The Confidence Man: His Masquerade* (1857) has almost four short chapters dealing with what is called "The Metaphysics of Indian Hating," a noteworthy phenomenon of the time. Melville's particular Indian-hater, a historical figure, Colonel John Moredock, is one who believes that it is right and just to kill Indians. Moredock's story, as its narrator makes clear, derives from John Hall's sketch, "The Indian Hater" (1835). Moredock is the son of a woman whose three successive husbands were killed by Indians on the frontier, before she herself, along with her nine children, succumbed to Indian attack. Only Moredock survived, and he has devoted his life to hunting down and killing the guilty Indians, occasionally dispatching without regret any other Native person he may encounter.

The Confidence Man is a complex and unsettling, indeed a strange book. Some critics have read Melville's chapters on Moredock as an allegory concerning Christianity, or any blind faith, trust, monomania, or "confidence" in general, with particular barbs in the direction of Ralph Waldo Emerson. Others have—quite incredibly, it seems now—read them as actually sanctioning the single-minded crusade against evil or savagery, as these are (apparently with reason!) represented by "the Indian." More likely is the suggestion that Melville's portrait of Moredock is meant to comment on the problematic advance of American civilization generally. "Indian-hating still exists," Melville's narrator affirms, "and no doubt will continue to exist, so long as Indians do" (1971, 124). Lucy Maddox quotes Carolyn Karcher's view that *The Confidence Man* may well be "Melville's most powerful indictment of nineteenth-century America," a nation engaged in "enslaving and massacring its nonwhite citizens while posing as a political and religious haven" (in Maddox 1991, 87). Maddox herself adds that the book can be read as an attack on contemporary writers who complacently expound on the distinction "between the civilized person and the savage" (87).

In his eulogy for Henry David Thoreau, Ralph Waldo Emerson remarked that "every circumstance touching the Indian [was] important in his eyes" (Norton 1993, 1243). Hawthorne had earlier commented that Thoreau "was inclined to lead a sort of Indian life among civilized men" (in Sayre 1977, 60). At his death, Thoreau left behind many notebooks focused on every aspect of Indian history and culture—some 2,800 handwritten pages—for what might or might not have been a book he intended to write on the Native peoples of America. Robert Sayre, in his book *Thoreau and the American Indians*, concludes that Thoreau's "savagism, naturalism, and classicism were all related" (1977, 35). This is to say that Thoreau's intense interest in nature and natural history inevitably drew him to an awareness of and admiration for Indian people who were already identified—sometimes detrimentally—with nature. Thoreau's general acceptance of the savagist view of Indians as incapable of "civilization," led him, curiously, to evaluate them *positively*, identifying them with our earlier ancestors the Greeks, a people whose "civilization" Thoreau saw as more robust than the "civilization" of his own time. As all his writings show, Thoreau did not think very highly of America's vaunted civilization, nor was he at all convinced that Christianity, as he knew it, contributed to a life of principle more than to a life of self-interest. In this regard, Thoreau's savagism seems to have operated independently of the racialism typical of his time.

When he moved to the cabin he had built by himself in the Walden woods, on July 4, 1845, Thoreau was, among other things, "playing Indian": exploiting his positive conception of "Indians" for his own purposes.[11] This use of Indians continued until the end of his life. And yet, as he grew older—and Thoreau was only forty-five when he died—he was able to keep an open mind about what he "knew," even to the point of depicting one living and breathing Indian, Joe Polis, an Abnaki guide to Thoreau on one of his three trips to Maine, as very much a complex *contemporary*. I believe Robert Sayre is correct when he writes that "Joe Polis is the most realistic and attractive native American" character portrayed by any non-Native writer in the nineteenth century (1977, 172). We can add to this Emerson's corroborating sense that the three men most important to Thoreau in the last years of his life were John Brown, Walt Whitman, and Joe Polis (Sayre 1977, 184).

The last trip of Thoreau's life was to Minnesota, where he was saddened by the degenerate state of the Indians he encountered. And yet he took the time to attend a government conference between leaders of the Minnesota Sioux, among them Little Crow, and the government agents.[12] Sometime earlier, he had gone with a friend to visit Martha Simons, the only surviving full-blood Indian in the New Bedford area.[13] And he had responded strongly to other Indian guides he had met on his trips to Maine. But not even from Thoreau can we get a revision of the comic narrative of civilization's progress and the tragic narrative of Indian decline; although Sayre (1977) entitles one of his chapters about Thoreau and the Indians "Beyond Savagism," I don't think Thoreau ever did get beyond savagism. At best, it seems to me, one can only call Thoreau's savagism (as so much else in Thoreau's thinking) an idiosyncratic and complex savagism.

Ralph Waldo Emerson made public a letter he composed in April of 1838 to President Martin Van Buren protesting the removal of the eastern Cherokees to Indian Territory (see chapter 4). (There is also some evidence that Thoreau's mother, Cynthia Dunbar Thoreau, was one of the people who urged him to write it.) But even as he sympathizes, Emerson persists in the racialized discourse of Indian "inferiority" typical of the period. His plea on behalf of the Cherokees notes that "we have witnessed with sympathy the painful labors of these red men to redeem their own race from the doom of eternal inferiority, and to borrow and domesticate in the tribe the art and customs of the Caucasian race" (in Emerson 2007, 1269). Inasmuch as the Cherokees had demonstrably managed to write, to plant, to govern themselves (adopting a constitution modeled on the constitution of the United States in 1827), and even to pray—as many of them did—in a manner similar to that of the Christian members of "the Caucasian race," it would seem that they *had* "redeem[ed]" their "race" from an "inferiority," which, if it ever existed, most certainly was not "eternal." *If* the Cherokees had somehow been "inferior" prior to, say, 1821 or thereabouts, surely they were quickly progressing to the level of the presumed superior race. Indeed, like many southern white planters, the Cherokees also owned slaves.

Virginia Kennedy has examined what is perhaps Emerson's most influential work, the extended essay called *Nature* (1836), for its references to the Native people of this continent, and we will look at only a few of these. In Emerson's chapter 3, "Beauty," Kennedy notes his imaginative reconstruction of Columbus's arrival to "the shore of America"—(Columbus never actually reached the North

American mainland; his first landing was Guanahani, in the West Indies, an island he renamed San Salvador)—where he sees "the beach lined with savages." She remarks on Emerson's assertion, in his chapter 4, "Language," that "children and savages use only nouns or names of things, which they convert into verbs" (in Kennedy 2000, 10). This is an extraordinary generalization when we consider that there was not, of course, an "Indian language," but, rather, hundreds of Native languages, that several of them have many more verb forms than English, and that Emerson in any case did not have the slightest knowledge of any Native language.

In later years, responding to the publication of Longfellow's *Song of Hiawatha* in an 1855 letter, Emerson praises Longfellow's achievement in writing a poem that is "sweet and wholesome as maize"—no small feat when writing about Indians, because, as Emerson continues, "the dangers of the Indian, are that they [sic] are really savage, have poor, small, sterile heads,—no thoughts; and you must deal very roundly with them, and find them in brains" (in Maddox 1991, 185n65). It's hard to guess what that last phrase means; or, rather, for it to mean anything, it must be referencing the "scientific racists" of the "American School of Ethnography," in particular those who followed Samuel Morton's commitment to cranial size as determining intelligence. (But if head size was important to Emerson, all he would have had to do was to look at George Catlin's paintings of Indians, reproduced from 1841 forward, in which he could have found representations of many Indians with quite substantial heads!)

Some years later, Emerson's attitude toward the Sioux—they seem to stand generally for the "wild" Indians of the Plains—would indicate no change of heart about the Indian's lack of brains. In a volume of verse called *May-Day and Other Pieces* (1867), there is a poem called "The Adirondacs" that recalls a hiking trip made by Emerson and some Boston friends in 1858. As the men walk, they meet someone who informs them that the trans-Atlantic cable has been completed and is in operation. Emerson is fascinated (in a manner Thoreau would not have been) by the possibility of trans-Atlantic communication, even as he appreciates his rural surroundings. He writes,

> We praise the guide, we praise the
> forest life: But will we sacrifice
> our dear-bought lore
> Of books and arts and trained experiment,
> Or count the Sioux a match for Agassiz? O no, not we!

(1929, 193)

Louis Agassiz, a professor of natural history at Harvard, Emerson's alma mater (and Thoreau's), came to believe in the theory of polygenesis, of multiple creations, as an explanation of what were taken, in the nineteenth century, to be innate racial differences. In 1850 Agassiz had written of "the submissive, obsequious negro" and "the indomitable, courageous, proud Indian" (in Dippie 1982, 92)—proud, perhaps, but at least in Emerson's view, obviously no match for his civilized company. Thus, Emerson again contributes to the triumphal comic narrative of American progress—in this case specifically, the progress of arts and science. The Sioux have not achieved the "dear-bought lore" of civilization, nor is there any likelihood that they could achieve it inasmuch as Emerson, like most of his contemporaries, perceives Indians as racially inferior to himself and his fellow Euro-Americans;[14] with their small brains, Emerson says, they are surely no "match for Agassiz."[15]

iii. The Representation of Indians in Other Writers of the Period

Washington Irving's essays "Philip of Pokanoket" and "Traits of Indian Character," originally published separately (1819–1820), appear together in *The Sketch-Book of Geoffrey Crayon, Gent.* (1998).[16] In "Traits of Indian Character," Irving is quite clear that, regrettably, "The eastern tribes have long since disappeared," and "in a little while, they [other tribes] . . . will vanish like a vapor from the face of the earth; their very history will be lost in forgetfulness" (248–49). At least Irving understands that if the disappearance of the Indians is certain, it will not come about as the result only of nature's laws but because the actions of the citizens of the United States are such as to drive them "to madness and despair by the wide-spreading desolation, and the overwhelming ruin of European warfare" (245).

Of "King Philip," Irving writes, "He was an evil that walked in darkness, whose coming none could foresee, and against which none knew when to be on the alert" (1998, 258). He deems Philip and his people "worthy of an age of poetry, and fit subjects for local story and romantic fiction" (251), but claims that they "have left scarcely any authentic traces on the page of history, but stalk, like gigantic shadows in the dim twilight of tradition" (251). This is oddly mistaken in that Irving knows some of the texts of the Puritan chroniclers of the war—although his republication of the essay on Philip does just barely precede the popularity of *Yamoyden* and other works about Philip in the 1820s and 1830s (see chapter 3). There is no question for Irving that the defeat of Philip and his people, like the destined vanishing of the other tribes, is a tragic story, sad-but-just. Irving writes that Philip had "heroic qualities and bold achievements that would have graced a civilized warrior, and have rendered him the theme of the poet and historian" (264), here anticipating the work of Eastburn and Sands, John Augustus Stone, and others (but not Hawthorne). Irving unequivocally confirms the tragedy of Philip's story in the conclusion of his essay, where he writes that Philip "lived a wanderer and a fugitive in his native land, and went down, like a lonely bark foundering amid darkness and tempest—without a pitying eye to weep his fall, or a friendly hand to record his struggle" (264). Irving pities Philip, weeps, and retrospectively offers him an ambiguously "friendly hand." But he never doubts that Philip's demise and that of his people was anything but just and necessary.

It is just and necessary because Philip and his people must fall before the advance of a higher and more able race, a perspective Irving develops in his 1836 celebration of John Jacob Astor, called *Astoria*. In contrast to Astor, whose "great commercial enterprises have enriched nations, peopled wildernesses, and extended the bounds of empire," Irving says of the Indians that they are people whose lives are "little better than a prolonged and all-besetting death," and, inevitably, tragically (and repetitively), "in a little while scarcely any traces [of them] will be left" (in Maddox 1991, 73).

A similar point of view, developed in much greater detail, appears in the work of Irving's contemporaries, Henry Wadsworth Longfellow and James Fenimore Cooper, writers less eminent than Hawthorne, Emerson, Melville, or Thoreau by our current reckoning (the same is true for Irving), but writers who were then and are now substantially identified with Indian subjects. Longfellow's *Song of Hiawatha* (1855) sold out its first printing of four thousand copies on the day of its publication and completed its first year in print with sales of thirty-eight thousand copies, extraordinary numbers for the time. As Helen Carr has written, "*The Song of Hiawatha* tells the story of a gentle doomed Indian in a vanished pre-colonial world, accepting and acknowledging the rightness of his people's fate" (1996, 106).[17]

Of course, Longfellow did not write about the Indians of his own day, nor did he, like many of his contemporaries, look to the history of earlier times;[18] rather, he worked from Native American stories and legends published by Henry Rowe Schoolcraft, an avid student of several Native peoples, a government researcher, and a man married to Jane Johnston Schoolcraft, whose mother, Ozha-guscoday-way-quay, was Ojibwe. Schoolcraft's *Algic Researches*, published in 1839, was the source for many of the characters and events in *Hiawatha*. But Longfellow got a good deal of Schoolcraft's material wrong. For one thing, although Longfellow's "song" deals with Algonquian peoples of the Great Lakes, his hero, Hiawatha, is a Mohawk from northern New York! Nor did Longfellow manage to distinguish between Hiawatha, probably a historical personage of the fourteenth century who established the Iroquois League of Peace, and Manabozho, a mythic trickster figure of the Algonquians (see chapter 1).

For his meter, Longfellow did not look to any of Schoolcraft's awkward but interesting experiments in translating Native song. Instead, he chose for his poem a sing-songy meter that he took from the Finnish epic *Kalevala*, first published in its entirety in 1849. Although Longfellow had, in fact, studied Finnish, he worked from the German translation of *Kalevala* by Anton Schiefner (1852). (The first English translation was not published until 1888.) A June 5, 1854, entry in Longfellow's notebook records that he read Schiefner's translation "with great delight." Then, on June 22, Longfellow notes, "I have at length hit upon a plan for a poem on the Indians.... I have hit upon a measure, too, which I think is the right one and the only one" (in Berg n.d., 3). He also took many scenes and incidents from the *Kalevala* for his "Indian" poem.

The point to be made here is that Longfellow spent some time with Schoolcraft (although not enough actually to understand the material—which Schoolcraft himself sometimes mangled), and considerable time with a Finnish epic in German translation, but the poem that resulted from these researches denies its relation to them.[19] Consider the following lines from the introduction to *Hiawatha*:

> Should you ask me, whence these stories?
> Whence these legends and traditions,
> With the odors of the forest,
> With the dew and damp of meadows,
> With the curling smoke of wigwams,
> With the rushing of great rivers, etc.
> I should answer, I should tell you,

> From the forests and the prairies,
> From the great lakes of the Northland,
> From the land of the Ojibways,
> From the land of the Dacotahs,
> From the mountains, moors and fen-lands,
> Where the heron, the Shuh-shuh-gah
> Feeds among the reeds and rushes. (in Berg n.d., 6–7)

Thus, Indian stories, legends, and traditions do not arise from cultural and intellectual work; rather, they arise from the land, the mountains, moors, and fen-lands. Indian "culture" is simply "nature," springing as it does, apparently fully formed, both from the land—forests, prairies, lakes, mountains, moors, and fen-lands—and its fauna (the heron, or Shuh-shuh-gah).

And just as nature must submit to cultivation, so, too, must the Indian, nature's creature, submit to "civilization." Longfellow dramatizes the general attitude of eastern progressive thought about Indians by having Hiawatha counsel his people to abandon the old ways, naturally charming as they may have been, and prepare themselves to "vanish" sadly-but-justly, in true tragic fashion, before the inevitable progress of cultivation and "civilization."

James Fenimore Cooper's five "Leatherstocking" novels (1823, 1826, 1827, 1840, 1841: see Works with Indian Subjects, below), like much other work of this period, deal with Indian-Euramerican relations of an earlier time, generally from around the mid-eighteenth century; only his *Wept of Wish-ton-Wish* (1829) is set in the seventeenth century, at approximately the time of King Philip's War. (His *Wyandotte*, not one of the "Leatherstocking" series, is set in 1758 and concerns a Tuscarora Indian whose name provides the title for the novel.) Although Cooper sometimes regretted the "inevitable" demise of the Indians, and, too, of Indianized whites like the old frontiersman Natty Bumppo, he was quite clear that there could be no future for the Indians. Typically, Cooper racializes the socio-historical encounter between white and red on this continent. He can grant a certain "nobility" to the "savage"—the broad options were "noble savage" (generally espoused by Easterners who had subdued local Indians a long time ago) or "murderous savage" (espoused by Westerners, wherever the West happened to be, who were still fighting the Native population)—but finds no future for him. Cooper's Indians, like Emerson's and Longfellow's, must make way for a "higher" race. As Cooper wrote in *Notions of the Americans* (1828), "As a rule, the red man disappears before the superior moral and physical influence of the white" (in Pearce 1953, 201). While the "superior moral . . . influence" of "the white" remains an open question, there was no doubt about the superior "physical influence of the white," the overwhelming force to which many Indian people did indeed succumb. To be sure, the whole thing is made a bit more palatable if force is referred to as "physical influence." I will say something more about Cooper below.

Lydia Maria Child's novel *Hobomok* (1824) took its inspiration either from James Wallis Eastburn and Robert Sands's narrative poem *Yamoyden* (1820), dealing with King Philip's war—or, as seems more likely, from John Gorham Palfrey's review of *Yamoyden* in the influential *North American Review* (1820). Making what was then an almost-inevitable reference to the historical novels of Sir Walter Scott, which represented, in heroic fashion, an earlier period on the Scottish border, Palfrey suggested that American writers could find more than the equivalent of Scott's settings and characters in the American Indians, "with all the bold rough lines of nature yet uneffaced upon them" (in Karcher 1986, xviii). (This is, again, the sort of work for which Hawthorne acknowledged himself unfit.) Palfrey believed that "whoever in this country first attains the rank of a first rate writer of fiction will lay his scene here. The wide field is ripe for the harvest" (in Karcher 1986, xviii).[20] And so the twenty-two-year-old Lydia Maria Francis produced a novel set in the seventeenth century, but one having to do neither with King Philip's War nor with the earlier Pequot War.

Bergland has gone so far as to assert that "*Hobomok* is central to American literature" (2000, 67), and Philip Gould's work convincingly shows that it is at least central to debates about the Puritan legacy in the early American republic.[21] "Nowhere," Gould writes, "were the exclusively masculine contexts for early republican behavior more saliently drawn than in early national narratives of the Pequot War of 1637" (1996, 59). And yet, as Gould notes in discussions of *Hobomok* and Catharine Maria Sedgwick's *Hope Leslie* (see just below), it was extremely difficult "*both* to critique republican manhood *and* fully humanize the Pequot for a dubious audience" (81, my emphasis). Child's novel seemed to suggest, in the union of Mary Conant and Hobomok, that intermarriage between whites and Indians might be an alternative to Indian disappearance. But when Mary's former lover, long thought dead, reappears, Hobomok leaves his wife and son to disappear into the West. Under the tutelage of his white mother and white stepfather, little Hobomok eventually becomes a Cambridge graduate. "His father," Child writes, was seldom spoken of, and by degrees his Indian appellation was silently omitted" (1986, 150).

But Child was only twenty-two when she wrote this, and for her the matter remained complex. In her 1828 history, *The First Settlers of New-England; Or, Conquest of the Pequods, Naragansets, and Pokanokets, as Related by a Mother to Her Children, and Designed for the Instruction of Youth*, for example, she writes, "It is, in my opinion, decidedly wrong to speak of the removal or extinction of the Indians as *inevitable*" (in Karcher 1986, my emphasis). Forty years later, Child's 1868 pamphlet, "An Appeal for the Indians," argues for justice toward Native American (and African American) people, claiming that Indians (and Africans) can attain the heights of white civilization given time and opportunity.

Linda Kerber has shown that Child was concerned with Indian issues before she became an abolitionist. As an abolitionist, she managed to oppose Cherokee removal by simply ignoring (cf. Kerber 1975, 282) the fact that the Cherokees were slaveholders, something other abolitionists sympathetic to the southeastern tribes found difficult to do. By 1868, however, Child could affirm that the "plain truth is, our relations with the red and black members of the human family have been one almost unvaried history of violence and fraud." Concerning the inevitability of the Indians' disappearance, she writes, "Yet, while we are perpetually robbing them, and driving them 'from post to pillar,' we go on repeating, with the most impudent coolness, 'They are *destined* to disappear before the white man'" (in Karcher 1986, 231).²² Anyone taking this view seriously must begin to see that the narrative of Native disappearance is a narrative in the ironic rather than the tragic mode.

With Lydia Maria Child we encounter the complex nineteenth-century intersection of concern for women's rights, for the abolition of slavery, and for Indian rights. As Kerber's work makes clear, the linkage of African Americans and Indians could have unfortunate consequences for the Natives in that the abolitionists' tendency to encourage individuality and Christian moral uplift was accompanied by a total lack of understanding of the importance of tribal membership, national sovereignty, and the continued vitality of Native religions.

Here I will only mention the work of Lydia Howard Huntley Sigourney, extremely popular from 1815, when her first book was published, until well past the middle of the century. The major works, for my purposes, are her "Traits of the Aborigines" (1822; its title would not, of course, immediately identify it as a poem), along with *Pocahontas and Other Poems* (1841). As Nina Baym, the most insightful of her critics, has shrewdly observed, "Sigourney faced the insoluble *political* and *moral* problem that the triumphs of Christianity and republicanism in America were achieved at the cost of their own basic tenets" (1990, 394). She was, Baym notes, "unwilling to adopt a tragic or ironic stance toward history." Thus, she is left with what Baym calls "an outright articulation of contradiction" (395). This was the best the sympathetic Sigourney could do; only William Apess will manage fully to achieve the ironic stance Baym finds Sigourney unwilling or unable to adopt.

Very likely inspired by Child's *Hobomok*, Catharine Maria Sedgwick's *Hope Leslie* (1827) is also set in the colonial period during the Pequot War. It, too, uses Puritanism, as Gould writes, as "an arena in which to debate the protean, gendered meanings of republican 'virtue'" (1996, 64). Because Puritan accounts of the Pequot War bequeath to the early republic what Gould calls "a narrowly masculine understanding of citizenship" (68), Sedgwick contests those accounts. Specifically, she describes Puritan violence against the Indians and Indian violence against the Puritans as equally *savage*. But here, too, we find an Indian rejected finally in marriage by a white woman, and, once again, the author cannot find any way to incorporate Indians into her view of America.

James Fenimore Cooper returned to Indian material in *The Wept of Wish-ton-Wish* (1829).[23] Cooper's only novel set in the Puritan era, *The Wept* does indeed treat King Philip's War, and specifically opposes Sedgwick's and Child's vision of what Gould calls "androgynous masculinity and sentimental republicanism" (1996, 136). But *The Wept*, Gould continues, also "critiques the canons of liberalism as they were written into the period's historiography of King Philip's War" (139). Writing about the time of Andrew Jackson's election as president, Cooper also critiques "frontier acquisitiveness" (1829, 141), recognizing that "the real issue of King Philip's War ... was the nation's economic potential" (142). Indeed, Cooper emphasized the frontier as an issue by giving the 1833 edition of *The Wept* the title *The Borderers*. While his rejection of any feminization of republican virtue only bolstered Jacksonian machismo, that is, the intensely cultivated image of Jackson as Old Hickory, Cooper nonetheless did expose what Gould calls "the power of early republican language to euphemize greed" (1996, 148).

Margaret Fuller, another champion of women's rights sometimes wary of the abolitionists but sometimes linking women's rights to the emancipation of blacks, also briefly wrote about Indians in her short life (she died in a shipwreck in 1850 at the age of forty), in *Summer on the Lakes in 1843* (1844), and, to a lesser extent, in journalism of the same period for the *New York Tribune*. Fuller's travels to the Great Lakes included encounters with Native peoples of various tribes (Potawatomis, Chippewas, and Ottawas); she also makes reference to the Sauk, Fox, and Cherokees and demonstrates some awareness of U.S.-Indian relations in her own time. When, for example, she walks along what she calls "Black Hawk's Trail," she speaks of the so-called Black Hawk War of 1832, and recalls a visit to Massachusetts by the Sauk chief, Keocuck (Fuller's spelling), who was addressed by Governor Edward Everett (1991, 114–19). (I will return to Everett in the following chapter.) Fuller does not seem to have read or even to have known of Black Hawk's autobiography published in 1833 (although a substantial part of her remarks on Indians is made up of rather cursory reviews of a number of books on Indian subjects), nor does she know that to Black Hawk Keokuk was an accommodationist who betrayed his people.

Near the end of her book, Fuller states, "Although I have little to tell, I feel that I have learnt a great deal of the Indians, from observing them even in this broken and degraded condition" (1991, 153). She congratulates herself on having become "acquainted with the soul of this race; I read its nobler thought in their defaced figures" (153). Fuller occasionally wrestles with the dominant discourse of "the unfortunately vanishing Indian"—Fuller's words—although she ultimately accedes to it. She can see that, in regard to the Indian, "the power of fate is with the white man" (71). For all that, shifting the blame or extenuating it, she remarks that "*nature* seems . . . to declare that this race [Indians] is fated to perish" (120, my emphasis). In any case, whether "fate" manifests itself through "the white man" or whether it is "nature" that is responsible for the Indians' "fate," there is no question that they must vanish. Indeed, as Lucy Maddox has shown, Fuller poetically redeems "the men of these subjugated tribes, now accustomed to drunkenness and every way degraded," by insisting that they can serve as reminders "of what *was* majestic in the red man" (in Maddox

1991, 143, my emphasis). "Fuller's own eye," Maddox writes, "is constantly turned to the past." As for the future, for Fuller, Indians face only "speedy extinction" (in Maddox 1991, 144).[24]

Fuller proposes "a national institute, containing all the remains of the Indians—all that has been preserved by official intercourse at Washington."[25] This will include "Catlin's collection [of paintings of Indians], and a picture gallery as complete as can be made, with a collection of *skulls from all parts of the country*" (1991, 143, my emphasis). Fuller, one may say with relief, was only partly prophetic: the National Museum of the American Indian, recently opened in Washington DC, is neither a mausoleum nor a repository of skulls. (A great many American museums did indeed keep collections of Indian skulls.)

In 1845 Fuller wrote a review of Henry Rowe Schoolcraft's book, *Oneota, or the Red Race of America* (1845) for the *New York Tribune*.[26] Fuller opens—my discussion here is based on Virginia Kennedy's work—with the standard observation that "the Red Race" has "well nigh melted from our sight." She endorses Schoolcraft's notion that Indian society might have been "re-organized"—except of course, as Fuller also writes, "it is too late for act . . . nothing remains but to write their epitaph with some respect to truth" (in Kennedy 2001, 33). As I have again and again noted, "sympathy" for the Indians' plight goes hand in hand with the racialized discourse of their inevitable disappearance. Lucy Maddox states this well: "For Fuller, clearly, what is best in the Indian 'type' is found only in those Indians who have, *by dying*, made themselves available to the poetic eye and the genteel imagination" (1991, 145, my emphasis).[27]

What I find extraordinary, as I bring this part of my survey to a close, is the degree to which, when it comes to the actual, detailed, year by year history of Native American removal and dispossession in the nineteenth century, both the canonical and the lesser authors of the period, have extraordinarily little to say. All of them reference Indians historically on occasion and symbolically somewhat more often, but they very rarely engage with them as contemporary historical, cultural, and social beings—and when they do, as we have noted even with Melville, Thoreau, and Fuller, it is still to see them as living anachronisms or last remnants. Even Child seems to believe that Native people must assimilate or die. The literary legacy of the nineteenth century in regard to Indians provides no Indian side to the two-hundred-year-long history of violent displacement. Everywhere the discourse of vanishment is built upon the rhetoric of "savagism" and "scientific racism." Regarded, for the most part, as racially inferior and incapable of civilization (even when civilization had demonstrably been achieved, for example, as in the case of the Cherokees, and other of the so-called Five Civilized Tribes), living, breathing Indian people were walking anachronisms whose present and presence were already the past. The story of the savages' passing is a tragic tale, and it balances quite neatly the comic narrative of the triumphant advance of American civilization.

This is the context in which I will consider two texts by the Reverend William Apess, a Pequot. Before doing that, however, it is necessary to return to a consideration of the Native American writers of this period.

iv. Native American Authors

Apart from William Apess, the Native American writers I am aware of in the half century under consideration are Elias Boudinot, George Copway, David Cusick, George Henry, Peter Jacobs, Peter Jones, Maris Bryant Pierce, John Rollin Ridge, Jane Johnston Schoolcraft, and Nathaniel Strong.[28] Black Hawk and Red Jacket could be added to this list, not as writers but as authors (I'll explain the distinction I intend in just a moment). Is it possible to offer an overview of the work of these writers and authors, an overview that would allow tentative generalizations concerning their representation of Native peoples, and of Indian–white relations? Is it possible to do for them what I have tried to do for the writers of the dominant society? I think not yet, not at this point in time.

Although Copway, Henry, Jacobs, and Jones had editions of their works published in the United States, they are Canadian First Nations people. The conditions to which they foremost respond, though equally difficult, are nonetheless different from those prevailing in the United States. On the basis of recent work by Donald Smith, Smith and LaVonne Brown Ruoff, and Maureen Konkle, I think it is beginning to be possible to offer tentative generalizations about their work, although, to repeat, their work appears in the context of Canadian history and literature.

Black Hawk was not a writer, although, as I have said, he might be included as an *author* of the period, one who, as the etymology of the word *author* makes clear, at one and the same time originates and augments. Although he was surely prodded in this direction, it does seem to be the case that Black Hawk initiated or originated the project that led to the publication of his autobiography; and he did so in the interest of augmenting the history of the recent "Black Hawk War" by recounting his people's side of the story. It is also the case that the life history that bore his name somewhat augmented the limited amount of cultural knowledge that whites possessed about his people. Although Black Hawk surely originated most of what appears in his 1833 autobiography, the book was undoubtedly augmented by its editor, J. B. Patterson, on the basis of materials provided by the (Potawatomi) interpreter Antoine LeClair. In addition to Donald Jackson's edition of Black Hawk's autobiography (1955), there are more recent editions— one by Roger Nichols (1999), and a Penguin edition ably edited by J. Gerald Kennedy (2008). Presently, there is a growing body of critical reflection on the text. I'll mention only my own very early work (Krupat, 1985) and that of Neil Schmitz (2001). Kennedy's new edition is sure to provoke further reflection on Black Hawk's autobiography. We are close to the time when it will be possible to offer some tentative generalizations about what Black Hawk meant by his book.

The great Seneca orator, Sagoyewatha, or Red Jacket, had some of his speeches published in this period and was sufficiently noticed to be considered an author, although he did no writing. Granville Ganter's fine edition of the collected speeches of Red Jacket appeared at the time of this writing (2006), and it should enable a good deal of further study. In the same way, it is also only recently (2007) that a scholarly and brilliantly edited volume by Robert Dale Parker of the complete works—or, surely, the great majority of them—of Jane Johnston Schoolcraft has appeared. In the future, as Parker has commented, it will be Jane Schoolcraft who is being referred to when one speaks of Schoolcraft, and Henry Rowe Schoolcraft will simply be Henry. Parker's research makes it possible for the first time to achieve an approximately full sense of the range of her work as a self-conscious writer and translator of "literary" material. But I think it is premature to generalize about or provide an overview of Jane Schoolcraft's work. She, too, wrote in relation to her Chippewa family, culture, and nation, and she was well aware of white denigration of Indians, for all that English poetry and prose were important to her as well.

Theda Perdue's *Cherokee Editor* collects many of the speeches and writings of Elias Boudinot, including representative selections of his work for the *Cherokee Phoenix*. I am not aware of any "collected works" as yet. Boudinot, of course, was a Christian progressive committed to the survival of the Cherokees in their homelands until 1832 or so, by which time he had begun to despair of staving off the onslaught of Jackson and Georgia (see chapter 4). Daniel Heath Justice's *Our Fire Survives the Storm* offers reflections on Boudinot and his relations with John Ross of the anti-Removal Party that are most helpful, although I think we are still in the early stages of achieving anything like a comprehensive view of Boudinot and his writing.

Maureen Konkle (2004) has offered commentary on Cusick, Pierce, and Strong, and also on the writings of John Ridge. Ridge's more-prolific son, John Rollin Ridge, became the "first" Native American novelist with his *Life and Adventures of Joaquin Murieta*

(1854); Ridge was also the author of a volume of posthumously published poems. James Parins, Ridge's biographer, writes that "John Rollin Ridge's *Life and Adventures of Joaquin Murieta* is not pure history, but it is not pure fiction, either. It is more like today's television "docudramas" or the currently fashionable news novels, productions based loosely on history but liberally sprinkled with embellishments and added emphasis designed to titillate the audience. There is no doubt that *Joaquin* was meant to be sensational... [and that] Ridge wanted a best-seller" (1991, 109–10). It remains to be seen what other commentators might do with that assessment.

The Native writers of the period 1820–1870 wrote for many reasons and to several audiences. Surely they wrote to preserve their culture, as David Cusick most explicitly did in publishing his translation/version of the Iroquois creation story. But Cusick also wrote to instantiate Iroquois history as a foundation for Iroquois political autonomy in the present and future. Given the special pressures on Native nations in this period in the United States, Native writers were virtually forced to *write back* against the prevailing racist insistence on Indian inferiority and inevitable disappearance. As Konkle has importantly shown, these writers offered not only a discourse of cultural difference but of political force. They were caught in the sorts of contradictions and tensions fairly well documented as the consequences of colonialism. Thus, they had to insist that they could become "civilized" and Christian while (at least in many cases) asserting the value of traditional culture. Konkle's emphasis on the political nature of these authors' texts is a useful corrective to those many readings of their work that were interested strictly in their cultural dimension, their attestation to varying degrees of Indian "difference" and "authenticity." Meanwhile, if restoring balance is important, so, too, is it important not to tip the balance too far in the other direction. I suspect many of these writers also wrote for some of the reasons that writers the world over and over all time have written. But to make that last, vague remark more specific will require just the sort of detailed study of each of these writers that, for the most part, remains to be done.

Appendix A: Works with Indian Subjects, 1820–1870
For A. LaVonne Brown Ruoff

I've compiled the list below to give some idea of the extent and variety of writing by and about Native Americans in the half century 1820–1870. I've called these "works with Indian subjects," an admittedly loose category that is meant to indicate the range of texts I am aware of—the reader will correctly guess that I haven't read them all—that describe or expostulate in some significant degree on Native people. Most of the authors in this listing, familiar or unfamiliar, are non-Natives, as one would expect, and, while many of the works are literary in the current sense of the word—novels, poems, plays, tales, romances, and autobiographies—others will serve as reminders of the degree to which the meaning of the category of *literature* has changed since 1820–1870.

In that period, for example, captivity narratives (many true stories, others fictitious) about persons captured and held by Indians qualified as literature. Even some of the "histories" are written in a style and a manner that today look more nearly literary than rigorously historical, that is, written with claims to empirical veracity. Melodramas and burlesques were also considered literature, although today the qualifying adjectives "popular," or perhaps even "bad" might be added. Also of note is the fact that most of those presently considered to be the major authors of the period are *not* represented on this list. I have tried to give the date of first publication, or, for theatrical works, the date of first performance.

This list makes no claim whatever to comprehensiveness. Indeed, as I have worked on it for more than five years, hardly a month has gone by that I haven't found a title or two to add. Friends have suggested titles, and very recently, Nina Baym kindly sent me a list of new entries from her own work on western American literature. And there are most certainly other titles that could be added. In much the same way, although I have tried to be as careful as possible, it is almost surely the case that I've made errors. Publication dates for materials of this period, for one thing, are sometimes clear and accurate, and sometimes contradictory or unclear; authors' names are spelled differently in different places, and so on. I haven't tried to include the enormous amount of material relating to Indians in periodicals or government publications in this period. I've listed only texts that were published in the United States, although occasionally I mention Canadian or English editions. It should also be noted that there were many reprints in this period of seventeenth-century texts by the Mathers, Daniel Gookin, John Eliot, and others, and they, too, played a part in the period's representation of the Indian—as do the reprints of Mary Rowlandson's seventeenth-century captivity narrative.

I want to note here that in regard to a number of Native authors of the period, in particular, whatever errors remain, there are fewer than otherwise might be found, thanks to the kind and careful attention of LaVonne Brown Ruoff, to whom this section is dedicated.

1820

>James W. Eastburn and Robert Sands, *Yamoyden, A Tale of the Wars of King Philip: in Six Cantos.*
>
>John Heckewelder, *Narrative of the Mission of the United Brethren among the Delaware and Mohegan Indians from Its Commencement in the year 1740, to the Close of the Year 1808.*

1821

>Elias Cornelius, *The Little Osage Captive* (captivity variant: Osage girl captured by Cherokees, "rescued" and raised by the author).
>
>Lewis Deffebach, *Oolaita; or, The Indian Heroine* (melodrama).

Joseph Doddridge, *Logan, The Last of the Race of Shikellemus, Chief of the Cayuga Nation* (play).

1822

John Neal, *Logan* (sensationalistic fiction).

Lydia Sigourney, *Traits of the Aborigines of America: A Poem* (published anonymously, and despite the odd title, indeed a poem in five cantos of four thousand blank verse lines).

Henry Whiting, *Ontwa, the Son of the Forest. A Poem.*

1823

Elias Boudinot (Buck Watie, Cherokee), *Poor Sarah; or, Religion Exemplified in the Life and Death of an Indian Woman* (religious tract attributed to Boudinot, who may not have written it, but did translate it into Cherokee).

Lewis Cass, *Inquiries, respecting the history, traditions, languages, manners, customs, religion, &c. of the Indians, living in the United States.* (This was an official survey by Cass, governor of Minnesota territory.)

James Fenimore Cooper, *The Pioneers; Or, the Sources of the Susquehanna: A Descriptive Tale.*

John Dunn Hunter, *Memoirs of a Captivity among the Indians of North America.* (An alternate title for a volume published the same year is *Manners and customs of several Indian tribes located west of the Mississippi.*)

James Kirke Paulding, *Konigsmarke; or, Old Times in the New World* (satirical novel).

1824

Lydia Maria Child, *Hobomok: A Tale of Early Times* (novel).

Epaphras Hoyt, *Antiquarian Researches: Comprising a History of the Indian Wars.*

James E. Seaver, ed. *A Narrative of the Life of Mrs. Mary*

Jemison, who was taken by Indians in the year *1755*, etc. (captivity narrative).

1825

Henry Rowe Schoolcraft, *Travels in the Central Portions of the Mississippi Valley, Comprising Observations on Its Mineral Geography, Internal Resources and Aboriginal Population.*

1826

Elias Boudinot (Buck Watie, Cherokee), *An Address to the Whites.* Delivered in the First Presbyterian Church [probably Philadelphia] on the 26th of May *1826* (an argument that Indians are capable of becoming as "civilized" as whites).

James Fenimore Cooper, *The Last of the Mohicans; Or, A Narrative of 1757.*

1827

Timothy Alden, *An Account of Sundry Missions Performed among the Senecas And Munsees, in a Series of Letters.*

Hendrick Aupaumat, *A Narrative of an Embassy to the Western Indians, from the Original Manuscript of Hendrick Aupaumat, 1791 and 1793.* (This is published by B. H. Coates for the *Pennsylvania Historical Society Memoirs*, 2, part 1. The author's name in the Library of Congress is spelled Aupaumut. The text includes autobiographical material about Aupaumat, a Mahican.)

James Fenimore Cooper, *The Prairie. A Tale.*

David Cusick (Tuscarora), *Sketches of the Ancient History of the Six Nations.*

George Washington Custis, *Pocahontas; or, The Settlers of Virginia* (play, first performance).

Thomas L. McKenney, *Sketches of a Tour to the Lakes and Character and Customs of the Chippeway Indians* . . . .

Sarah Savage, *Life of Philip the Indian Chief.*

Catharine Maria Sedgwick, *Hope Leslie; or, Early Times in the Massachusetts* (novel).

1828

Lydia Maria Child, *The First Settlers of New-England; or, Conquest of the Pequods, Naragansets, and Pokanokets, as Related by a Mother to her Children, and Designed for the Instruction of Youth.*

1829

William Apess (Pequot), *A Son of the Forest* (autobiography).

James Fenimore Cooper, *The Wept of Wish-ton-Wish* (novel; the English edition of 1833 was titled *The Borderers; or, The Wept of Wish-ton-wish*).

Jeremiah Evarts, *Essays on the Present Crisis in the Condition of the American Indians.*

John Augustus Stone, *Metamora; or, The Last of the Wampanoags* (play, first performance).

1830

Henry Rowe Schoolcraft, *Indian Melodies.*

John Tanner, *A Narrative of the Captivity and Adventures of John Tanner*, ed. Edwin James.

1831

Nathaniel Deering, *Carabasset* (play, first performance).

Richard Peters, *The Case of the Cherokee Nation Against the State of Georgia.*

B. B. Thatcher, *Tales of the Indians; being prominent passages of the history of the North American natives. Taken from authentic sources.*

Henry Whiting, *Sannilac, A poem, by Henry Whiting. With notes by Lewis Cass and Henry Rowe Schoolcraft, esqs.*

1832

Rufus B. Anderson, ed., *Memoir of Catherine Brown, A Christian Indian of the Cherokee Nation* (biography and collected letters).

Samuel G. Drake, *Biography and History of the Indians of North America* (this appeared in at least eleven editions).

James Hall, *Legends of the West.*

James Kirke Paulding, *Westward Ho! A Tale.*

B. B. Thatcher, *Indian Biographies; or, An Historical Account of Those Individuals Who Have Been Distinguished among the North American Natives, as Orators, Warriors, Statesmen, and Other Remarkable Characters.* (This went through many editions over many years).

1833

William Apess (Pequot), *The Experiences of Five Christian Indians of the Pequ'd Tribe* (autobiography and biography).

Black Hawk (Sauk), *Life of Ma-Ka-Tai-Me-She-Kia-Kiak or Black Hawk*, ed. J. B. Patterson (autobiography).

1834

Richard Emmons, *Tecumseh* (play, first performance).

1835

William Apess, *Indian Nullification of the Unconstitutional Laws of Massachusetts; or, The Pretended Riot Explained.*

Edward Everett, *An Address Delivered at Bloody Brook in South Deerfield, September 30, 1835, in Commemoration of the Fall of the 'Flower of Essex,' at that Spot in King Philip's War, September 18, (O[ld]. S[tyle], 1675)* (Celebrates the Puritan victory over Philip).

Samuel G. Goodrich, *The Captive of Nootka; or, The adventures of John R. Jewett* (captivity narrative).

James Hall, *Sketches of History, Life, and Manners in the West* (contains the sketch "The Indian Hater").

James Hall, *Tales of the Border.*

Washington Irving, *A Tour of the Prairies.*

William Gilmore Simms, *The Yemassee, A romance of Carolina.*

1836

William Apess (Pequot), *Eulogy on King Philip.*

Benjamin Franklin Hallett, *Rights of the Marshpee Indians.*

George Turner, *Traits of Indian Character; as Generally Applicable to the Aborigines of North America.*

1837

Robert Bird, *Nick of the Woods; or, The Jibbenainosay; A Tale of Kentucky* (novel).

Robert Dale Owen, *Pocahontas: A Historical Drama* (play).

Crane Simmons, *Sketches of the Indian War in Florida . . . Together with the Life of Mrs. Simmons, Who Has Been Twice Taken by Indians.*

1838

Benjamin Drake, *The Life and Adventures of Black Hawk: With Sketches of Keokuk, the Sac and Fox Indians, and the Late Black Hawk War.*

Alexander Macomb, *Pontiac* (play, first performance).

Louisa H. Medina, *Nick of the Woods* (melodrama).

William L. Stone, *Life of Joseph Brant—Thayendanegea: Including the Border Wars of the American Revolution . . . with the Indian Relations of the United States and Great Britain from the Peace of 1783 to the Indian Peace of 1795.*

1839

Samuel G. Drake, *Tragedies of the Wilderness; or, True and*

Authentic Narratives of Captives, Who Have Been Carried Away by the Indians from Earliest to the Present Time. Illustrating the Manners and Customs, Barbarous Rites and Ceremonies, of the North American Indians, and their Various Methods of Torture Practised Upon Such as Have from Time to Time, Fallen into Their Hands. (At least one more edition appeared in 1841.)

Anna Brownell Jameson, *Winter Studies and Summer Rambles in Canada.* (This is the first American edition of a three-volume work originally published a year earlier in London. Although it speaks of Canada, Mrs. Jameson visited the John Johnston family of Sault Ste. Marie, and wrote of Jane Johnston Schoolcraft.)

Samuel G. Morton, *Crania Americana; or, A Comparative View of the Skulls Of Various Aboriginal Nations of North and South America: To Which Is PreFixed an Essay on the Varieties of the Human Species.*

Maris Bryant Pierce (Seneca), *Address on the Present Conditions and Prospects of the Aboriginal Inhabitants of North America, with Particular Reference to the Seneca Nation.*

1840

James Fenimore Cooper, *The Pathfinder; Or, The Inland Sea* (novel).

1841

George Catlin, *Letters and Notes on the Manners, Customs, and Condition of the North American Indians, by George Catlin. Written during Eight Years' Travel amongst the Wildest Tribes of Indians in North America. In 1832, 33, 34, 35, 36, 37, 38, and 39, with Four Hundred Illustrations Engraved from His Original Paintings* (also published in London and reprinted many times with varying numbers of engravings of the paintings).

James Fenimore Cooper, *The Deerslayer; Or, The First War-Path: A Tale.*

Benjamin Drake, *Life of Tecumseh, and of his Brother the Prophet; with a Historical Sketch of the Shawanoe Indians.*

Samuel Drake, *Book of the Indians.*

Lydia Sigourney, *Pocahontas and Other Poems.*

William L. Stone, *Life and Times of Red-Jacket, or Sa-go-ye-wat-ha; Being the Sequel to the History of the Six Nations* (several later reprints).

Nathaniel Strong (Seneca), *Appeal to the Christian Community on the Condition and Prospects of the New York Indians, in Answer to a Book, Entitled The Case of the New-York Indians, and Other Publications of the Society of Friends.*

James Winer, *Events in Indian History Beginning with an Account of the Origins of the American Indians . . . Concise Biographies of the Primary Chiefs . . . with Narratives and Captivities . . . and an Indian Vocabulary.*

1842

William L. Stone, *Uncas and Miantonomah: A Historical Discourse Delivered at Norwich (Connecticut) on the Fourth Day of July, 1842, on the Occasion of the Erection of a Monument to the Memory of Uncas, the White Man's Friend, and First Chief of the Mohegans.* (This book is 209 pages long, so presumably Stone did not "deliver" all of it on July 4, 1842.)

1844

Margaret Fuller, *Summer on the Lakes in 1843* (travel account with references to Black Hawk and the "Black Hawk War").

Josiah Gregg, *Commerce of the Prairies.*

Thomas L. McKenney and James Hall, *Indian Tribes of North America* (several other editions).

1845

Henry Rowe Schoolcraft, *Oneota; or, The Red Race of America* (popular version of his collection of Indian myths and legends).

William Gilmore Simms, *The Wigwam and the Cabin* (novel).

1846

Thomas James, *Three Years among the Indians and Mexicans.*

Henry Rowe Schoolcraft, *Notes on the Iroquois* (report to the government on the possibility of "civilizing" the Iroquois).

1847

John Brougham, *Metamora; or, The Last of the Pollywoags* (burlesque).

George Copway (Ojibwe), *The Life, History, and Travels of Kah-ge-ga-gah-bowh (George Copway), a Young Indian Chief of the Ojibwa Nation in Regard to Christianity and Their Future Prospects.* (This appeared in several editions.)

Henry Rowe Schoolcraft, *Historical and Statistical Information Respecting the History, Condition, and Prospects of the Indian Tribes of the United States . . . Prepared for the Bureau of Indian Affairs.* (Further volumes of this massive work were issued between 1851–57.)

———. *Notes on the Iroquois.*

1848

Charlotte Barnes, *Forest Princess* (play, first performance).

Maungwudaus (George Henry, Ojibwe), *An Account of the Chippewa Indians, Who Have Been Travelling among the Whites, in the United States, England, Scotland, France and Belgium . . .* (The English edition of the same year has the title as *An Account of the North American Indians, Written for Maun-Gwu-Daus.* Maungwudaus was the younger half-brother of the Reverend Peter Jones or Kahkewaquonaby.)

———. *An Account of the Ojibway Indians.* (This also appears the same year as *An Account of the Chippewa Indians.*)

Washington Irving, *The Sketch-Book of Geoffrey Crayon, Gent.* (This is the author's revised edition of the work that had originally appeared in pamphlet form in 1819–20; it reprints "Philip of Pokanoket" and "Traits of Indian Character.")

1849

Mary Henderson Eastman, *Dahcotah: Or, Life and Legends of the Sioux Around Fort Snelling.*

Francis Parkman, *The California and Oregon Trail: Being Sketches of Prairie and Rocky Mountain Life.*

William Gilmore Simms, *The Cassique of Accabee. A Tale of Ashley River. with Other Pieces.*

Elbert H. Smith, *Ma-Ka-Tai-Me-She-Kia-Kiak, or Black Hawk, and Scenes in the West: A National Poem in Six Cantos.*

Alfred B. Street, *Atotarho of the Iroquois, a Metrical Romance.*

1850

Emerson Bennett, *The League of the Miami* (fiction).

George Copway, (Kahgegagahbowh, Ojibwe), *The Ojibway Conquest, A Tale of the Northwest.* (Although this is called a tale, it is actually a long poem by Julius Clark, who allowed Copway to publish it under his own name, with some revisions and the addition by Copway of a short poem to his wife.)

———. *Organization of a New Indian Territory, East of the Missouri River. Arguments and Reasons Submitted.*

———. *The Traditional History and Characteristic Sketches of the Ojibway Nation* (reprinted 1858 as *Indian Life and Indian History, by an Indian Author* . . . .).

Lewis H. Garrard, *Wah-to-yah and the Taos Trail; or, Prairie Travel and Scalp Dances with a Look at Los Rancheros from Muleback and the Rocky Mountain Camp-Fire*. (An extraordinary account by a seventeen-year-old from Cleveland who was part of a militia that helped retake Taos after the uprising of 1847.)

1851

Emerson Bennett, *The Pioneer's Daughter: A tale of Indian Captivity* (fictional captivity narrative).

John DeForest, *History of the Indians of Connecticut from the Earliest Known Period to 1850*.

G. H. Hollister, *Mount Hope; or, Philip, King of the Wampanoags, An Historical Romance*.

Lewis Henry Morgan, *League of the Ho-Do-No-Sau-Nee or Iroquois* (full-scale study of the Iroquois).

Francis Parkman, *History of the Conspiracy of Pontiac, and the War of North American Tribes against the English* (many more editions).

Henry Rowe Schoolcraft, *Personal Memoirs of a Residence of Thirty Years with the Indian Tribes on the American Frontiers . . . 1812–42*.

1852

John Frost, *Thrilling Adventures among the Indians . . . as well as . . . Incidents . . . in Mexico and Texas* (history and captivity narratives).

John A. McClung, *Sketches of Western Adventure* (includes many captivity narratives).

Francis Parkman, *The Oregon Trail* (travel writing).

1853

Emerson Bennett, *Clara Moreland; or, Adventures in the Far South-west [among the Wepecoolah Indians]* (fiction).

Mary Henderson Eastman, *The Romance of Indian Life* (poems, tales, and chromolithographs).

Peter Jacobs (Pahtahsega, Ojibwe), *Journal of the Reverend Peter Jacobs, Indian Wesleyan Missionary, from Rice to the Hudson's Bay Territory, and Returning. Commencing May 1852* (at least two more editions appeared).

Henry Rowe Schoolcraft, *Information Respecting the History, Conditions and Prospects of the Indian Tribes of the United States: Collected and Prepared under the Direction of the Bureau of Indian Affairs.*

1854

B. F. Ellis, *The Book of American Indians* (history).

John Rollin Ridge (Chees-quat-a-lau-ny or Yellow Bird, Cherokee), *The Life and Adventures of Joaquin Murieta, the Celebrated California Bandit* (novel).

1855

Henry Wadsworth Longfellow, *The Song of Hiawatha* (epic poem).

John Brougham, *An Original Aboriginal Erratic Operatic Semi-Civilized and Demi-Savage Extravaganza, Being a Per-Version of Ye Trewe and Wonderfulle Hystorie of a Rennowned Princesse Pocahontas; or, The Gentle Savage.*

1856

James P. Beckwourth, *The Life and Adventures of James P. Beckwourth, Mountaineer, Scout, and Pioneer, and Chief of the Crow Nation of Indians*. Written from his own dictation by T. D. Bonner.

John Frost, ed. *Indian Battles, Captivities, and Adventures, from the Earliest Period to the Present Time.*

Juliette Kinzie, *Wau-Bun: The "Early Days" in the North-West.*

Henry Rowe Schoolcraft, *The Myth of Hiawatha, and Other Oral Legends, Mythologic and Allegoric of the North American Indians.*

1857

Charles M. Walcot, *Hiawatha; or, Ardent Spirits and Laughing Water, A Musical Extravaganza.*

Royal B. Stratton, *Captivity of the Oatman Girls: Being an Interesting Narrative of Life among the Apache and Mojave Indians.*

1858

Sylvester Crakes, *Five Years a Captive among the Black-Feet Indians . . . Endured by John Dixon* (fictitious captivity narrative).

Teresa Vielé, *"Following the Drum:" A Glimpse of Frontier Life.*

1859

Nelson Lee, *Three Years among the Camanches: The Narrative of Nelson Lee, the Texan Ranger.*

Randolph Marcy, *The Prairie Traveler; A Hand-book for Overland Expeditions* (with maps, illustrations, and itineraries of the principal routes between the Mississippi and the Pacific).

William Gilmore Simms, *The Cassique of Kiawah: A Colonial Romance.*

1860

Horace Greeley, *An Overland Journey from New York to San Francisco in the Summer of 1859.*

Daniel P. Thompson, *The Doomed Chief; or, Two Hundred Years Ago* (novel about King Philip).

1861

Peter Jones (Kahkewaquonaby, or Sacred Feathers/Sacred Waving Feathers, Ojibwe), *History of the Ojibway Indians, with Especial Reference to Their Conversion to Christianity.* (This was published after his death, in an edition prepared by his wife.)

1863

Sarah Wakefield, *Six Weeks in the Sioux Tepees.* (An expanded edition appeared the following year.)

1864

> J. Ross Browne, *Adventures in the Apache Country: A Tour through Arizona and Sonora.*
>
> *Miss Coleson's Narrative of Her Captivity among the Sioux Indians . . . a Victim of the Late Indian Outrages in Minnesota.*
>
> Harriet B. McConkey, *Dakota War Whoop: Indian Massacres and War in Minnesota.*

1867

> Albert Richardson, *Beyond the Mississippi: From the Great River to the Great Ocean, Life and Adventure on the Prairies, Mountains, and Pacific Coast.*

1868

> Margaret Carrington, *Ab-Sa-Ra-Ka; Home of the Crows: Being the Experience of an Officer's Wife on the Plains, and Marking the Vicissitudes of Peril and Pleasure during the Occupation of the New Route to Virginia City, Montana, 1866–7, and the Indian Hostility Thereof; with Outlines of the Natural Features and Resources of the Land, Tables of Distances, Maps, and Other Aids to the Traveler; Gathered from Observation and Other Reliable Sources.*
>
> Lydia Maria Child, *An Appeal for the Indians.*
>
> John C. Cremony, *Life among the Apaches.*
>
> John Rollin Ridge (Chees-quat-a-lau-ny, or Yellow Bird, Cherokee), *Poems* (published after Ridge's death, in an edition prepared by his wife).

1870

> Albert W. Aiken, *Metamora, the Forest King* (novel).
>
> Francis Parkman, *The Conspiracy of Pontiac; and the Indian War after the Conquest of Canada* (history).
>
> Frances Fuller Victor, *The River of the West. Life and Adventure in the Rocky Mountains and Oregon; Embracing Events in*

the Life-time of a Mountain-man and Pioneer; with the Early History of the North-Western Slope, including an Account of the Fur Traders, and Indian Tribes, the Overland Immigration, the Oregon Missions, and the Tragic Fate of Rev. Dr. Whitman and Family. Also, a Description of the Country, Its Condition, Prospects and Resources; Its Soil, Climate, and Scenery; Its Mountains, Rivers, Valleys, Deserts, and Plains; Its Inland Waters, and Natural Wonders. With Numerous Engravings (in the running for longest title in this half century).

3

Resisting Racism
William Apess as Public Intellectual

For Scott Richard Lyons

i.

Almost forgotten until the late 1970s,[1] William Apess, a Pequot, exists today in a volume of "complete works," Barry O'Connell's superbly edited *On Our Own Ground: The Complete Writings of William Apess, a Pequot* (1992), and in a body of critical work that is growing daily.[2] For those not yet familiar with Apess, I'll quickly summarize some of what is known. Apess was born in Colrain, Massachusetts, in 1798. Early in his life he was put in the care of his alcoholic grandparents, who beat him severely and then sold him as an indentured laborer when he was only four or five years old. Apess eventually ran off from his master's house and participated in the unsuccessful U.S. attack on Montreal in the War of 1812. He had taken up drinking in the army, and, after leaving it in 1815, he wandered about and held a number of odd jobs. In 1813 he had had a religious experience, and he turned to evangelical Methodism to help him regain control of his life. He was baptized into the church in 1818, and was ordained a minister in 1829. By 1834, however, he had left Methodism, founding his own "Free and United Church." Around that time, Apess went to Cape Cod to work on behalf of the Mashpee tribe, whose rights had been much curtailed by the State of Massachusetts. Although he contributed substantially to the Mashpees' achievement of a greater degree of sovereignty, for reasons not yet fully established, he fell out of favor with the tribe. Twice in January of 1836, Apess delivered a "eulogy" of the Wampanoag leader called King Philip to an audience in Boston, and in January of 1839, Apess and his second wife, Elizabeth, moved to New York City, where he died four months later of "apoplexy"—of a cerebral hemorrhage, and/or the unfortunate administration of botanic remedies by a physician. Testimony by Apess's wife and others also suggests that he had on occasion been drinking heavily.[3]

Apess's first publication was a book-length autobiography, *A Son of the Forest: The Experience of William Apes, a Native of the Forest* published in 1829, the first such text by a Native American person to be produced without the participation of a translator, amanuensis, or editor.[4] Apess followed this with an abbreviated version of his life story along with short biographies of his first wife and four other Native converts to Christianity in *The Experiences of Five Christian Indians of the Pequ'd Tribe* (1833).[5] The original edition of this book concluded with an extraordinary essay called "An Indian's Looking-Glass for the White Man," a powerful indictment of what Apess called color prejudice and what we would today call racism. (He did not reprint this essay in the 1837 edition of *The Experiences.*) Apess's account of his activism on behalf of the Mashpee Indians of Massachusetts is documented in his 1835 *Indian Nullification of the Unconstitutional Laws of Massachusetts Relative to the Marshpee Tribe; or, The Pretended Riot Explained.* In 1836 Apess published the last of his works, the text of his "eulogy" for King Philip, whom he claimed as a distant ancestor. My focus in this chapter will be on "An Indian's Looking-Glass" and the *Eulogy on King Philip* as texts directed against American racism as it most particularly oppresses American Indians and African Americans. Apess's texts work against the dominant, racialist construction of Indians as an inferior race,[6] and they contest the dominant narrative of the Jacksonian period in the tragic mode, the story of the sad-but-inevitable disappearance of the Indians. Apess insists that Native people and people of color generally are equal to the whites in the sight of God and in their intellectual and moral capacities as well. Indeed, he relies quite intensely on the notion, still debated in his time, that the American Indians derive from the Ten Lost Tribes of Israel, and that the Indians share Adam's complexion. In both texts he employs *religious* discourse to contest politically and culturally "*scientific* racism's" presumptions of Indian inferiority. Far more strongly than the Cherokee memorialists and such later-nineteenth-century writers as Lydia Maria Child, Apess makes the case that if Indian peoples were, indeed, to vanish from the East and eventually from the earth, the story of their disappearance would not be a tragic narrative of sad-but-just inevitability, but, rather, an ironic narrative in which justice is mocked as might alone makes right.[7] In his *Eulogy on King Philip*, with particularly intense awareness of the imminence of Cherokee removal, Apess offers a revisionist history of America from the Puritans to the Jacksonian period, demonstrating that the racism and greed then forcing removal upon the eastern tribes are the direct legacy of America's revered founders, the Puritans.[8] Apess was the earliest producer of Native American writing in resistance to colonialism, and he remains one of the most powerful *literary* writers—although he was not a novelist or a poet.[9] Nonetheless, as I hope to show, the worldly effectivity of his texts are in large measure the result of their powerful *language* and *style*.

In his speeches, his activism, and his writing, Apess took upon himself the role—common in his time, but only later to be more fully theorized—of the public intellectual, specifically, the oppositional public intellectual.[10] This was a role very different from the one that Hawthorne, Melville, or Washington Irving, among others, were attempting to create and embody, the role of the American man of letters. To contextualize Apess's work historically, I'll make brief mention of some of Apess's contemporaries, who, in the 1820s and 1830s also functioned as public intellectuals.

First among these was surely Ralph Waldo Emerson, Apess's contemporary and probably the most prominent public intellectual of the age. Two of Emerson's texts—both of them, like so many in this period, were first delivered as public lectures—have been mentioned as possible influences upon Apess, despite the fact that both "The American Scholar" (1837) and "The Divinity School Address" (1838) appeared later than Apess's "Indian's Looking-Glass" and *Eulogy*. But there is little doubt that some of the ideas Emerson expressed were in the air. Nonetheless, as I read both Emerson and Apess, I find it difficult to believe that Apess would have found much to inspire him in Emerson. Of greater importance to Apess, I believe, were the examples of David Walker, Frederick Douglass, Elias Boudinot, and even, tangentially, as Sandra Gustafson has suggested, Joseph Smith, who founded Mormonism, and the less well-known Mordecai Manuel Noah, who, in 1825, sought to found an independent Jewish state in New York to be called Ararat.

One of the epigraphs to Gustafson's essay is from Emerson's "Divinity School Address." She cites his observation that the "need was never greater of new revelation than now" (1994, 31), and she refers to Emerson's "discomfort with the Puritans' heritage of racial violence" (32), an issue, as we shall see further, that a number of progressive New Englanders would also confront. Mild as one may now find some of Emerson's assertions, they were considered radical enough at the time to provoke outrage in newspapers and pamphlets, and even a book-length attack, *The Latest Form of Infidelity* (1839). Emerson's alma mater, Harvard, was sufficiently upset by his "divinity school" address to withhold invitation for him to speak again for a full thirty years! In 1837, in the address published as "The American Scholar," Emerson had written that "action is with the scholar subordinate, but it is essential. . . . Without it thought can never ripen into truth" (2003, 1140). He further asserts that "he who has put forth his total strength in fit actions, has the richest return of wisdom" (1141). Emerson must surely have understood that the intellectual or "scholar's" action might have material consequences beyond the scholar/actor himself, and yet his intense focus on the self very nearly blocks that understanding. Although Emerson was most decidedly opposed to slavery, and acquainted with many of the New England abolitionists, he could not persuade himself to act on behalf of their cause until the 1850s.

In regard to the American Indians, Emerson certainly shared the general eastern distaste for President Andrew Jackson's removal policies, although it is only in his letter to Jackson's successor, President Martin Van Buren, that he committed himself publicly to the attempt to prevent the Cherokees' forced removal (this, in spite of the fact that, as noted in the preceding chapter, he could not divest himself of the notion of the Indians' racial inferiority). Emerson seems to have become aware of the imminent forced removal of the Cherokees only on April 19, 1838, writing agitatedly in his journal for that day, "I can do nothing. Why shriek? Why strike ineffectual blows?" Yet the very next day he composed the first draft of his letter to Van Buren, noting, "the amount of [it], [to] be sure, is merely a Scream but sometimes a scream is better than a thesis." A journal entry for the following day records his sense that having written the letter was "a deliverance that does not deliver the soul." Obviously, even this level of public action—writing a letter to the president—was not easy for him. The letter does not seem actually to have been sent to Van Buren. Rather, it was first published in the issue of May 14, 1838, of the *National Daily Intelligencer*, whose proprietors acknowledged that they published it "with some reluctance."

Far more important contemporary models for Apess as oppositional public intellectual, I believe, were Elias Boudinot, David Walker, and Frederick Douglass. I will make only brief reference to them in order further to contextualize Apess's work. I'll then move forward in time to look at some of the writers who would more fully theorize the situation of the oppositional public intellectual.

Elias Boudinot was born about 1804 at Oothcaloga, a Cherokee "progressive" town, in northwestern Georgia. His birth name was

Gallegina, and he was also called Buck Watie. At the age of six, his father, Oo'watie, or David Watie, sent him to a nearby Moravian Mission School, where he continued until the age of seventeen, at which time he set out for the East, again to a mission school, this one in Cornwall, Connecticut.[11] It was on this trip that Buck Watie met the elderly Elias Boudinot (1740–1821), who had been a member of the Continental Congress and was at the time president of the American Bible Society. The elder Boudinot had written a book whose complete title is not often cited. I am referring to *A Star in the West; or, a Humble Attempt to Discover the Long Lost Ten Tribes of Israel, Preparatory to Their Return to Their Beloved City, Jerusalem* (1816). In it he developed the still-prevalent theory that Native people were descended from the Ten Lost Tribes of Israel. Consistent with an old Cherokee practice of changing names and also with a newer Cherokee practice of adopting the names of prominent whites, Buck Watie took the name Elias Boudinot.

Although his family was staunchly progressive, Boudinot opposed removal until sometime in 1832. In what is probably his best-known work, "An Address to the Whites," delivered in Philadelphia in 1826, he makes the same case that the Cherokees would make for themselves in their "Memorials" to Congress, opposing removal and insisting that his people are not only able to attain Christian civilization, but that they are well on the way to that attainment. He concludes, in Maureen Konkle's words, by noting that Indian "extinction is a possibility, not an inevitability, the result of the actions of Euro-Americans, not the nature of the Indians" (2004, 56). As I have said, this was very much the point of some of the Cherokee memorials to Congress, just as it was much later (as we noted in the preceding chapter) of texts such as Lydia Maria Child's *An Appeal for the Indians* (1868).[12]

Boudinot took on the job of editing the *Cherokee Phoenix*, the first American newspaper to print articles in an Indian language (in the syllabary Sequoyah had invented in 1821), and also in English. In his 1827 "Prospectus" for the paper, Boudinot indicates in his very first sentence that this "paper [is] published exclusively for [the Cherokees] and under their direction" (in Perdue 1996, 89). And in the first issue, dated February 21, 1828, he alerts his readers to the fact that "the design of this paper . . . is the benefit of the Cherokees" (in Perdue 1996, 91). He does note that the paper is also addressed to "those who wish well to the Indian race." Boudinot continued as editor until 1832, when the Cherokee Council asked him to withdraw because of his support for removal.

This is to say that, soon after the passage of the Indian Removal Act in 1830, and, in particular, once Georgia had instituted a lottery to dispose of Cherokee lands to white citizens of the state, Boudinot, along with other members of his family and several well-to-do Cherokee planters, concluded that further resistance to removal was hopeless (see chapter 4). In 1835, he; his uncle, Major Ridge; and a distinct minority of wealthy Cherokees met at the Cherokee nation's capital, where, on December 29, they signed the Treaty of New Echota, agreeing to exchange Cherokee lands in the Southeast for land in Indian Country, present-day Oklahoma, thus giving Jackson the required legal authority to remove the eastern Cherokees. In the late spring of 1839, when the last of the Cherokee people to survive the Trail of Tears (see chapter 4) arrived in Indian Country, several Cherokees came to Boudinot to ask for medicine. Two followed him as he led them to the mission dispensary, and they attacked him with a knife and a tomahawk, leaving him to die. On the same day, his relatives Major Ridge and John Ridge were also killed for their part in signing the treaty. The murderers may have acted in accord with a traditional practice of vengeance, taking lives in recompense for the lives lost by those who had died on the Trail, and also to fulfill the law passed by the Cherokee Council in 1829 making it a capital crime to cede Cherokee lands.

Apess (who had died of natural causes, more or less, only a few months before Boudinot) surely knew of Boudinot's work, and, indeed, Konkle's extensive research has unearthed a letter suggesting that in 1832 "an evening of oratory on behalf of the Cherokees . . . included" not only Boudinot, but also the minister Lyman Beecher, "the Massachusetts congressman Edward Everett [to whom we shall return], and an unnamed native orator who was William Apess" (2004, 99).[13] Apess had earlier replaced John Ridge as a speaker in Boston, and "in May, June, and July several notices appeared in the *Liberator* [William Lloyd Garrison's abolitionist newspaper] for sermons or lectures Apess would give," on a variety of subjects, among them "an Address on the subject of Slavery" (100). Apess's association with Garrison, such as it was, makes it possible that he might have known David Walker, and, perhaps even Frederick Douglass—although Walker died in 1830, and Douglass did not escape from slavery until 1838, nor did he come to New Bedford, Massachusetts, until shortly before Apess would have left for New York.[14]

David Walker was born a free black in Wilmington, North Carolina, but his exact birth date has not yet been established. The Boston Index of Deaths lists him as dying on August 6, 1830, of consumption at the age of thirty-three—I am relying mostly on Peter Hinks's fine book, *To Awaken My Afflicted Brethren: David Walker and the Problem of Antebellum Slave Resistance* (1997), to calculate that Walker was born only a year before William Apess. Who his father was is another matter of some debate, and his early years in the South are also not well documented. He seems to have been in Boston by 1826, and, according to James Turner, "Walker's *Appeal* was written originally as a series of articles that he used as the text of speeches and presentations that he delivered in Boston and around the New England region in defense of the abolition of slavery" (1993, 10). Among other antislavery publications, Garrison's *Liberator* was one to which Walker contributed for a time. His own short book, with its lengthy title, *David Walker's Appeal to the Coloured Citizens of the World, but in Particular, and Very Expressly, to Those of the United States of America*, was published in 1829 and surreptitiously was distributed along the eastern seaboard, even in the slave-holding South. A third, revised, and somewhat expanded edition appeared in 1830, the year of Walker's untimely death.[15] Apess seems not to have been much involved with Garrison and the abolitionist movement before 1832, but it seems fairly certain that he would have been aware of the *Appeal*. Indeed, Maureen Konkle has suggested that the first paragraph of *An Indian's Looking-Glass* is similar to the first paragraph of the *Appeal*, a matter to which I will return (2004, 116).

Before addressing Apess's texts, I want further to develop the conception of the public intellectual by looking at some of those who have theorized the concept in the twentieth century. I will consider Edward Said's Reith Lectures of 1993, published as *Representations of the Intellectual* (1996); comments by Antonio Gramsci in his *Prison Notebooks* (1971), written between 1929 and 1935; and Jean-Paul Sartre's preface to Frantz Fanon's *Wretched of the Earth* (1961), which first appeared in English translation in the United States in 1968.[16] For these writers, the term *public intellectual* is, in a certain sense, a tautology, for the category of the intellectual, they make clear, has meaning only in social, which is to say public, terms.

To cite Gramsci's homely example, although we all may occasionally fry some eggs, that doesn't make us chefs. Likewise, although all humans think, that doesn't make all humans intellectuals. What makes the intellectual is his or her social function, the speech, action, and writing undertaken publicly on behalf of a class, a group, a people, a nation. Gramsci offered an important distinction between what he called the "traditional intellectuals" and the "organic intellectuals." The former are a professional class, of clerics once, of academics, and others, later, who disseminate, in a presumptively neutral fashion, the ideology sustaining a society's dominant or ruling class. A newer professional class derives from the media. These "intellectuals," ranging from those who today report what Fox Network outrageously calls "fair and balanced" news, to such deeply learned men as, among others, Bill O'Reilly, Rush Limbaugh, or Michael Savage, assume, in a new (and astoundingly vulgar) fashion, the role of traditional intellectuals. Organic intellectuals are those who rise—sometimes even from the ranks of clerics and professors—to provide a rationale or ideological legitimacy for an emerging group, a people, a nation. (Thus, Philip Deloria, in a recent essay, refers to "the existence of any number of organic Indian intellectuals" (2003, 670), in addition to academic Indian intellectuals.)

The emerging groups for whom organic intellectuals speak may themselves be elites vying to replace a dominant class or group. But Gramsci, Said, and Sartre are most interested in those who work on behalf of the dispossessed and oppressed, organic *oppositional* intellectuals who, in the phrase Said takes from Michel Foucault—it has, curiously, begun to show up regularly in the speeches of members of Congress and on television—"speak truth to power." In a colonial situation, whether that of Fanon's Algeria in the late 1950s, of Said's Palestine in the 1990s and to this day, or of Apess's United States in the 1830s and indeed in the present as well, speaking truth to power can, at the very least, induce a measure of shame, and "shame," as Sartre notes, "is a revolutionary sentiment" (1979, 14).

Thus, during the Algerian revolution against French colonial rule, Sartre, in 1961, wrote, "It is not right, my fellow countrymen, you who know very well all the crimes committed in our name . . . that you do not breathe a word of them to anyone, not even to your own soul, for fear of having to stand in judgment of yourself" (1979, 30).

We will soon quote a number of extraordinary passages from Apess in which he also insists that white Americans must take their crimes to heart. (It must be noted that this is a point of special importance to Americans, who "know very well all the crimes committed" at Abu Ghraib, Guantanamo Bay, Haditha, and in the secret prisons to which we "render" suspects to be tortured.) The point of such speech, whether by Sartre and Fanon or by William Apess, as Said notes, is that "in writing and speaking, one's aim is not... to show everyone how right one is but rather to try to induce a change in the moral climate whereby aggression is seen as such, the unjust punishment of peoples or individuals is either prevented or given up (1996, 100).

Said continues that the intellectual, by his or her speech, writing, and action seeks to "give greater human scope to what a particular race or nation suffered, to associate that experience with the sufferings of others" (1996, 44). I have referred elsewhere to such practices as cosmopolitan comparativism in the fight against colonialism,[17] and Said's words seem to me to describe quite exactly William Apess's procedure, for he often links the suffering of his Native American people to the suffering of African Americans, a linkage that I have already noted and that I will examine further below. Sandra Gustafson also points to Said's phrase—in his book, *Culture and Imperialism* (1993)—"the voyage in," by which colonized people "enter into the discourse of Europe and the West, to mix with it, transform it, to make it acknowledge marginalized or suppressed or forgotten histories" (in Gustafson 1994, 34). Scott Stevens suggests that some of Apess's work is best "understood as a chapter in the history of an ethnic group written from within. His task is to create an alternative, and in many cases a corrective, historical model" (1997, 78). This very well describes Apess's rhetorical strategy.[18]

ii.

Although *An Indian's Looking-Glass* was not delivered orally by Apess, its oratorical style is immediately apparent. The regular use of direct address—the address is, here, to the "reader"—and the number of insistent interrogatives—Now I ask; Now I would ask, and so on—all suggest a situation in which a speaker stands before an audience, sometimes sharply pointing a finger. It is tempting to ponder the influence on Apess of some form of oral traditional performance, but he nowhere writes of Pequot—or any other Native—oral performances. Thus, without entirely ruling out the possibility that Native oral performance of one sort or another *might* have been an influence on Apess, one can still point to the fact that impassioned public address—Boudinot, Walker, Emerson, Douglass, in addition to Daniel Webster and Edward Everett (Apess specifically mentions these last two, see below)—and a strong reliance on oratorical power was an important aspect of the work of public intellectuals in his time.

Well aware that Indian peoples had regularly been consigned to passivity (because they are inferior to the ever-active whites) and the past (they are a last remnant, a doomed and dying race), Apess opens with a sentence that insists upon the presence, agency, and equality of at least one Indian person, the author himself. "Having a desire to place a few things before my fellow creatures," Apess begins, asserting, with the participial "Having," and the characterization of his audience as his "fellow creatures," the activity, contemporaneity, and equality of the Indian writer,[19] Apess continues: "*Now* I ask if degradation has not been heaped long enough upon the Indians?" (1992, 155, my emphasis). The number of interrogatives, as I have said, is high, with the present indicative tenses of the beginning mixing with conditionals.[20]

Let me turn here for a moment to Apess's diction. It is in his third paragraph that he writes of the neighbors of the Indians that they are people "who have no principle" (1992, 156), while the second sentence of his fourth paragraph asks whether Indians are not "said to be men of talents" (156). Principles and talents are, of course, moral and intellectual qualities. But, as Thoreau would soon establish (learning this, I am increasingly convinced, from Apess among others), both of these words also reference the economic and financial: principle and interest ("talents" appear in the Bible as monetary units). Apess will develop the notion that the materially well-off whites are not at all superior to the Indians from a religious and moral perspective because they are unprincipled—bankrupt—when it comes to dealing with those of a different skin color: his fourth paragraph, for example, has five uses of "principle" or a variant, and in every case this is to establish the *un*principled actions of white in regard to red (156).

Apess uses "black" as an adjective to describe morals—principles—that have become corrupted by an aversion to black or colored *skin*. Apess speaks of "the impure black principle . . . as corrupt and unholy as it can be" (156), leading to his notation of the "black inconsistency that you place before me," the extremely bad "principle," of considering "skins of color—more disgraceful than all the skins that Jehovah ever made" (157). Not only is this bad, but it is absurd and ludicrous as well, inasmuch as God "has made fifteen colored people to one white" (157).[21]

All of this, obviously enough, is delivered with a full freight of irony; Apess's use of irony—here, as a rhetorical device rather than a structuring principle—is something notable even earlier in his text. Apess's first strong irony, for example, appeared in his seventh paragraph, where he wrote: "But, reader, I acknowledge that this is a confused world, and I am not seeking for office, but merely placing before you the *black* inconsistency that you place before me—which is ten times *blacker* than any skin that you will find in the universe" (157, emphasis added).

This is the paragraph that includes the ironic observation noted just above, that if skins of color, "black or red skins or any other skin of color" were disgraceful in God's eye, "it appears that he has disgraced himself a great deal—for he has made fifteen colored people to one white and placed them here upon this earth" (157). Apess will use ironic discourse again and again to induce the sort of shame in his audience that might produce a revolution in its moral feeling, and, so, in its future behavior.

Apess goes further with his speculations concerning skins of color. Making the point that only the Indians retain Adam's color, he insists throughout that the Jews were a colored people and that, as I've noted, the Indians must derive from the Ten Lost

Tribes of Israel. Sandra Gustafson links this sort of commentary with Emerson's attempt to reformulate "the Puritan sense of an Hebraic American identity" (Gustafson 1994, 34), part of a project "to create a usable Puritan past for the entire nation" (35). She continues, "Emerson's plea for justice to the Cherokees, like Garrisonian abolitionism, reflects the separatist strain in Puritan culture" (35). It's in this context that she mentions Mordecai Manuel Noah, who attempted to establish Ararat, a kind of state within a state for Jews, in Buffalo, New York. The project failed. Gustafson also mentions Joseph Smith's publication of the Book of Mormon in 1830 (the year, coincidentally, of the passage of the Indian Removal Act), and, of course, the Mormons' attempts to establish themselves as an autonomous community. But, as David Hollinger points out, as early as 1818 Congress had rejected the "notion of legally protected territorial enclaves for nationality groups," including those "[for] Irish immigrants in Ohio . . . and thirty years later for German immigrants in Texas" (1995, 91). Georgia, would, of course, soon attempt to extinguish Cherokee sovereignty within its borders.

Gustafson relates Apess to the tradition of "taking up the Israelite origins theory [for Native people] as a means of validating non-European, non-Christian cultures . . . , in the course of his life transform[ing] it into a justification for native independence" (Gustafson 1994, 36). This is intriguing, although I think the situation is somewhat more complex. In regard to the Mashpees, Apess worked successfully to obtain for the tribe a greater degree of sovereignty, and he spoke and wrote on behalf of Cherokee sovereignty. In regard to Philip's Wampanoags and his own Pequot people, any claims to "native independence" seem to me not immediately cultural or political in the specific sense of the issue of national sovereignty but, rather, first and foremost, moral and Christian: these people are and were as good as you, and they are entitled to the same justice you would want for yourself. If that is accurate, then his position is hardly "separatist." Meanwhile, I think Gustafson is surely correct in reading Apess as someone who spoke for peoples, groups, nations—particularly Indian nations. It is in the eighth paragraph that Apess launches his bitter and powerful indictment of the white man's crimes, a strong challenge to the whites' presumptive racial superiority. Echoing the strategy with which he began, he poses a rhetorical question: "Now let me ask you, white man. . . ." He then offers the truly horrifying possibility that if all the world's "different skins were put together, and each skin had its national crimes written upon it—which skin do you think would have the greatest?"[22] I have noted earlier Apess's linkage of the outrageous mistreatment of Indians because of the color of their skin to the mistreatment of blacks. In the paragraph here at issue, Apess's charge against the white citizens of the United States is not only that they have robbed "a *nation* almost of their whole continent, and murder[ed] their women and children," but as well that they have robbed "another *nation* to till their grounds and welter out their days under the lash with hunger and fatigue under the scorching rays of a burning sun" (1992, 157, emphasis added).

The verb choice—"welter"—is interesting in that Apess knows well that "the lash" raises *welts* on one's back. Perhaps most extraordinary in this particular indictment of the U.S. Americans is Apess's repeated use of the word "nation" and his complete avoidance of the word "race." Indians and Africans are *nations*, a political term, not races, a putatively scientific term.[23] As noted in the last chapter, the word "race" was in common usage in a great deal of American writing by 1833—it would become even more common later in the century—but it does not appear even once in "An Indian's Looking-Glass." This is surely no accident. Apess here engages in what Linda Tuhiwai Smith has called "reframing." "Reframing," she writes, "is about taking much greater control over the ways in which indigenous issues and social problems are discussed and handled" (1999, 153).

Apess's linkage of blacks and Indians as subjects of oppression has abundant precedent in his period. Linda Kerber writes that "in the decade of the 1820s... the slavery issue was largely muted in the public press; but the Indian issue was not" (1975, 271). Kerber traces the ways in which concern for the abolition of slavery and for Indian rights persists in a number of important writers (e.g., Lydia Maria Child, as already noted, but also the poets John Greenleaf Whittier and James Russell Lowell, among many others) and public figures (William Lloyd Garrison; James G. Birney, who served briefly in the 1820s as a lawyer for the Cherokees; and former president John Quincy Adams).[24] And, to be sure, Apess himself was involved with some of the abolitionists and had given antislavery lectures.[25]

Apess's counter-discourse, I have said, grounds itself in religious authority, something even the presumptive scientists had to take seriously into account.[26] Thus Apess can rhetorically ask, "Is not religion the same now under a colored skin as it ever was? If so, I would ask, why is not a man of color respected?" (1992, 158). He then goes on to adduce scriptural support for these arguments, after which, again directly addressing his audience, he throws out the challenge: "But you may ask: Who are the children of God? Perhaps you may say, none but white. If so, the word of the Lord is not true" (159). At this point, Apess boldly engages what he knows may be for some the unacknowledged heart of these matters: "Perhaps you will say that if we admit you to all of these privileges you will want more. I expect I can guess what that is— Why, say you, there would be intermarriages" (159). This "would be nothing strange or new to me," Apess writes, and he virtually taunts his audience, noting, "I do not wonder that you blush, many of you, while you read," becoming as *red* as those against whom those "many" discriminate. He continues with this irony—an irony of the sort, once more, that Thoreau would later exploit—assuring the reader that he is "not looking for a wife, having one of the finest cast" (160).

The penultimate paragraph repeats what has been central to

Apess's argument thus far, as the author again addresses the reader directly: "By what you read, you may learn how deep your principles are. I should say they were skin deep" (160). He assures the reader that many "men of fame" advocate the cause of the Indians, among them Daniel Webster, Edward Everett, and William Wirt, and he takes pains to conclude on a positive note, exhorting his readers to be hopeful: "Do not get tired, ye noblehearted—only think how many poor Indians want their wounds done up daily; the Lord will reward you, and pray you stop not till this tree of distinction be leveled, and the mantle of prejudice torn from every American heart—then shall peace pervade the Union" (160–61).[27]

iii.

Apess's *Eulogy on King Philip* was orally presented twice in Boston, on January 8, 1836, and again on January 26 of the same year, "in a shortened form" (O'Connell 1992, 275). Maureen Konkle has noted that January 8 was the anniversary of President Andrew Jackson's defeat of the British at the Battle of New Orleans, and thus Apess spoke "on the day most identified with Jackson" (131) in order to tell "the story of how one gets from the Puritans to New Echota" (133), the treaty enabling Jackson legally to remove the eastern Cherokees.[28] Publication of the first performance also occurred in 1836, while the second, shorter version, appeared in print in 1837. Both editions had as their epigraph, "Who shall stand in after years in this famous temple [presumably the Odeon, in Federal Street] and declare that Indians are not men? If men, then heirs to the same inheritance"—as all other men, it would surely seem. The epigraph is true to the address Apess's Boston audience would have heard, in that Apess reiterated in the *Eulogy* what I have observed in "An Indian's Looking-Glass," a passionate insistence on the equal value of all in the eyes of God, regardless of the color of their skin. What Apess will add to his attack on nineteenth-century American racism is the insistence that it derives directly from the Puritans, an interpretation of American history in the early republic that, if not unique, is nonetheless radical.

For Puritanism, as Philip Gould has noted, was "a protean metaphor for the early republic" (1996, 8), serving as "an arena in which early nationals negotiated the contemporary meanings of republican virtue" (9). What Gould calls "'metaphorical Puritanism' constituted a political-cultural act of recuperation of a traditionally conservative ideology" (28), and Puritan "'virtue' serviced a larger cultural project of social and political containment" (31). Historical fiction of the sort I have discussed in the previous chapter—*Hobomok, Hope Leslie* and Cooper's *Wept*, among others—emerged in the 1820s and was " bracketed," as Gould remarks, "by the bicentennial commemorations of the founding of Plymouth and the Massachusetts Bay colony" (17). Cooper, as already noted, was highly critical of the Puritans and—once more in Gould's words—he exposed "the unmitigated greed contemporary New England historians [and literary authors] rationalized in order to defend their Puritan ancestors" (18), attacking "The Discourse of Puritan Empire" (47). But Cooper also abhorred the "androgynous masculinity" and "sentimental republicanism" (Gould 1996, 136) suggested in the work of Child, Sedgwick, and others. This left him in the contradictory position of advocating the martial prowess and masculine virtue of Puritan warriors—whose acquisitiveness he thoroughly disapproved. So, too, did he disapprove of Jackson—whose martial prowess and masculine virtue explicitly derived from the Puritans.

Apess, to the contrary, is entirely consistent in his interpretation of American history from the Puritan period to his own Jacksonian era. He rewrites the dominant, comic narrative of the progress of civilization and its parallel narrative of tragic Indian decline in the ironic mode. His is neither the happy story of the progress of white "civilization" nor the sad-but-just story of the decline of Indian "savagery." Rather, it is an ironic narrative in which white triumph is an unjust consequence of force and greed.

Apess's decision to extol Philip as exemplary American—he calls him the "greatest man that ever lived upon the American shores" (1992, 290)—is surely carefully calculated.[29] In his very first publication, *A Son of the Forest* (1829), his autobiography, Apess had written that his "grandfather was a white man and married a female attached to the royal family of Philip, king of the Pequot tribe of Indians" (3); indeed, he asserted that his "grandmother was . . . the king's granddaughter and a fair and beautiful woman" (4).

But Philip was not a Pequot. Barry O'Connell, in his introduction to the complete works of William Apess, writes that "Philip was not king of the Pequots, a culture located in the southeastern part of what is now Connecticut, but the sachem of the Pokanokets located in and around Mount Hope in Rhode Island" (1992, 4).[30] Pokanoket seems to have been the name for Wampanoags living in Rhode Island, and, as noted earlier, Washington Irving's influential essay, originally published in 1814, was titled, "Philip of Pokanoket." But from the seventeenth century until the nineteenth century, in which Apess wrote, Philip was regularly referred to as Wampanoag. Kim McQuaid, who identifies Philip as Wampanoag (1977), also calls the Mashpees Wampanoags, and Jill Lepore has noted that there was a community of Wampanoags living in Mashpee (1998, 184) (although the ancestors of the Mashpee Wampanoags were not involved in King Philip's War; see Lepore 1998, 236). John Augustus Stone's enormously popular play about King Philip of 1829, "performed until at least 1887, and one of the most widely produced plays in the history of nineteenth-century theater" (191), was called *Metamora; or, The Last of the Wampanoags*. Other writing of the period (e.g., John Greenleaf Whittier's poem, "Metacom"), along with imitations and parodies of Stone's play (e.g., John Brougham's *Metamora; or, the Last of the Pollywogs* [1847]), regularly spoke of Philip as Wampanoag.[31]

Why, then, does William Apess call Philip a Pequot? He may simply have been unclear on this matter, or, as noted, simply mistaken.[32] I think it more likely, however, that the young—then just past thirty years old—but already very accomplished rhetorician had some strategic intent in appropriating Philip to his own Pequot people. At the least, Apess might have chosen to call Philip a Pequot simply to imply his own descent from a "royal" line; this son of the forest, that is to say, is not just a vaguely "noble savage," but one descended from royalty.

Additionally, inasmuch as Apess's purpose in eulogizing Philip is to revise the narrative of the European invasion of the Americas from the Puritans to his own time, he may wish to associate "King Philip's War" with an earlier war against his own Pequot people. In the Pequot War of 1637, Apess's ancestors were "the objects" of what Barry O'Connell has called "the first deliberately genocidal war conducted by the English in North America" (1992, xxv). The Puritans' later aggression against "King Philip," precipitating what they called *his* "War," might therefore be seen to descend in a direct line from earlier Puritan aggressions, aggressions—if Philip is thought of as a Pequot—against the living descendants of the same people barely fifty years later.[33] Finally, if, as I suspect, Apess is aware of the fact that his own Pequot people, along with the Mohegans and some Christian Indians, fought on the side of the English *against* Philip (see Lepore 1998, 118) in the seventeenth century, he may here also be engaged in a different sort of revisionist history. As the self-appointed eulogist of Philip, Apess, himself a Pequot, might want to claim not merely kinship (his grandmother may have been Philip's granddaughter) but a tribal-national connection to Philip, and to make this connection he must blur the fact of historical conflict between the Pequots and the Wampanoags in the last quarter of the seventeenth century. This, to be sure, is speculation.

Apart from any presumed relation to Philip, Apess surely was drawn to him as a subject because of the very considerable amount of attention—we have already noted some of it—that had been paid to Philip in a body of literary, historical, and oratorical work from the Puritan writers of the seventeenth century to his own early nineteenth century. Linda Kerber makes the point that the decade 1820–29 opened with the publication of *Yamoyden: A Tale of King Philip* and ended in 1829 with the publication of *Metamora*, a play that continued to be performed for some forty years, as already remarked.[34] Its hero, Kerber writes, is "the same King Philip, who is shown as valiantly resisting white encroachment" (1975, 272). Jill Lepore has done the most substantial recent study of American attention to King Philip in her *The Name of War: King Philip's War and the Origins of American Identity*. King Philip's War and King Philip's fate are exactly what Apess examines in order to offer major revisions of the construction of "American identity" in the Jacksonian period.

King Philip's War, as Gould asserts, was seen as "a conflict of extremely high stakes where the winner would control the destiny of New England" (1996, 157). Although Puritan authors had demonized Philip, a considerable number of Apess's white contemporaries instead chose to represent him as a sympathetic, if inevitably doomed, patriot and protector of his people and his lands, a tragic hero whose fate was ordained if not by God (as the Puritans, and some later writers, would have it) then by the "laws of nature."[35] We have no study of Apess's reading, and it is not likely that materials for such a study will be found (although Konkle refers to the contents of his library in 1836; see Konkle 2004, 153). But I believe there is one text centering on Philip and the war with the Puritans that Apess not only knew but that his *Eulogy* specifically wishes to engage and contest. I am referring to Edward Everett's "Address Delivered at Bloody Brook, in South Deerfield, September 30, 1835."[36] Although we cannot know for sure, it is even possible that Apess was among Everett's audience on that day.

Everett's talk follows in a long line of "bicentennial commemorations of the founding of Plymouth and the Massachusetts Bay Colony" from the 1820s, as Philip Gould has noted (1996, 17). Thus, we have such texts as Noah Porter's "Forefather's Day Oration" of 1820, called "A Discourse of the Settlement of New England," and the eminent Lyman Beecher's "Sermon Delivered at Plymouth, on the 22d of December, 1827," along with texts by Daniel Webster and others. Everett's "Address" is specifically "In Commemoration of the fall of the 'Flower of Essex,' at that spot, in King Philip's War, September 18, (O[ld] S[tyle]) 1675." The "Flower of Essex" are "her hopeful young men" (Everett 1835, 24). Everett's lengthy speech on the occasion of the dedication of a monument to these fallen Puritan warriors emplots the colonists' struggle against Philip and his people in the comic mode, as had the Puritans themselves. Thus, a representative quotation from Everett's address states that "if we turn our thoughts to the grand design with which America was *colonized*, to the *success* with which, under *Providence*, that design has been *crowned*, I own I find it difficult to express myself in terms of moderation" (35, my emphases).

Everett's narration of the Puritans' victory as triumphal comedy implies a counternarrative, the tragic story of Philip and his people's defeat. Another representative quotation from Everett has him imagining "the *ill-starred* chieftain, who, hunted to his last retreat, . . . seized his gun," at which point, after an Englishman fires and misses, "an Indian fires and shoots the fallen chief through the heart. . . . Such was the *fate* of Philip" (Everett 1835, 27, my emphases).[37] Acting as organic, oppositional, public intellectual, Apess writes against Everett's performance as traditional intellectual. He insists that Philip's defeat and the subsequent dispossession and degradation of the Native population is a story that is not comic, as Everett and the Puritans emplot it (happily, the good is triumphant and an admirable society is established). Neither is it tragic for Philip and his descendants, as emplotted by Everett and a great many writers more sympathetic to Philip and his people (sadly, but inevitably, a "noble savage" and his people meet their fated end). Rather, Apess will insist that the defeat of Philip and its consequences for America constitute a narrative that is ironic in the extreme (greed and treachery are unjustly rewarded). As I have noted above, this is the same ironic story the

Cherokees' "Memorial to Congress" of February 1830, which petitioned against the Indian Removal Bill, sought to substitute for the Jacksonian narrative of the Native's tragic disappearance before the white man's triumphant, comic progress.

Apess had twice been an autobiographer, and his first approach to Philip is biographical: "The first inquiry," he proclaims on the second page of his text (but this is indeed the text of an oral performance), "is: Who *is* Philip?" He begins to answer this question by noting that Philip "*was* the descendant of one of the most celebrated chiefs in the known world" (1992, 278, my emphases). But the present tense of the question is crucial. For Apess had insisted in his second paragraph that just as "the immortal Washington lives endeared and engraven on the hearts of every white in America, never to be forgotten in time—even such is the immortal Philip honored, as held in memory by the degraded but yet grateful descendants who appreciate his character (277).[38]

Apess insists upon equating Washington and Philip (he will return to this later) and insists, as well, upon the equality, so far as their common humanity is concerned, of whites, Indians, and all persons of color. As Washington presently lives in the hearts of white America, so, too, does Philip presently live in the hearts of red America. He has not tragically vanished, nor—however "degraded" by the depredations of the settlers—have the Natives.

To understand better who Philip was and is, Apess, as several times noted, offers a revisionist history of the Puritan invasion of America.[39] He documents the Puritans' many "inhuman" acts (282) and rhetorically asks his audience, "And who, my dear sirs, were wanting of the name of savages—whites or Indians? Let justice answer" (283).[40] He develops this line of argument by describing further savage acts on the part of the "lewd Pilgrims," citing, in particular, "one Standish, a vile and malicious fellow!" (284). Apess then asks, "And do you believe that Indians cannot feel and see as well as white people? If you think so, you are mistaken. Their power of feeling and knowing is as quick as yours. . . .

But if the real sufferers say one word, they are denounced as being wild and *savage* beasts" (285, emphasis added). Considering the treatment of Native people at the hands of the Puritan colonizers, Apess says "to the sons of the Pilgrims (as Job said about the day of his birth) let the day be dark, the 22d day of December 1622; let it be forgotten in your celebration, in your speeches, and by the burying of the rock that your fathers first put their foot upon" (286).[41]

Apess's vehemence, here, seems very much a response to what he would surely have taken as outrageously insulting remarks made by Everett, for example, Everett's claim, "That the settlers made as near an approach to the spirit of the gospel, in their dealings with the Indians, as the frailty of our natures admits, under the circumstances under which they were placed, is clear" (Everett 1835, 32).[42]

Apess continues his narration of Philip's life history, urging that we see clearly the ways in which Philip was *not* treated in "the spirit of the gospel," but, to the contrary, was insulted and abused by the putatively God-fearing Puritan invaders. From this perspective, Apess rhetorically asks, "Is it not certain that the Plymouth people strove to pick a quarrel with Philip and his men?" (1992, 293). He is referring here to the Puritans' sponsorship of the Indian preacher, John Sassamon, who, Apess has no doubt, was "a traitor . . . the more to be detested than any other" (293). When Apess comes to an account of the war that finally broke out between the settlers and the Indians, he insists upon Philip's military prowess, in spite of his having stated in the first moments of his *Eulogy* that he did not "approve of war as being the best method of bowing to the haughty tyrant" (277).[43] Describing Philip's death, Apess is at pains to insist that he was "fired upon by an *Indian* and killed dead upon the spot" (302, emphasis added), so that "the Pilgrims did not have the pleasure of tormenting him" (302). The Puritans do, however, have the grim pleasure of quartering Philip's body, then giving his head and one hand "to the Indian who shot him," later displaying the head for twenty years "upon a gibbet" in Plymouth, while the hand goes to Boston "where it was exhibited in *savage* triumph" (302, emphasis added). I do not know whether Apess had read Montaigne, but he nonetheless echoes him, remarking, "I can rejoice that no such evil conduct is recorded of the Indians, that they never hung up any of the white warriors who were head men" (302–3).[44] This leads Apess back to his critique of Cotton Mather and his bloody-minded rejoicing at Philip's fate, a most unfortunate precedent for the subsequent history of Indian-white relations in America.

Everett had made no mention whatever of this Puritan butchery, although he does bemoan the fate of Philip's wife and son, "sold into slavery; West Indian slavery!—an Indian princess and her child, sold from the cool breezes of Mount Hope, from the wild freedom of a New England forest, to gasp under the lash, beneath the blazing sun of the tropics!" (1835, 28–29). Yet Everett's lament does not extend itself to criticism of the noble Puritans who effected this sale. No wonder, then, that Apess will forthrightly state, "I do not hesitate to say that through the prayers, preaching, and example of those pretended pious has been the foundation of all the slavery and degradation in the American colonies toward colored people. Experience has taught me that this has been a most sorry and wretched doctrine to us poor ignorant Indians" (1992, 304).

The irony of this last self-description is intensified as Apess further illustrates how it is that the Puritan foundation of America is the condition for the color prejudice he finds everywhere in nineteenth-century America. He tells his audience that he will mention "two or three things to amuse [them] a little." Returning to the autobiographical mode for a moment, the personal anecdotes he narrates are bitter, full of a dark ironic humor. Apess recalls a time "about 15 years ago" when he was passing through Connecticut, "where they are so pious that they kill the cats for killing rats, and whip the beer barrels for working upon the Sabbath"

(304). It happened that he called upon a rich man, "very pious," a member of his own church, to ask if he could stay the night. The man does not outright refuse, but allows Apess, on "a severe cold night," only "a little wood but no bed, because [Apess] was an Indian" (305). "Another Christian," Apess says, was so very Christian as to ask him "to dine with him," but not at the same table: "I thought this a queer compliment indeed" (305). A third anecdote involves a man at an inn in Lexington, who, unaware that Apess is himself an Indian, "began to say they [Indians] ought to be exterminated." Apess writes, "I took it up in our defense, though not boisterous but coolly; and when we came to retire, finding that I was an Indian, he was unwilling to sleep opposite my room for fear of being murdered before morning" (305). "These things I mention," Apess says, not boisterously but with cool irony, "to show that the doctrines of the Pilgrims has [sic] grown up with the people" (305). As ye have sown so shall ye reap: the racialist legacy of Puritanism must be rejected before justice can prevail in America.[45]

Apess returns to Philip's history in a manner that will show its present relevance to Andrew Jackson and his legal assault on the Georgia Cherokees. He invites his audience to imagine the "deep ... thought of Philip, when he could look from Maine to *Georgia*, and from the ocean to the lakes, and view with one look all his brethren withering before the *more enlightened* to come; and how true his prophecy; that the white people would not only cut down their groves but would enslave them" (306, emphasis added).

It is no accident that Apess imagines the trajectory of Philip's gaze extending beyond his own lands to the south, specifically to Georgia—at that very moment working actively, in its great "enlightenment," to "enslave" the Cherokees within its borders by bringing them under Georgia law. Apess indirectly refers to this just a few sentences later, writing, "Look at the deep-rooted plans laid, when a territory becomes a state, that after so many years the laws shall be extended over the Indians that live within their boundaries" (306).

But here, too, Apess seems quite specifically to be rewriting Everett's address. Consider, for example, the moment when Everett seeks to bolster the view of Philip's story as a tragedy by inviting his audience to "think of the country for which the Indians fought!" remarking, "Who can blame them?" (1835, 29). Everett then offers the following imaginary tableau: "As Philip looked down from his seat on Mount Hope, that glorious eminence, . . . and beheld the lovely scene which spread below . . . could he be blamed, if his heart burned within him, as he beheld it all passing, by no tardy process, from beneath his control into the hands of the stranger?" (29).

Earlier, Everett had, also indirectly and somewhat elliptically, *denied* any linkage between the treatment of the New England Indians in Philip's time (and, by implication, at least, in his own) and the treatment of the Cherokees in Georgia. In a note on the migration "farther west and north" of the New England tribes defeated by the colonists and their "advancing settlements," Everett had said that: "It can be scarcely necessary to state that considerations of this kind have no applicability to the questions recently agitated in the United States, relative to the rights acquired by Indian tribes under solemn compacts, voluntarily entered into by the United States, at the instance and for the benefit of an individual state" (1835, 10).[46]

Apess will have none of this. In the paragraph I have been examining, he continues his attack on the treatment of the Cherokees, remarking that "even the president of the United States tells the Indians they cannot live among civilized people, and we want your lands and must have them and will have them" (1992, 307). He then turns the tables, doing to President Jackson what had so often been done to Indian people, ventriloquizing him.[47] Apess has the (unnamed) president say, "We want your land for our use to speculate upon, it aids us in paying off our national debt and supporting us in Congress to drive you off" (307).[48] Consistent with his firm belief that the treatment of the Indians of his own day descends in a direct line from Puritan treatment of Indians in an earlier day, Apess has the president conclude, "This has been the way our fathers first brought us up, and it is hard to depart from it; therefore, you shall have no protection from us" (307). Georgian and Jacksonian rapaciousness are only the most recent version of Puritan greed.

Relentless in his revision of the national master narrative of comic progress, the story of civilization's inevitable advance, Apess once more poses the rhetorical question to his audience, "Does it not appear that the cause of all wars from beginning to end *was and is* for the want of good usage? That the whites have *always* been the aggressors, and the wars, cruelties, and bloodshed is a job of their own seeking, and not the Indians?" (307, emphases added).[49] Before returning to name Philip "the greatest man that was ever in America" (308), Apess exhorts his audience, "Give the Indian his rights, and you may be assured war will cease" (307). Until such a time, the triumphal progress of the white invaders and the dispossession of Native tribal nations for more than two hundred years cannot accurately be emplotted as comedy (for the whites) or as tragedy (for the Indians), for American history, as Apess portrays it, is a painfully ironic story of unrelieved injustice.

In very nearly an anticlimactic gesture, Apess returns to scriptural quotation (308) and to anecdotes from American history, instancing the famous, if possibly spurious, speech of Logan, and recalling a massacre of Christian Indians by "a party of two hundred *white warriors*" (308, emphasis added) in 1757. So, too, has it been suggested that Apess's conclusion, in its rather bland statement of the speaker's unworthiness ("many thanks is due from me to you, though an unworthy speaker, for your kind attention") and his reference to himself as "a poor Indian" (310), is rather anticlimactic as well. Both statements, to be sure, may be ironically intended but, if so, it is a much more muted irony than appears elsewhere. Nonetheless, the substance of Apess's concluding paragraph is forceful. Just as the great scholar of "savagism,"

Roy Harvey Pearce, insisted that while we are not responsible *for* history we must be responsible *to* it, so does Apess assure his audience, in a gesture toward a future reconciliation between whites and Indians, that "you and I have to rejoice that we have not to answer for our fathers' crimes; neither shall we do right to charge them one to another." Instead, what we must do is "to regret . . . and flee from it [the crimes]; and from henceforth, let peace and righteousness be written upon our hearts" (310). What is needed is a strong turn away from the legacy of the Puritan forefathers and the ruthless continuation of that legacy in the policies of Andrew Jackson. It is nothing less than that which William Apess calls for in his powerful *Eulogy on King Philip.*

And yet, neither Apess nor anyone else succeeded in deterring Jackson from removing the eastern Cherokees.

4

Representing Cherokee Dispossession

For Daniel Heath Justice

On February 21, 1828, the Cherokees published the first issue of the first newspaper in America to contain writing in an indigenous Native language. The paper was called "Cherokee Phoenix —Tsalagi Tsu-le-hi-sa-nu-hi, or something like 'I will arise' in the Cherokee language."[1]

(Wilkins 1988, 196)

On August 1, 1838, Chief John Ross "assembled his Cherokee followers and led them in a pledge that, despite the loss of their homeland, the Cherokee Nation would never die."

(Hoig 1998, 171)

It is useless to attempt to describe the long, wearisome passage of those exiled Indians.

(Wahnenauhi [Mrs. Lucy L. Keys] 1966, 207)

Granma and Granpa wanted me to know of the past, for "If ye don't know where your people have been then ye won't know where your people are going." And so they told me most of it.

Forrest Carter, *The Education of Little Tree: A True Story* (1976, 40)

"Grandpa," I said, suddenly excited. "Grandpa, I can hear them. They're singing."

Robert J. Conley, *Mountain Windsong:
A Novel of the Trail of Tears* (1992, 218)

> I regarded this new birth as not just the end of our suffering but also as the dawn of a new day–the first day of our new life in the promised land.
>
> Glenn J. Twist, "The Promised Land (1837)" in *Boston Mountain Tales: Stories from a Cherokee Family* (1997, 143)

Full Circle: The Connecticut Casino

> . . . all the gold stolen from the Cherokees
> in Georgia seeming to return now to the
> Pequots in Connecticut . . .
>
> William Jay Smith, *The Cherokee Lottery: A Sequence of Poems* (2000)

MARITOLE

> "The baby who had been born was crying.
> "Luthy took my arm. 'It's a new voice that won't grieve for our old land in North Carolina.'"

QUATY LEWIS

> "Some night I'd listen to the wind in the pines. Only there weren't pines here. I looked around. They were oaks, a different kind of oak than we'd had in North Carolina, but they would sound the old truth of the pines."

LUTHY

> "As for the trail—it's over—Tanner and my boys are alive."

MARITOLE

> "Maybe someday love would come."
>
> Diane Glancy, *Pushing the Bear: A Novel of the Trail of Tears* (1996, 228, 229, 233)

i.

Not William Apess, not Ralph Waldo Emerson, neither Chief Justice John Marshall, nor Cherokee Principal Chief John Ross could prevent the removal of the Cherokees from their southeastern homelands. But how might this terrible dispossession be represented in writing? How might words convey the experience of "*Nunna daul Tsunyi*... 'the trail where we cried'" (Mankiller 2000, 46),[2] the Trail of Tears, on which, from the summer of 1838 until March 1839, of some thirteen thousand people, black slaves and intermarried whites among them, more than a third, perhaps four thousand people, died?[3] Difficult as it surely is to represent this climactic event of Cherokee dispossession, it is not very difficult to say how it came about. Even in an age wary of "facts," the facts in this instance are very little contestable. Set out as a "Chronology of the Cherokee Removal," they can be listed, as Theda Purdue and Michael Green have done, in little more than two pages of text. Except as noted, what follows is based on Perdue and Green (1995, 176–79).

About 1700 the Cherokees first encountered Europeans in the persons of British traders.

In 1776 the American colonists invaded Cherokee towns.

After the American Revolution, the Treaty of Hopewell (1785) pledged peaceful relations between the new United States and the Cherokee Nation.

In 1800 Moravian Fathers from Germany established a mission among the Cherokees, to further their Christianization.

In 1802 in exchange for a land cession from the State of Georgia, the U.S. government promised to extinguish Creek and Cherokee title to lands in the State of Georgia.

A first major migration of Cherokee people west of the Mississippi occurred between 1808 and 1810.

In the Creek War of 1813–14 the Cherokees fought on the side of Andrew Jackson and the United States against hostile Creeks.

In 1821 Sequoyah invented a syllabary by which the Cherokee language could be written, and in 1828 the *Cherokee Phoenix* began publication, in English and in Cherokee.

In 1828 Andrew Jackson was elected president; immediately after, in 1828 and 1829, the State of Georgia refused to acknowledge Cherokee sovereignty within the state, extending its laws over the Cherokees in 1830.

In 1830 the Indian Removal Act, granting the president the authority to enter into treaties with the Eastern Indians that would provide for their "removal" west of the Mississippi, was passed by Congress and signed into law by Jackson.[4]

In 1832 the Supreme Court, in *Worcester v. Georgia*, upheld Cherokee sovereignty in the state. But Jackson did not act to protect the Cherokees from individual Georgians and from officers of the state.

In 1832 Georgia organized a lottery to assign Cherokee lands and property to "fortunate drawers" (Wilkins 1988, 225).

In 1835 a small number of Cherokees, led by the Ridge family, believing further resistance to Georgia and Jackson was doomed to failure, signed the Treaty of New Echota, pledging the Cherokees to remove west of the Mississippi by May of 1838.

In 1836 the Senate ratified the Treaty of New Echota.

In 1837 a party of 466 wealthy Cherokees, with considerable property, including African slaves, migrated west of the Mississippi to Indian Territory (Foreman 1976, 273). Others, but not the vast majority of the Nation, would follow.

On May 23, 1838, federal troops under the command of General Winfield Scott, began forcibly to round up the Cherokees, driving them into what Grant Foreman, writing in 1932 (i.e., before Hitler's implementation of the "final solution" to the "Jewish question"), called "concentration camps" (Foreman 1976, 290 and 300).

In June, General Scott sent the first contingent of resisting Cherokees west, but as the summer progressed, heat and drought took such a toll on the travelers that Principal Chief John Ross persuaded Scott to allow the Cherokees themselves to oversee the Removal once the worst of the summer had passed.

The first party under Cherokee direction left on October 1, 1838; eight more left in October, and another four in November.

By March of 1839, all those who survived had reached Indian Territory, present-day Oklahoma. For more than a century, the figure of four thousand deaths in a population of some thirteen thousand, as I have noted, has been generally accepted as a more or less accurate statement of the number who died on the Trail. Russell Thornton (1984) estimates that between 1835 and 1839 the overall death toll was probably as high as eight to ten thousand persons.[5]

How to represent collective trauma of this magnitude? The question has been asked again and again in Holocaust studies considering the fiction and autobiographical production of Jews and others who found themselves swept into the Nazi death camps. So, too, has the question been considered by Armenians reflecting on the Turkish genocide of 1915, and, more recently, by Cambodians remembering the mass killings between 1975 and 1979. Rwandans must come to terms with the murder of some eight hundred thousand people, mostly Tutsis, in 1994, and the genocide in Darfur goes on as I write. Will it one day come to representation?[6] This essay focuses on the work of four contemporary Cherokee writers—Robert J. Conley, Glenn J. Twist, Wilma Mankiller, and Diane Glancy—each of whom, in the last quarter of the twentieth century, attempted to represent their ancestors' dispossession in writing. I also briefly consider work by two non-Cherokee writers, William Jay Smith, who is part Choctaw, and Forrest Carter, a pretend Cherokee, and not even the particular white man he claims to be (see below). They, too, write of Cherokee Removal, and I include them to provide some further context for the work of Conley, Twist, Mankiller, and Glancy. I am once more interested in the intersection of literary style and literary functionality, representation as esthetic object and social act.

ii.

Wahnenauhi, Mrs. Lucy L. Keys, granddaughter of the eminent Cherokee leader and statesman Major George Lowrey, wrote "Historical Sketches of the Cherokees, Together with Some of Their Customs, Traditions, and Superstitions," in 1889. Wahnenauhi was, as her editor, the contemporary Cherokee scholar Jack Kilpatrick, noted, a member of the "planter class of mixbloods." "English was its first language, evangelical Christianity its religion, and acculturation its code" (1966, 181). But that "planter class of mixbloods," as Kilpatrick makes clear, was "indissolubly bound" to more conservative, traditional, full-blood people "by the only ties that Cherokees ever understood or still understand—a fierce loyalty to common ancestry" (182). Nonetheless, as she looked back, Wahnenauhi seems to have thought it "useless" to attempt to convey the pain and suffering, the *trauma* of the forcible dispossession of the Cherokees. Perhaps it had also seemed useless, or, more likely, impossible, to those Cherokees who endured and survived it to convey the day-to-day experience of the Trail, at least in writing. Although many of them were literate in English and/or in the Sequoyah syllabary, not one seems to have left a detailed account of the terrible ordeal. Cherokee letters and brief remembrances from before and after the Trail exist, but the "only daily record of the Trail of Tears yet found" is that of the Reverend Daniel

Butrick, a white minister who accompanied the Cherokee detachment led by Richard Taylor (Hoig 1998, 171).[7]

We must set beside this observation, however, James Mooney's testimony that, even near the end of the nineteenth century, there were Cherokee people who not only vividly recalled, but harrowingly could relate some of the worst moments of the winter of 1839. Mooney writes, "In talking with old men and women at Tahlequah [still Indian Territory, not yet Oklahoma] the author [Mooney] found that the lapse of over half a century had not sufficed to wipe out the memory of the miseries of that halt beside the frozen river [the Mississippi], with hundreds of sick and dying penned up in wagons or stretched upon the ground, with only a blanket overhead to keep out the January blast" (1900, 132–33).

And the contemporary Cherokee writer Marilou Awiakta (1995) tells of meeting "Maggie Wachacha, an eighty-eight-year-old member of the Eastern Band [of Cherokees]" in 1984.[8] Maggie Wachacha's grandson informs Awiakta that his grandmother remembers hearing "her elders tell how they walked the Trail of Tears" (33). But very few of these people, as I have said, *wrote* of these experiences.[9]

At the end of the nineteenth century, James Mooney observed that "unlike most Indians the Cherokee are not conservative . . . the Cherokee mind . . . is accustomed to look forward to new things rather than to dwell on the past" (1900, 229 and 232).[10] A more nuanced generalization comes from Jack and Anna Kilpatrick, who, just past the middle of the twentieth century, write of "the amazing ability of the Cherokees to maintain an equilibrium between two opposing worlds of thought." The Kilpatricks offer as an illustration the image of a "Cherokee businessman, on the way to his country club," wrapped "in deep speculation as to the exact height of the slant-eyed giant, Tsuhl'gul'," as well as "the television set in the cabin of his fellow tribesman," behind which "lurk the Little People." *Both* "the Bible *and* Thunder share Cherokee reverence," the Kilpatricks assert. I would amend this only to suggest that "the amazing ability of the Cherokees" to which the Kilpatricks refer is perhaps better described as the capacity to maintain two *different* rather than "two *opposing* worlds of thought," another instance of both/and rather than either/or perspective 1964, v, my emphases).[11] This seems to be the case with Conley, Twist, and Glancy, three of the four contemporary Cherokee writers under consideration. Their representation of the trauma of dispossession references Christian and classical images and concepts of rebirth, return, and renewal, but it also sets these *non*-Cherokee materials in relation to very *different*, traditional Cherokee images and concepts.

Robert Conley is the author of some thirty books, at least ten of which comprise "The Real People" series, novels documenting virtually every aspect of Cherokee life and history. In *Mountain Windsong: A Novel of the Trail of Tears* (1992), Conley tries to represent at least some of "the long, wearisome passage of these exiled Indians" (Wahnenauhi 1966, 207), from Georgia and North Carolina to Indian Territory, by telling the story of a fictional Cherokee conservative, named Waguli or Whippoorwill, and his love, Oconeechee. Resisting removal from the start, Waguli is beaten and manacled, yet he repeatedly tries to escape as his party wends its way overland, and by paddle-wheeler down the Tennessee and Ohio rivers to Mississippi, before trekking into Indian Territory. A broken man, Waguli succumbs to alcoholism and despair before being rescued by an aged white man, Titus Hooker or Gun Rod, someone who had fought with the Cherokees beside Andrew Jackson at Horseshoe Bend in the Creek War. Hooker, after a lengthy series of adventures that threaten to obscure the main lines of the narrative, is successful in bringing Waguli back, largely detoxified, to his ever-loyal beloved, Oconeechee. Conley's unabashedly sentimental account regularly fills itself out with long quotations from C. C. Royce's 1887 *Cherokee Nation of Indians*, the 5th Annual Report of the Bureau of American Ethnology, and from James Mooney's "Historical Sketch of the Cherokee People," the first section of Mooney's *Myths of the Cherokee*, also a Bureau of American Ethnology Report, published in 1900. Other documents of interest, for example, almost twenty pages of the Treaty of New Echota (1835), and Ralph Waldo Emerson's 1838 letter to President Van Buren protesting Cherokee removal, are dropped in as efficient, if esthetically jarring, means of conveying the facts and feel of the period. (But, of course, there is a real problem in trying to write about these matters for an audience who may know little or nothing about them—a problem to which my own solution was the provision of the list of "facts" above.)

Conley's novel is narrated by a young man whose name is LeRoy or Sonny, although he is referred to by his folksy, mountain grandpa as *chooj* or boy. At the beginning of the novel, the boy and his grandfather take a walk in the hills, and the boy hears a "windsong," which, his grandfather explains, is "a lovesong" (1992, 6). To explain the lovesong, Grandpa tells the story of the love between Waguli and Oconeechee, and he sets it against the background of Removal. As already noted, that story ends happily for the two nineteenth-century lovers, and, in an epilogue to the novel, Conley has *chooj* ask his Grandpa, "What happened . . . after that?" Grandpa says that the couple lived and had children and "By and by, they died. That was all a long time ago" (218). This observation causes *chooj* to recognize, in a fairly standard trope of the "coming of age" novel, that his Grandpa and Grandma will also one day die. But the sadness of this realization is lessened when the boy looks up into a tree, hearing a sound on the wind. The "wind picked up some more, and [chooj] heard that sound again." "Grandpa," he says, suddenly excited, "Grandpa, I can hear them. They're singing" (218).

So Whippoorwill and his beloved live on, in a sound, a song in the wind through the trees. And, doubtless, when Grandma and Grandpa also pass away, they, too, will live on. It will return, it will survive, it will rise again—not as bird or God, but as a "windsong" in the trees. Conley here risks perpetuating the stereotype of the intimate connection between the Native and nature; nonetheless, the ongoing existence of Waguli and Oconeechee is entirely a matter of Cherokee history and culture. This particular "windsong" is a Cherokee song for Cherokee ears. It will always sound and, it is strongly suggested, there will always be Cherokees to hear it.

Curiously, Conley's *chooj*, and his situation—he is spending the summer with his traditional grandfather and grandmother in the North Carolina hills—strongly echo the by-now-notorious *Education of Little Tree: A True Story* (1976) by Forrest Carter. Forrest Carter's real name was Asa Earl Carter, and we know for certain that Asa Carter grew up in Alabama (not Tennessee), that he was not Cherokee, and that he was not orphaned. Thus, *Little Tree*, although it is subtitled *A True Story*, must be considered a novel.[12] Its narrator, Little Tree, is a five-year-old orphan. "Ma lasted a year after Pa was gone," the novel begins, "That's how I came to live with Granpa and Granma" (1) up in the Tennessee hills. Granma is a full-blood Cherokee but Granpa is mixed-blood, the child of a marriage between his full-blood Cherokee father, whose family took to the "mountains" (42) in order to escape Removal, and the daughter of white mountain men, considered outlaws. Contrary to historical fact, Carter insists upon an alliance between these two peoples based upon their strong opposition to "guvmint" (44, 46);[13] this alliance forms the cornerstone of his racial mythology of the past (Carter had been a Ku Klux Klan member and speechwriter for the segregationist governor of Georgia, George Wallace). Granpa's father, we learn, will join "the Confederate raider, John Hunt Morgan, to fight the faraway, faceless monster of 'guvmint,' that threatened his people and his cabin" (44). Before developing these matters, however, Carter first has Granpa offer an account of the Trail of Tears, although his people did *not* themselves walk the Trail. This account, too, seeks to create a mythology of the Trail at odds with history.[14]

The great villains of Cherokee dispossession for Carter are "the government soldiers" (40, 41), a phrase repeated some five times in the first two pages of the chapter called "To Know the Past." The soldiers bring "wagons and mules" (41) for the Cherokees to ride in, but the Cherokees refuse as a matter of pride. Then, when the Cherokees begin to die in greater numbers than can be buried, the soldiers tell the Cherokees to put their dead in the wagon. The Cherokees resist, and we are offered a strange picture of people walking the Trail with the bodies of their dead in their arms. Carter insists that "the Cherokee did not cry" (42). The migration route to Indian Territory was called the Trail of Tears because "it sounds romantic and [it] *speaks of the sorrow of those who stood by the Trail*" (42, my emphasis). Thus, the Cherokees who submitted to the "government soldiers" are not even the originators of history's name for their dispossession! The Trail of Tears commemorates not the sorrow of the Cherokees, but of the *whites* who watched the Cherokees pass! Grandpa's Pa's greatest loyalty, in the end, is *not* to his fellow Cherokees removed to Indian Territory but to the slaveholding rebels with whom he shares a hatred of "guvmint."

Glenn J. Twist, a Cherokee writer (d. 1995) whose name will be unfamiliar, I suspect, to most readers, tried to give some sense of the pain of the Removal period in two texts called "The Dispossession (1837)" and "The Promised Land (1837)," the second and the ninth (and final) story in a collection called *Boston Mountain Tales: Stories from a Cherokee Family* (1997). Twist's name derives from his nineteenth-century ancestor, Ganu'teyo'hi, which translates as "twist" or "twister" and describes the man's ability to braid fine rope from animal hair or vegetable fibers. Ganu'teyo'hi; his white wife, Rachel; and other members of his family are "thought to have traveled to the West with the B. B. Cannon wagon train" (Twist 1997, xiii). The party reached "the base of [a then-] unnamed mountain, Cherokee Nation, Indian Territory side, on 27 December 1837" (xii).

In "The Dispossession (1837)," Twist offers the only contemporary text I know to represent and re-imagine in detail the humiliation of Cherokee "dispossession" as first occasioned by the Georgia lottery, which granted to lucky white Georgians specific tracts of Cherokee lands with all buildings, livestock, and improvements upon it. (Smith's *Cherokee Lottery*, as we'll soon see, also treats this period.) It is after Ganu'teyo'hi and his family are driven off their land that they eventually make the journey to Indian Territory chronicled in "The Promised Land (1837)." After a long and difficult journey, during which many members of the party perish, "the Cannon train arrived in Indian Territory approximately one year prior to the so-called *Trail of Tears*" (Twist 1997, xii). (Twist regularly precedes reference to the Trail of Tears with "so-called." I haven't discovered the reason for this.)

Traveling, as I have noted, a year earlier than the first detachments forcibly sent upon the Trail, and traveling voluntarily, as it were, Twist's ancestors were free to proceed at whatever pace they could, to stop where they chose, and so on. But the story does give a strong sense of the extraordinary difficulties involved in removing west to Indian Territory. Twist assigns the narration to the only white woman in the Cherokee family, Rachel, Ganu'teyo'hi's wife; her way of making sense of the dispossession and the pain of the journey—Glenn J. Twist's way, very likely—also involves the concept of renewal.

As the party finally enters Indian Territory, somewhat ironically but also hopefully referred to as "the promised land," Little Flower, wife of Ganu'teyo'hi's cousin, Smokehouse, dies, as do the last children of an unfortunate white family named Timberlake.[15] But, says Rachel, "still we were blessed." As if to balance the deaths, Jess Half Breed's wife, Sally, gives birth to a "big healthy-looking boy" who "came into this world hungry." Rachel concludes, "If the others were like me they would see the birth of Half Breed's son in much the same light as I did, a good omen. I regarded this new birth as not just the end of our suffering, but also as the dawn of a new day—the first day of our new life in the promised land" (Twist 1997, 143).

Here, any irony associated with the phrase "promised land" drops away; much has been lost, but, quite literally, a new day dawns and brings new birth.

A prolific poet, William Jay Smith, part Choctaw, published *The Cherokee Lottery: A Sequence of Poems* (2000) in his eighties. The book is constructed around meditations on the 1832 Georgia lottery that was used to determine which whites were to appropriate which lands of the Cherokees. In the final poem of his "sequence," Smith has a vision of history coming "Full Circle" as the roulette wheels go 'round and 'round at the Pequots' multimillion dollar casino, Foxwoods, in Mashantucket, Connecticut. Smith's sense of "return" or regeneration is rather different from that of Conley and Twist and seems worth a moment of attention. Smith writes, "High above that table where the spinning ball comes to rest on the red and black numbers of the roulette wheel, I hear the faint ghostly creaking of the clumsy wooden wheel, designed more than a century and a half ago for the Cherokee Lottery in Georgia" (87).

This eighteenth and final poem of the sequence, perhaps the very best thing in Smith's slim volume, gathers past and present, myth and history, stereotypes and their ironic revisions.

At one point in the poem, the speaker thinks he is having a vision of a herd of *buffalo*, only to see not buffalo but "steaming *buses* queuing up to deliver / their anxious occupants / to the gambling tables of the great Foxwoods Resort Casino" (W. J. Smith 2000, 85). The recent success of that casino and of the Pequots who own it will be referenced further, as we shall see. The last part of the poem introduces the Native American trickster, Coyote, here, *Ms.* Coyote, fully and brilliantly described:

> From the thin lascivious full-reddened lips
> drawn back under the black round rubbery tip of her
>   nose
> in a wry sinister smile over the pointed teeth
> emerges a voice neither male nor female

> but one having a somewhat unsettling sexless and
> timeless quality
> and the cold compact clarity of a computer chip.
> The voice announces,
> All those who are willing and eager to relinquish
> territory
> obtained illegally from Indian tribes at any time
> in the past
> will kindly record their property identification
> numbers on their Wampum
> Cards and leave them at the Cherokee Lottery
> Roulette table.
> When their numbers are called, they are requested
> to proceed
> to the Holding Area in front of the Casino. There
> the
> Native American Escort Service will help
> facilitate their departure on fully-monitored
> Buffalo Buses by providing
> each one with a TRAIL OF TEARS Passport printed
> in Cherokee
> that will insure their safe passage on the Tall
> Ships that await them at the principal ports of
> the Eastern Seaboard. (89–90)

The past is not past; the past lives—in transformed and also in transformative fashion—at least in the poet's imagination. Postmodern trickster ironies here rewrite the past, and some justice, ironic justice, to be sure, is done, as those whites who have obtained Indian lands illegally sail back to Europe, with "all the gold stolen from the Cherokees in Georgia / seeming to return now to the Pequots in / Connecticut" (90).

It returns, at least in some fashion. (I will soon consider Diane Glancy's use of a somewhat similar irony in *Pushing the Bear*, conveyed by the phrase, "It comes back" [1996, 237].)

iv.

Wilma Mankiller, principal chief of the Cherokees from 1985 to 1994, in her autobiography, *Mankiller: A Chief and Her People* (1993), discusses the Removal period, but she doesn't at all represent it in terms of the figures of renewal, rebirth, and return that the Cherokee novelists use.[16] On the one hand, this may be because Mankiller does not offer her book primarily as a work of art, but, rather, as the testimony of a public person. That is to say, her autobiography consistently portrays her life in terms of the growth of her will and ability to serve her people. She presents herself foremost as a woman of action, and, much as she values words and language, it seems clear that for her "actions speak louder than words." On the other hand, it may be that Mankiller is not drawn to *figurative* images of return because although her family left its home (in Oklahoma), in time, she literally *did* return, as her ancestors *did not* return to Georgia or North Carolina. In any case, for her the Trail is not, as it seems to be for the Cherokee fiction writers we are considering, perceived in terms of rebirth, return, and renewal, but only in terms of loss; for Mankiller, the Trail was nothing other than a "tragedy" for the Cherokees. In a chapter called "Genesis of Removal," Mankiller speaks of the "sesquicentennial" commemoration of the journey west by the eastern Cherokees. "There were no festivities," she writes, "Nobody smiled. There was absolutely nothing to be happy about. It was a solemn observance, a very emotional time. We regarded the removal as something that happened to our family—something very bad that happened to our family. It was a tragedy. It brought us pain that never seemed to leave" (Mankiller and Wallis 2000, 47).[17]

When Mankiller thinks about Removal today, it is *not* because some good came from it (the lovers still sing; after much pain Indian Territory became a kind of promised land, and so on), but, rather, because it is a benchmark against which to measure subsequent federal assaults upon the Cherokees, in her own case, the termination and relocation programs of the fifties that led her family from Mankiller Flats in Oklahoma to inner-city San Francisco.

Mankiller begins her chapter "The Trail Where They Cried" with a version of a traditional story about trickster Rabbit's escape from the wolves, noting that after her family relocated in San Francisco, she felt like the rabbit surrounded by wolves only without Rabbit's power to escape. This is how she introduces her account of the Trail:

> I experienced my own Trail of Tears when I was a young girl... the United States government, through the Bureau of Indian Affairs, was again trying to settle the "Indian problem" by removal. I learned through this ordeal about the fear and anguish that occur when you have to give up your home, your community, and... move far away to a strange place.
>
> I cried for days, not unlike the children who had stumbled down the Trail of Tears so many years before.[18] (Mankiller and Wallis 2000, 62)

When Mankiller refers to the Cherokee *Phoenix*, she calls it "*Tsa la gi Tsu lehisanunhi* or the *Cherokee Phoenix*" (83). The reader might well assume that the second part of the phrase I've quoted, *Tsu lehisanunhi*, translates to "Phoenix." But as Wilkins noted in the first epigraph I've provided for this chapter, that is not the case. Mooney translated the syllables (I don't know whether they constitute one word or two) after *Tsa la gi* as "Resurrected One," "I was resurrected," or, more literally, "I was down and I have risen" (1900, 539). Mankiller knows, of course, that the Cherokee newspaper *was* called the *Phoenix*, but she is quick to leave "Phoenix" behind, translating the newspaper's name back into Cherokee terms. She writes, "The name given to the newspaper was a fitting choice" because "the power of that mythical bird... *reminds us of the Cherokees' eternal flame*" (Mankiller and Wallis 2000, 83, my emphasis), the Keetoowah fire. With no traditional *Cherokee* Phoenix imagery to invoke (and apparently not tempted here to use

Christian imagery), Chief Mankiller focuses on the Cherokees' "eternal flame," stating, "According to *our* legend, as long as that fire burns, our people will survive" (83, my emphasis).[19] Her account of the Trail firmly details its horrors and forthrightly insists on what other accounts either ignore (Conley, Twist) or mention merely in passing (Glancy): "It should be remembered," Chief Mankiller writes, that "hundreds of people of African ancestry also walked the Trail of Tears with the Cherokees during the forced removal of 1838–1839. Although we know about the terrible human suffering of our native people . . . during the removal, we rarely hear of those black people who also suffered" (95).

For the Cherokees, red and black, the Trail was a place and a time of suffering that must be remembered for itself and also as an event against which to measure assaults on the people in the present and the future. But Wilma Mankiller does not remember it as having led to a promised land, to birth after death, or to some sort of renewal. As I have noted, its commemoration, 160 years later, was a time of pain, when "nobody smiled" (Mankiller and Wallis 2000, 47). (Mankiller writes about the 1984 reunion of the Eastern and Oklahoma Cherokee, mentioned above, as a much happier occasion.)

v.

I come at last to *Pushing the Bear* (Glancy 1996). The account that follows limits itself, for the most part, to the representation of the Trail, even if this inevitably slights aspects of the novel. This is to say that just as Robert Conley set the love between Waguli and Oconeechee against the background of Removal, so, too, does Glancy set the deterioration and possible amelioration of the marriage between Maritole, and her husband, Knowbowtee, against the experience of the Trail. Much could be said about their relationship. The novel does indeed conclude with Maritole thinking of Knowbowtee and hoping that, "Maybe someday love would come" (233). I chose Maritole's words for the last of the epigraphs to this chapter because her hopefulness regarding her marriage also works with other gestures of renewal and rebirth in the last pages of the novel to produce a potentially comic interpretation of the Trail—in the very specific structural and ideological senses of the comic as I have discussed them: I am most certainly *not* saying that Glancy finds anything *funny* here.

Pushing the Bear consists of eight chapters, each marked by a date, a place, and a map for each stage of the journey west. Glancy will attempt the formidable task of imagining the Trail in its entirety. The novel begins in late September, 1838 in North Carolina, and concludes on February 27, 1839 in Indian Territory.[20] Each of the chapters is composed of a number of separate sections, for the most part headed by an individual's name, and, also for the most part, consisting of an interior monologue.[21] There is a section headed "James Mooney" (1996, 34)—although, as Glancy surely knows, Mooney did not travel the Trail with the Cherokees; in fact, in 1838 he had not yet been born. The "James Mooney" section is a very slightly altered version of the account Mooney gives in his "Historical Sketch of the Cherokee Nation" (1900, 221) of the stockades into which the Cherokee were driven before being sent off on their journey. Other sections are called "Voices as They Walked" and "The Soldiers." There is no section devoted to an African voice or voices.[22]

There are a number of sections that do not represent the thoughts of characters along the Trail. These have titles like, "A Government Teamster's Journal" (Glancy 1996, 191–93), "The Baptist" (110–11), or "A White Traveler from Maine" (122–23). There is a section that consists of a tally of the expenses incurred by Principal Chief John Ross (23–24), and a catalogue of Ross's lost personal property (77–79); there is also a list of items required for the journey that was submitted by the Reverend Jesse Bushyhead (196–201). These sections offer *writing* of one sort or another rather than speech or thoughts.

The words printed under the names of individuals historically present at the time of the story may be, as I have suggested, spoken words, or, perhaps, thoughts (interior monologues).[23] Meanwhile, Maritole's words in English, whether they are words thought or spoken, must be a translation from the Cherokee, in that Maritole is represented as understanding little or no English. (This is surely true for others who have their names at the head of one or another section.) There are also words and phrases in the Sequoyah syllabary, which Glancy sometimes translates and sometimes leaves untranslated (cf. "SONG WE SANG ON——THE TRAIL OF BLOOD, 1996, 129). Although she prints the syllabary among the materials appended to the novel, I have not been able to decode some of the words in the text that are in the syllabary.

Glancy's use of the syllabary would seem to be a way of conveying some specific Cherokee-ness or *difference* to her text, a kind of resistance to any transparency of thought and experience. The syllabary was for *writing* Cherokee, but in the novel it often appears to convey speech or thought, oral narrative or song. This latter issue, the difference (in function, in value) between spoken and written words, frequently comes up in contemporary Native American writing, and this is the case in *Pushing the Bear*, as well—although there is no space to pursue this matter here.

Along with meditations on the spoken and written word come speculations about the uses and powers of stories, both traditional stories, which Glancy on at least one occasion composes in the Sequoyah syllabary (1996, 194–95; we shall return to this below), and the story as testimony to personal experience that is also quite self-consciously recognized as historical experience. For example, Maritole says, "I would have the tongue of a leaf. I would tell our story, I thought" (172–73). Someone called "The Basket Maker" says: "The baskets hold fish and corn and beans. Just like our stories hold meaning." Baskets "copy our stories" (153).[24] Maritole's mother says or thinks: "Tell stories. . . . Riding on your stories you can walk" (72). Knowbowtee, Maritole's estranged husband, echoes this when he says, "The stories fueled my walk" (144). He may also echo Maritole when, near the end of the novel, he says, "Could the trees also mean something about words?" (227–28). But his monologue then goes on to speculate further about the differences between spoken and written words, in particular words on documents used to betray the Cherokees (cf. 224). There are also meditations on the Sequoyah syllabary and the fact that it made it possible to write in Cherokee; words can be used in different ways, to different ends, and that is true for both the written and the spoken word.

I'll turn now to the metaphor of "pushing the bear," which provides the title of the novel and operates from perhaps page 15 to page 233, the novel's last page. The "bear" is Maritole's foremost image for the oppression of the Trail. The bear is the weight, the pain, the violence of the journey; the bear is that which can destroy us by devouring us. It is mostly Maritole who feels the bear or pushes it, suffers from it, is nearly devoured by it, and, finally, perhaps, overcomes it. Others, it should be noted, are also aware of the bear. Maritole remarks, "When we stopped at midday, I heard someone telling the story of the bear" (Glancy 1996, 102).

But it is only later in the novel that Glancy specifically offers "The Story of the Bear" (176). Set in italics, the story appears to be told by one of the *Ani' Tsa'guhi*, a member of an ancient Cherokee clan that long ago chose to go into the woods and become bears so that the people, in times of famine, might hunt them and have food to eat. Glancy's version may derive from Mooney's "Origin of the Bear: The Bear Songs" (1900, 325–27; see also Mooney, "The Bear Man," 1900, 327–29), although, she gives no references to works she has consulted.[25] *If* her story is based on the one Mooney published—and I think it is—it is much abbreviated and impressionistically altered. Here is the story as Glancy presents it:

> **The Story of the Bear**
>
> A long time ago the Cherokee forgot we were a tribe. We thought only of ourselves apart from the others. Without any connections. Our hair grew long on our bodies. We crawled on our hands and

knees. We forgot we had a language. We forgot how to speak. That's how the bear was formed. From a part of ourselves when we were in trouble. All we had was fur and meat to give. (1996, 176)

This differs considerably from Mooney's publication of traditional Cherokee oral stories about bears, which begin with a boy who decides life is easier in the woods than at home. He persuades his parents and all the members of their clan to join him, and, although people of the other towns try to dissuade them from going, they do go into the woods to live. (There are no bear stories of this type in the Kilpatricks' collection from Oklahoma Cherokees in the early 1960s.) Their bodies grow hairy; they become and are henceforth to be known as *yanu*, bears. They give their fellow Cherokees songs with which to call them so that they may come and sacrifice themselves for those who are hungry.

Glenn Twist, in "Na'Ci'e and the Ani'-tsa'ghui (1814)," the eighth of his *Boston Mountain Tales* (1997), offers a similar account to that collected by Mooney. Twist has Na'Ci'e (she is Ganu'teyo'hi's mother) begin the story as follows: "Long before the memory of anyone living today, a great famine prevailed among the Ki- to'hwa people. They were starving. The spirit of Selu [the corn-giver] . . . called upon one clan of the Ki- to'hwa to go into the forest and become bears. As bears they were to sacrifice themselves by becoming food for the rest of the clans" (113).

In neither Mooney's version nor Twist's is there anything like Glancy's sense of a fall from community (the Cherokees forgetting that they were a tribe) or what appears to be the *punishment* of crawling on hands and knees, a kind of regression, rather than an importantly positive *transformation*. The bears of the traditional story do not *lose* language; although they surely will no longer speak human words, their brother and sister Cherokees can always call them with song. Nor is there the sense that the *yanu* came "from *a part of ourselves* when we were in trouble" (Glancy 1996, 176). In any case, Glancy's "Story of the Bear" comes fairly late in the novel, and it is not developed further. In the novel as a whole, the bear image is essentially a metaphor for the enormous difficulty and oppression of the Trail.

About halfway through the novel (but not halfway through the journey; this occurs on the first leg of the journey, in Tennessee), Maritole feels herself being eaten by the bear: her toes, her legs, her stomach, her chest, until she "was inside him" (114). But then she feels "the shaman" over her, "sucking [her] out of the bear" (114). Although she resists him, apparently the shaman is successful in his doctoring. Maritole wakes and she will be well. Other than stating that the shaman sucked her out of the bear, Maritole gives no information about his practice.

Elsewhere in the novel, however, Glancy includes healing formulas from James Mooney's "Swimmer Manuscript," published in 1932.[26] The format for the healing formulas in the Swimmer collection is: Cherokee text with an interlinear, literal translation into English, then a "Free Translation," followed by an "Explanation." Although Glancy does not identify Mooney/Swimmer as the source, *Pushing the Bear* has a section entitled "A Holy Man," which comes from Swimmer's formula 21, "This (is) to cure (them) with whenever they have lost their voice" (Mooney 1932, 198). Glancy calls it "This (Is) to Cure (Them) with Whenever They Have *Forgotten* Their Voice" (128, my emphasis), and she gives a slightly rewritten version of Mooney's "Free Translation" that also includes some of the "Explanation" following the "Free Translation." That is, Glancy combines the formula and Swimmer/Mooney/Olbrechts's explanation of it. For reasons that are unclear to me—unless she wants to convey here that someone who speaks in English is really speaking Cherokee—Glancy puts the formula into pidgin English. Where Mooney has (in the "Explanation"), "Some of the liquid is also rubbed on his throat and neck" (199), Glancy writes, "Some of it rub on neck" (128). Mooney: "The bark, as usual, is from the east side of the tree" (199). But Glancy: "The bark from east side of tree" (128). Glancy does this a few pages later when she has someone named "Kakowih" think/speak of Maritole and the bear also in pidgin: "[Maritole] got eat by bear. She have bear strength." This has been preceded by "Womens cry and make sad wails" (131). This is odd, inasmuch as Maritole, who also speaks no English, is nonetheless "translated" grammatically. Perhaps the brief bits of awkward "Indian" are meant to distinguish the traditionalists of that time from the Christians?

On another occasion, in a section called "Healing Song," Glancy combines and rewrites parts of *Swimmer*, "This is for the Purpose of (Curing) Children When They Constantly Cry" (Glancy 1996, 138; Mooney 1932, 284). Here, Swimmer gives two formulas, numbers 59 and 60, for "whenever their feet are frost bitten" (Glancy 1996, 257–58), both of which might surely have aided the Bushyhead detachment of Cherokees as they marched through the coldest part of winter. Bear imagery in the novel continues as Maritole observes that "at times my own body was the bear I pushed on the trail" (191). This is extended, in a manner, when Lacey Woodard calls Jesus "the man who pushed the bear" (220), the man who was nailed to the cross "with claws" (220). In much the same vein, Tanner (Maritole's older brother) meditates on "the story of Jesus that could hardly be understood," recalling that it was the "blood of Selu, who gave us corn, who also gave us strength to walk," and also that the Reverend Bushyhead had said that "inside it was another blood" (182), the blood of Christ they had as well.

I think the Reverend Jesse Bushyhead, leader of the party in which Maritole and her family walk the Trail, is the character who enunciates Glancy's own belief in the necessary coexistence of traditional Cherokee and Christian thought and belief. Bushyhead says, "I would not be one of those ministers who tried to rid the Cherokee of their stories. It would take everything we could muster to start again" (186). He thus echoes what Maritole herself had concluded, that the minister who "preached Christ as the corn god, the giver of life along with Selu," was right because "if any one of us made it to the new land, then it must be true. Both Christ and myth. It would take both" (112). Later, Maritole will say, "I heard the conjurers. I heard the Christians. I believed them both" (215).²⁷ Again, I think this is the position toward which Glancy herself strives. I'll return to this point by way of conclusion.

vi.

As the Bushyhead detachment approaches Indian Territory, and the novel moves to a close, a good deal of material about death and loss being balanced by birth and renewal is introduced. I will cite only some of it. In the sixth chapter, "Missouri," Reverend Bushyhead's sister, Nancy, dies and, Bushyhead notes, "As Nancy died, my second daughter, Elizah Missouri Bushyhead, was born January 3, 1839, in a clump of trees" (Glancy 1996, 166). In the seventh chapter, Arkansas, Knowbowtee says to O-ga-na-ya, "Everything is broken.... Even my wife loved a soldier—She's broken for me, too."²⁸ O-ga-na-ya answers, "We're all torn and hurt. ... But we're nearing a place where we have to start over. Maybe what Maritole did doesn't matter" (217). In the final chapter, "Indian Territory," in a section given to Maritole—I have quoted it among the epigraphs—we learn that "the baby who had been born was crying," to which Luthy responds, "It's a new voice that won't grieve for our old land in North Carolina" (228). This same section has Maritole also feeling the signs of renewal: "I feel something happen in me as I walk. Something small and strong begins to grow" (228). Affirming that she will "hold the memory of this trail," she turns to the future: "We'll have the new Keetoowah fire to light our hearth. We'll have our stickball games again ... somewhere deep inside me I carry a tiny piece of joy like a ball" (229). Quaty Lewis, whom I have also quoted in the epigraphs, affirms that the oaks she sees growing in Indian Territory "would sound out the old truth of the pines" of South Carolina; no new pines does not mean no old truths. Luthy adds, "As for the trail—it's over—Tanner and my boys are alive" (229). The novel concludes, as it began, with Maritole: "At night the children slept against us ... Knowbowtee and I held them between us. Maybe someday he would touch me. Maybe someday love would come" (233). Maybe, for all the pain, for all the loss, maybe something good will come from the suffering of the Trail.

It is by imagining such possibilities of renewal, return, and rebirth, as I have said, that Robert Conley in his *Mountain Windsong* and Glenn J. Twist in two of his *Boston Mountain Tales* also try to understand Cherokee dispossession. Glancy's turn to these images and concepts as a way of understanding the Trail, however, is very specifically a commitment to *both* the "conjurers *and* the Christians" (1996, 215, my emphasis), and it is that dual commitment that governs the materials Glancy appends to her novel after the narrative has concluded.[29]

After the close of the story, Glancy offers, first, an "Author's Note" and then "A Note on the Written Cherokee Language." This latter gives the eighty-five symbols of the Sequoyah (Glancy spells it Sequoia) syllabary presumably so that the reader can go back and decipher some of the untranslated words in the syllabary that appear at various places in the novel. (I have admitted to little success in doing this.) And it also reprints, with only the addition of "an English phonetic version, . . . the story of the boxturtles and deer that Quaty told on pages 194 and 195" (240).

This story is a version of the tortoise and the hare tale. It appears in Mooney's *Myths of the Cherokee* as "How the Terrapin beat the Rabbit" (1900, 270–71), and, more recently, in Jack and Anna Kilpatrick's *Friends of Thunder: Folktales of the Oklahoma Cherokees*, in versions in which the Terrapin races either the Rabbit, the Deer, or the Fox. I have not been able to find a source that prints this story in the Sequoyah syllabary. Glancy, who, as I have said, gives no references of any kind, seems to have chosen to reprint the story she had already printed in the novel, to remind the reader that Maritole has been thinking of it in her final monologue. Maritole: "Sometimes I thought about Quaty's story of the Trickster Turtle. I had heard Luthy telling it to her boys again. I told it now to the orphans. There was a turtle at the starting line in the old territory.

There was a turtle at the finish line in the new. Our Cherokee nation had become two to survive" (Glancy 1996, 233).

Once again, this is a rewriting of the traditional tale in which Terrapin wins out over the speedier animal not by *becoming two*, but, rather, by placing other Terrapins at various points along the trail so that whenever the Rabbit or Deer looks ahead of him, to the next stage of the race, he already sees a Terrapin there— and, of course, yet another Terrapin simply steps to the finish line ahead of the swifter animal. Glancy's version here, like her version of "The Story of the Bear" earlier, offers traditional material filtered through a powerfully Christian perspective.

If the attention paid to Quaty's story gestured in the direction of the "conjurers" and their worldview, the "Author's Note" gestures more nearly in the direction of the Christians and their worldview. (But we have already seen that these presumptively disparate "views" are not at all incompatible, nor have they been for over a century.) Glancy begins by telling of a trip she and her daughter took "in 1977 or 1978" to see a dramatization of the Trail of Tears. Just before the play begins, Glancy sees "two rainbows in the sky above the amphitheater" (1996, 235). "In the summer of 1995," she said she saw the two rainbows again, this time on the Rosebud Reservation in South Dakota. This marks for her "the closure of [her] work on *Pushing the Bear*, some seventeen or eighteen years after it began" (236). She next offers thanks and acknowledgments, *after* which Glancy notes that she "knew this wasn't going to be a good Indian/bad white man story. You know there has to be both sides in each" (237). She informs the reader that the "dried-up land" the Cherokees once sold to some Osages turned out to have oil on it. "It comes back," Glancy observes in a single-sentence paragraph. Similarly, the farms General Sherman burned in Georgia during the Civil War were farms taken from the Cherokees. It comes back. Glancy concludes her "Note" by saying, "Maybe, in the end, our acts cause little energy fields that draw their likenesses toward them" (237). I think this is fairly close to a restatement (and a recommendation) of the Golden Rule. Be that as it may, although I have treated the "Note on the Written Cherokee Language" before the "Author's Note," it is the former that actually concludes the book; Quaty's story in the Sequoyah syllabary gets the last word.

Before I comment on that, let me note that although Wilma Mankiller in her treatment of the Trail was not interested in parceling out blame, she most certainly didn't offer "both sides" to the story of Cherokee dispossession. Robert Conley and Glenn J. Twist are determined to believe that not only bad but some possible good—in Conley's case, a kind of continuance, an eternal return; in Twist's, arrival in the promised land—came to the survivors of the trek to Indian Territory.[30] Neither one of them is interested in demonizing whites, but neither one of them is interested in urging a two-sides-to-the-story approach. *Pushing the Bear* is not very much interested in doing this either—although as Glancy in her "Author's Note" thinks back on how her work on the novel began and concluded under the sign of two rainbows—doubling the sign of God's covenant with Noah—she most certainly wants to emphasize the message that "maybe someday love would come" (1996, 233), and not only between Maritole and her husband, Knowbowtee, but between conjurers and Christians, whites and Indians, both sides. If our acts draw their likes to them, then do unto others as you would have them do unto you. It seems to have been necessary for Glancy to believe this in order to re-create the long and painful journey of the trail where they cried. But it seems also to have been necessary to believe in clever turtle, a shrewd survivor, from a time far antecedent to Cherokee Removal.

5

Atanarjuat, the Fast Runner and Its Audiences

For Patricia Penn Hilden and Shari Huhndorf

i.

Part of the resistance to colonialism around the globe, as is well known, was and continues to be cultural; art of a variety of kinds works to counter the repressive hegemony of the European metropolis by presenting and re-presenting the world in ways that challenge colonial representations. The aim has been to unsettle the ideological, indeed, the epistemological perspectives underpinning Western sociopolitical hegemony. In the case of Native American artists, from at least 1968–1969 and the beginnings of what has been called the Native American Renaissance, indigenous artists have tried, to borrow a phrase from Leslie Marmon Silko's *Ceremony*, to show "the world as it always was,"[1] the world as Native people may have seen it traditionally, and the world as Native people might still see it beyond what the novel called the "entanglements" brought by the European invasion.[2] This vision of the world runs strongly counter to Euramerican representations of the world: To refer again to a quotation from Eric Cheyfitz, "Practical social power, not aesthetic originality or genius, is the category of understanding in Native art, [so that] for a Native community the beauty of expressive oral culture is synonymous with its practical social power" (2006, 68).[3]

This seems also to be true of contemporary Native American writing,[4] and for much contemporary Native film. It is intensely true, as this chapter hopes to show, for the recent Inuit film, *Atanarjuat, the Fast Runner*.

Native people who read the work of Silko and a range of Native fiction writers, "insiders," let me very loosely call them, may be able to see these writers' representations of the world as it always was with little or no effort. Non-Native readers, "outsiders," will usually have to make a considerably greater effort to see the world this way if they are to become adequate readers for a novel like *Ceremony* or the many postcolonial works of art that seek to challenge Euramerican perceptions of the world.[5] These works ask the "outsider" audience if not to alter then at least to relativize its habitual perspectives, ultimately, in the phrase of Ngugi wa Thiong'o, to which we will return, to "move the center."[6] Those who can't or won't participate in such movement are surely many, even a majority; but postcolonial artists and critics don't usually say much about these people. For the most part, in the face of such intransigence, we just throw up our hands, or perhaps realize that we'll all just have to work harder.

But what about a contemporary, Native artistic production that is contextualized in such a way as to appeal to and apparently to welcome not two but three fairly distinct audiences? It seems to me that *Atanarjuat* first and foremost addresses a local and quite specific contemporary indigenous community for whom it will help provide answers to the question, Who are the Inuit today?[7] One of the ways in which the filmmakers answer that question—as Julie Cruikshank and Elaine Jahner, among others, have demonstrated—is by defining the Inuit today as a community that tells certain stories, in this film, a particular version of the traditional story of Atanarjuat.[8] This self-definition has much to say about the complex ongoing relationship between the Inuit and Canada, the dominant nation-state in which they live. For this audience, the expressive force of the film, its "beauty," is very strongly "synonymous with its practical social power." The film's beauty, in part, is that it does good things for the Inuit.

Second, *Atanarjuat* also wishes to address a southern—French and English Canada and the United States, but also a more generally metropolitan—audience, which it challenges to see with a Native eye, to relativize its usual perspectives, and indeed to move the center. By representing the world as it always was to the Inuit, by refusing to represent the world as the South, with its entanglements, represents it, the film powerfully challenges this audience to see *differently*. The film works in ways that urge its audience to bracket—"abandon" may be too strong a verb—its familiar habits of response. To engage in such bracketing, I would suggest, is already to move in the direction of linking the film's beauty to its "practical social power." This is not an easy task, and I have no idea to what degree the filmmakers imagined that their film, for all its extraordinary power, could, in fact, move an audience to do this.

But the filmmakers also and quite unusually seem to welcome and willingly acknowledge a third audience. Numerically the largest by far, this audience consists of southerners who are either unwilling or unable to alter their habits of perception. This audience manages successfully to ignore or reject the film's challenges to think *differently* by systematically translating the film's world into familiar categories. Rather than relating the film's beauty to its "practical social power," this audience responds to the film's production of the beautiful as a purely formal matter giving rise to an experience at best to be contemplated, or else simply consumed. And yet, although the film itself is uncompromising in its refusal to accommodate the South, the filmmakers have nonetheless provided elaborate and substantial materials—Web sites, press releases, interviews, speeches, and a published screenplay with many supplements—that accommodate or actively encourage translation of the film into familiar (but largely irrelevant) Western categories. This, to repeat, is unusual.[9]

Although there have been some few attempts to monitor the responses of audiences of the first type—attempts, for example, to ask Cherokee people which Cherokee writers, if any, they read and admire—postcolonial criticism knows best the texts and films that appeal to the second audience I have so generally described.[10] Indeed, it may be the case—I do not say this cynically or triumphantly—that postcolonial critics comprise a near-majority of this second audience. Meanwhile, the third audience, as I have said, is usually dismissed with something of a groan. Thus, Lucas Bessire writes, "Films such as *Atanarjuat should* force many viewers to confront the depth of their own ethnocentrism" (2003, 836, my emphasis). But what if "many viewers" resist this confrontation? Patricia Penn Hilden notes that the film gives "non-Inuit viewers not a single respite, no glimpse of the Euro-known, no concessions to cultural ignorance" (2006, 7). But what if "non-Inuit viewers" don't feel culturally ignorant because they quite comfortably impose "the Euro-known" on the film? Shari Huhndorf, noting the abundant tendency of reviewers to relate the film to what I will later generalize as the *epic* and the *ethnographic*, states quite clearly that "these interpretations render *Atanarjuat* meaningful *solely* in relation to European narrative conventions or by explaining its purpose as translating Inuit culture for outsiders" (2003, 822, my emphasis). But what if "outsiders" remain quite secure in their belief that *Atanarjuat* is indeed consistent with "European narrative conventions," and moreover, that "translating Inuit cultures for outsiders" is exactly what the film should be doing? I fully share these critics' positions and their concerns. But the makers of *Atanarjuat*, as I will try to show, seem to see these matters rather differently.

It seems beyond doubt that Zacharias Kunuk, Norman Cohn, and others involved with Isuma Productions have made their film first for Inuit people, whose perception of its beauty is very likely to involve an understanding of its potential social power.[11] Kunuk, Cohn, and Isuma would also be pleased, I believe, if outsiders made the effort to see the film to some degree in the way that the people of Igloolik, Kunuk's hometown, did; indeed, they say as much in a variety of places.[12] What their film does, as the critics I have cited note, is present just the sort of challenge, just the sort of postcolonial resistance of which I have spoken. And yet Kunuk and Cohn not only accommodate, but, surprisingly, even encourage southerners—Canadians and U.S. Americans—to appreciate their film by translating it into their habitual interpretative comfort zones.

Of course, artists often say odd things about their work; they are artists, after all, not critics. Perhaps then we should just discount some of the filmmakers' remarks. But on the several *Atanarjuat* and Isuma Web sites, in interviews Kunuk and Cohn have given, in a few publications, and in the published screenplay and its many supporting materials, there is an enormous amount of material encouraging and apparently validating responses to the film that haven't at all approached one step nearer to anything like an Inuit perspective.[13] All of this can't just be odd, or off, perverse, or simply mischievous. But that's not to say that it is consciously and carefully premeditated either.[14] If I am at all correct, we have something different here, and the difference, I will speculate, has something to do with the establishment of Nunavut in 1999 as a Canadian territory with home rule for the Inuit.

ii.

If Silko's *Ceremony* insists upon the "entangled" nature of the people's world since the arrival of the Europeans, Kunuk's *Atanarjuat, the Fast Runner* works very differently. For almost three hours, the film represents a northern world in which *nothing* European exists: no machines, no electric or telephone lines, nothing—and where no European person, name, or word exists; indeed, every one of the characters in the film is Inuit, and the dialogue is entirely in Inuktituk, the language of the Inuit. *Atanarjuat*, in this regard, could well be criticized for indulging the fantasy that Europe had never invaded the North. This criticism would be understandable, but it would also be mistaken, for what the film shows finally is that its representation of an Inuit sense of the way the world always was and still is can only be realized in relation to a world other than the Inuit world. This other world—call it the South, Europe, the West, modernity, or colonialism—is invoked by the text that appears for several seconds on the screen at the outset, by the texts superimposed upon the film's first images, and by the outtakes that appear after the story proper has ended. I'll consider these later on. These framing devices must be read in relation to the body of the film as offering a comment on contemporary Inuit identity.

Set in Igloolik, the "place of houses," in northeastern Canada off Baffin Island, where Kunuk himself grew up, the film opens some two decades before the main body of the story, with what A. O. Scott (2002), writing in the *New York Times*, called a "prologue to the main narrative." We are first shown a lone man out on the snow with a sled and dogs;[15] then, as the film moves inside, we hear someone say—it is a woman named Panikpak, and she will be important to the story—"I can only sing this song to someone who understands it." We hear an unidentified man note his pleasure in songs. He is a stranger to the community, in fact, a mysterious and evil shaman from the North. This shaman, Tungajuak, engages Kumaglak, the camp leader, in a shamanic contest that leads to the latter's death, sowing dissension in the Inuit community.[16] Indeed, Kumaglak's son, Sauri, is accused of complicity in the death of his father, because he has served as Tungajuak's helper.[17] Sauri becomes the new leader, and he humiliates an old rival and formerly influential man called Tulimaq. Sauri has a son, Oki, and a daughter, Puja. Tulimaq has two boys, Amaqjuat, the elder, known as the strong one, and Atanarjuat, the younger, known as the fast runner. We see these boys first as toddlers. Then the film moves some twenty years forward.

For a number of reasons, sexual rivalry among them, Oki and his friends try to murder the brothers. They succeed in killing Amaqjuat, but, in an extraordinary scene, Atanarjuat escapes by running naked across the spring ice. Atanarjuat finds refuge with an old couple, Quilitalak and his wife, Niriuniq, and their adopted daughter, Kigutikarjuk, people who had some time ago fled the evil that the shaman had introduced into the community at Igloolik. They first conceal Atanarjuat from his pursuers and then nurture him back to health—his run had left his feet battered and bloody—and he eventually returns home, as do his hosts.

Atanarjuat then invites Oki and his companions to a feast in an igloo whose floor he has glazed with ice. Atanarjuat has hidden a club just outside, along with footgear to keep him from slipping. He retrieves these, then attacks and beats Oki and his friends, but he does not kill them, announcing that the "killing stops here." As the film approaches its ending, Quilitalik and his sister, Panikpak, the grandmother of the murderous Oki, perform a shamanic ceremony for expelling evil. Panikpak proclaims that Oki and Puja, along with some others, must leave so that the community may again live in order and harmony. Then the voice of the dead Kumaglak is heard requesting that his wife (Panikpak) sing his song, one in which all the remaining community members join, and the story concludes with an intact Inuit community (in some ways like the intact Laguna community at the end of *Ceremony*). The evil has been expelled for now, and the world is as it always was; everything is as it should be, at least for now.

The film is based on a traditional Inuit story that Kunuk and the scriptwriter, Paul Apak Angilirq, have said they had heard early in their lives. For the film project, the story was recorded in Inuktitut in versions told by seven or eight or ten elders (different interviews and publications have given different numbers). Before his early death from cancer in 1998, Paul Apak wrote the screenplay in English and also in the Inuktitut syllabary invented in about 1840 by James Evans, a Wesleyan missionary.[18] The published screenplay—which is clearly not the shooting script—is in Paul Apak's Inuktituk and in English; the English version is credited to Norman Cohn, the Isuma videographer and a longtime associate of Kunuk.

iii.

The earliest ethnographic account of the legend was published by Franz Boas in 1901, from a version taken down by the Quebec-born American sea captain and amateur ethnographer, Captain George Comer.[19] Titled "*Armuckjuark*," it is number twenty-eight of a group of tales from the "West Coast of Hudson Bay." The story tells of the trouble caused by the brothers' wives, to the point that the women, at the behest of "a number of people" (Boas 1901, 330), aid the brothers' enemies. At the time of the attack, the brothers are in different tents. Most of the assailants descend upon and kill Armuckjuark in his tent, while many fewer attack Artinarjuark, who escapes and makes his way to his parents, who protect him and heal his wounds. Finally, Artinarjuark returns to the village and kills "two men who had stabbed him" (331).

The story next appears in a version published by Knud Rasmussen, who heard it sometime between 1921 and 1924, in or near Igloolik, as told by Inugpasugjuk, known as a prodigious storyteller. Titled "Aumarzuat and Atanarzuat," and listed by Rasmussen among "tales of killing and vengeance," the story has Atanarzuat killed by unidentified "enemies" (1929, 298), while the wounded Aumarzuat escapes to the house of his parents. Later, he returns and slays two of the attackers and also one man who "meant no harm to him." "He had, as it were, got into the way of killing; and thus he avenged the slaying of his brother" (299).

A very brief version of the story appeared in Inuktitut for the first time in 1964, "written down in syllabic characters," as Bernard Saladin d'Anglure, the ethnographer for the Isuma screenplay, tells us, by Jimmy Ettuk, who also did four small drawings of scenes from the story (2002, 197). Saladin d'Anglure notes that he himself collected "the second Inuit-language version of the legend . . . while interviewing Michel Kupaaq, who was born in the mid-1920s." Kupaaq told the story again in 1987, 1990, and 1991, and "these four versions rounded out" by five other contemporary tellings, Saladin d'Anglure notes, "were the main sources for the film" (199).

Although the Boas/Comer version is called *Armuckjuark*, it is indeed the brother named Artinarjuak, who, when the two brothers are attacked, escapes (by wading through a stream, not by running over the ice), is healed (by his parents), and returns to challenge and kill the men who had killed his brother. The version published by Rasmussen has Atanarzuat killed, with his brother returning to avenge him. In Ettuk's brief version, it is again Atanaaqjuat who avenges the death of his unnamed brother, and it is he who "clubbed all his enemies to death" (Saladin d'Anglure 2002, 132). At the conclusion of Saladin d'Anglure's composite version in English, it is Atanarjuat who clubs "to death all those who had attacked him and killed his brother" (203).

In the question-and-answer period following his Spry lecture at McMaster University, in 2002, Kunuk was asked, "Did you make any changes to the original legend?" Kunuk answered that, at Paul Apak's suggestion, "we all changed the ending." Regarding the killings that are a consistent element of the story, Kunuk said, "Paul felt that doesn't make any sense. That is going to go on and on. We also knew that they used to just send people away instead of killing them and that was a better ending so we chose that" (9).

Kunuk added that Paul Apak "even asked the elders, is it all right to change the end?" and said, "I remember one of the elders answering him, 'We are storytellers'" (2002, "Spry," 9). I take that to mean that storytellers always make changes even though the story is always the same. Thus, the filmmakers arrived at a version at once true to the traditional story—and yet different, not at all a contradiction in terms. (Indeed, tradition, as Marshall Sahlins long ago noted, often means culturally consonant *change*.) In the same way, as we shall see, their film defines Inuit identity as always the same, even when inevitably different.[20]

But there is one other important change that I will note here and comment upon later. Not one of the extant versions has any mention whatever of shamanism.[21] Whatever it may be that leads to conflict in the community between fathers and sons, husbands and wives, and so on, it is not the appearance of an evil shaman from the North or from anyplace else. Nor is the problem resolved by any shamanic activity, as it is in the film. This particular change, an important one, will require some further commentary. But now let me consider broadly the audiences of *Atanarjuat*.

iv.

Inasmuch as Paul Apak and Zach Kunuk heard the story in their youth and inasmuch as eight or ten Inuit elders were able to tell it in Inuktitut toward the end of the twentieth century, it would seem that the story of Atanarjuat was still current in the culture of Igloolik and Nunavut. So what did these Inuit people make of the film? Speaking in Sydney, Australia on the occasion of a special screening of the film in 2001, Paul Okalik, premier of Nunavut, said, "Personally, it was wonderful, as an Inuk, watching the legend come to life on the big screen.... Never did I feel that a barrier existed between the story and myself.... I was impressed at how true the story was to the legend" (3).[22] So, too, it would seem, was there "no barrier" between the story and the people of Igloolik, the initial audience for the film. I'll quote Zacharias Kunuk at some length, again from his 2002 Spry lecture at McMaster University, as he describes what happened the first time he showed the film to his community. Kunuk says,

> The first screening in Igloolik in December 2000 was my scariest moment because we finally put it on the table to the people what we are making. We have no theatres in Igloolik. We found the biggest room we could find, which was a gymnasium. We bought a video projector, a wide screen. We put out four hundred chairs, and when we opened the gym, kids were running, pouring in. They were sitting on the floor. Elders were sitting and people were standing in the back for almost three hours. Sometimes there was silence, sometimes there was laughter, and then silence again. And when the credits rolled, people were clapping and crying and shaking our hands. That day

I knew we did our job right. For three screenings each night, about five hundred people came, out of twelve hundred people. Inuit loved it. Kids loved it. Kids were even playing Atanarjuat on the street. Every household in Igloolik had a copy of the video. We made a thousand VHS copies and sent them to the co-op stores in other communities to distribute it throughout Nunavut. Nunavut doesn't have a theatre system. This was the only way, the fastest way, so that they wouldn't be left out when we launched it.[23] (5–6)

Here, we might say, are the reviews from Nunavut, and most particularly from Igloolik. Perhaps it is no wonder, then, that the Atanarjuat Web site's production diary states that "the goal of Atanarjuat is to make the viewer feel inside the action, looking out, rather than outside looking in." Certainly the viewers from Igloolik, and the premier of Nunavut, felt this way, and the mere possibility that other viewers, outsiders, might experience the film in anything like this way is surely powerful and exciting. Nonetheless, as I have said, for outsiders to view the film in a manner even approximating the way in which Inuit insiders saw it would constitute a substantial moving of the center, a significant altering of consciousness and cognition.

The Web site quotation given above continues with the assumption that this goal has been achieved. It asserts that the film "lets people forget how far away they really are, and to identify with the story and the characters *as if they were just like us*" (my emphasis). This quotation—there are many others like it—does indeed acknowledge the fact that many people who see the film really are far away, and, in point of fact, that they are *not* "just like us," the people of Nunavut. And, again, their distance from the Inuit is not only spatial but perspectival. What can it mean, then, to encourage their identification "with the story and the characters *as if they were just like us*?" (my emphasis). Is this meant to endorse a by-now-disreputable "family of man" view that "we are really all the same?" that southerners are "just like us?" That seems mistaken or wishful thinking at best.

In any event, postcolonial criticism has quite thoroughly dismantled such a view, insisting, rather, on a difference that is—take your pick—either negotiable and reconcilable or absolute, but certainly not negligible. Recent postcolonial work has been concerned—to cite the title of a book published in 1997 examining a court case involving the Canadian Coast Salish—to insist upon the fact that *We Are Not You*. Which also means that you are not just like us. Does a comment like this from the Web site then testify to Kunuk's faith that his film really did "move the center," that it has provoked outsiders into seeing the film, at least to some degree, as the people of Igloolik saw it? Perhaps, at least for some—the second audience I have described above. How it might work for this audience, a relatively small audience, as I have said, will require much consideration. In the meantime, what about the larger audience of outsiders?

v.

As Kunuk notes in his Spry lecture, the film won many prizes and it did indeed attract an audience far beyond Igloolik and Nunavut—a global audience, in fact. Submitted to the international Cannes Film Festival in 2001, *Atanarjuat* won the prestigious Caméra d'Or award for best first feature film, going on to win prizes in Scotland, Belgium, and Canada as well. This led to its distribution in "thirty countries" (6).[24] *Atanarjuat*'s U.S. distributor is Lot 47 films, and I will later relate the curious anecdote that gave rise to the distributor's name and also look at how the Lot 47 logo is used as one of the framing devices of the film. On its Web site, Lot 47 has no fewer than seven pages of positive excerpts from Southern reviewers. Patricia Penn Hilden, Shari Huhndorf, and Lucas Bessire, whom I've already cited briefly, have reviewed some of these reviews, noting that they tend to praise the film for its epic and "universal" qualities, and also for its ethnographic qualities, that is, that it translates a foreign, exotic culture (that of the far North) for "us." These critics, and some few others, have pointed out that these reviews make sense of the film in Western terms exclusively; they valorize it by Homerizing or Shakespearizing it, as it were, on the one hand, and Nanook-ing it—the reference is to Robert Flaherty's 1922 silent film, *Nanook of the North*—on the other. A look at some of the reviews indicates that these very positive responses are thoroughly dependent upon a translation of the film's difference into these familiar Western categories.[25] Here, I'll go through some of the comments Lot 47 has collected, in addition to some few others that I have found. Of course these are all taken out of context, but my sense is that the selections are indeed representative of what the reviewers thought.

To authorize an estimate of *Atanarjuat*'s "universality," a few reviewers dredge up Joseph Campbell. Thus, Desson Howe in the *Washington Post* writes that the film is in "the spirit of Joseph Campbell," while Paul Malcolm of the *L.A. Weekly* sees it as a frontrunner for "Campbell's sense of mythomania," whatever that means. Arthur Salm of the *San Diego Union Tribune* generalizes that the film is "majestic, timeless," a sentiment shared by Eric Harrison of the *Houston Chronicle*, who writes, "A beautiful, timeless and universal tale."

Referencing Shakespeare is Robert Denerstein of the Denver *Rocky Mountain News*, who writes that the film has "a plot that rivals Shakespeare for intrigue, [and] treachery." From another Web site comes a quotation identified with radio station KCRW which calls *Atanarjuat* "a Shakespearian tale of love and vengeance, of magic and bawdy humor." An online reviewer who uses the name "misterbaby" says that this is a story "that would make Shakespeare proud; love, adultery, revenge, murder." That particular foursome, as we'll see, either derives from or is supported by the Atanarjuat/Isuma official Web sites, in addition to a number of comments offered by Kunuk and Cohn. Dennis King of the *Tulsa World* also refers to "Shakespearian themes of romantic rivalry, clan chicanery." Peter Ritter of the *Minneapolis City Pages* proclaims that the film has "the same cosmic sweep, the same sense of . . . Shakespeare and the Iliad." A similar pairing is that of Chris Hewitt on TwinCities.com, who also affirms that "'The Fast Runner' has the simple, timeless quality of Greek Tragedy or Shakespeare." Arion Berger of the *Washington City Paper* offers the view that the film "is like a roiling, passionate Shakespearian [play] . . . told with the engrossing intimacy of a documentary." Here we combine the epic with what might be the ethnographic, a category we shall consider in a moment. Chris Wiegand of *Boxoffice Magazine* references a different epic when he notes that the film has much "in common with Beowulf," although he also mentions the *Odyssey*.

The absurdities to which these comparisons can lead are epitomized in an excerpt from a review by the novelist Margaret Atwood, who gushed, in the *Globe and Mail*, "Homer with a video camera!" It seems clear that she means to praise Zach Kunuk by comparing him to Homer, although my sense is that it was mostly Cohn who held the camera. But wait! Is it not the case that we conventionally imagine Homer to be *blind*? In the rush to assimilate the film to Western epic, here is a serious writer who tells us that she admires this film because a blind bard held the camera! The quotation from Atwood, however, does not appear among those collected by Lot 47 Films. Where, then, did I find it? Nowhere else than on the first page of the screenplay published by Isuma Productions![26] Nor do I think they put it there to mock it. Before I say anything further about this willingness to validate responses that do *not* move the center, let us take a look at some of the ethnographic references.

There is, for example, Eric Harrison, who saw the film as not only "beautiful, timeless" but worth comparing to another "terrific Eskimo movie." He recalls, "In 1922, it was *Nanook of the North*," and now it is *Atanarjuat*. Michael Wilmington of the *Chicago Tribune* proposes that the film's "sweep and high drama" suggests "Nanook of the North done by a Kurosawa disciple," an interesting reference to a canonical figure in world cinema. Matt Zoller Seitz of the *New York Press* says the film "combines [?] . . . with

Nanook of the North." Scott of the *New York Times*, in a comment not quoted by Lot 47, also mentions *Nanook* at the beginning of his review, although, in fairness, he does so only in order to note the difference between Flaherty's silent Eskimos and the Inuit who are given voice in *Atanarjuat*.[27] Scott, however, also looks to epic, although he turns to the nineteenth-century novel, noting that the rivalry between Atanarjuat and Oki "is as violent and stirring as anything in Victor Hugo." Shari Huhndorf (2003), foremost among other postcolonial critics, has provided a detailed and thoroughly convincing critique of Flaherty, in addition to a brief history of the display of "Eskimos" from at least 1897 to the present.[28] But as early as 1927, in a quirky but often stunning little book called *The Standardization of Error*, Vilhjalmur Stefansson begins by noting that "the *Nanook* story was at least as true as that of Santa Claus" (1927, 67); he then proceeds systematically through a checklist of the film's "errors."

But when we finish reading the screenplay—Paul Apak's Inuit syllabics, and Norman Cohn's English—we find that Isuma has indeed provided an ethnographic commentary by Saladin d'Anglure to interpret Inuit culture for "us." And what is the image that appears on the very first page of Saladin d'Anglure's text? Nothing other than a still from *Nanook of the North*! But this should come as no surprise. In response to a question from the audience at his Spry lecture about the possible influence of *Nanook* on *Atanarjuat*, Kunuk said, "Yes, I have been asked this question a lot of times. Robert Flaherty did his documentary about 500 miles south of our community. . . . *I am really glad he did record that culture at the time. We are doing ours further north*" (9, emphasis added).[29]

Kunuk, thus, would indeed seem to offer, if not an invitation, at least full permission to compare his film to *Nanook*, and not necessarily as an antidote to *Nanook*, notwithstanding that postcolonial critics, myself included, see it as very different from *Nanook*.[30]

As I noted above, Kunuk, in his Spry lecture, named prizes won by the film, and noted its widespread distribution and robust ticket sales. How has all this come about, he was asked? "First of all," Kunuk said, because *Atanarjuat* "was a really good film—exciting, entertaining, with good action, love, sex, good camera work, good music. . . . Our legend is a universal story: about love, jealousy, murder, revenge, forgiveness[31]—the same for everybody everywhere. Not like Hollywood films. It was shot, acted, edited in our own style. Everything is authentic. The audiences really get the story" (6).

Cohn is also on record to the effect that the film "teaches a very *universal* lesson. . . . Don't mess around with your family. Don't let your personal pride or needs destroy your community" (Camhi 2001, my emphasis).[32] He is quoted by *Village Voice* reviewer Leslie Camhi, who herself notes what she calls the film's "Shakespearean plot." In another interview, Paul Apak (2002), remarking, "Yes, I am sure that this movie will help promote the culture" of the Inuit, described the intended audience as "anybody, no matter who they are and where they are from. We are thinking about the same audiences that would go to see movies in the South. You know, the movies with movie stars, or whatever. Anyone who watches the movies" (Angilirq 2002, 3).

Isuma's Web site describes *Atanarjuat* as "an exciting action thriller set in ancient Igloolik, the film unfolds as a life-threatening struggle of love, jealousy, murder and revenge." These "official" sentiments, as I have shown, have been picked up by reviewers. Those involved in the production of the extraordinarily different and difficult *Atanarjuat* here speak as though it were not so extraordinarily different and difficult at all. They invite the faraway viewer to feel close to the material—just like "us." This, as I have said, is unusual.

If moviegoers who like "the movies with movie stars," see the film as an "exciting action thriller," "the same for everybody everywhere," then surely any sense they might have of feeling "inside the action, looking out, rather than outside looking in" could only be the result of their having translated the film and assimilated it to what they already know. How else could they believe that traditional Inuit people then and now really were "just like us?" Of course, it is true that love, jealousy, murder, and so on are indeed "universal," that they are known in some form to humans in all times and all cultures. And yet, love, jealousy, and murder in *Atanarjuat*, as Kunuk also says, appear "in our own style. Everything is authentic" (2002, "Spry," 6). But the Inuit "style," in its full authenticity, can't possibly be universal any more than any culture-specific "style" can be universal. Moreover, for all that Kunuk's remark is dismissive of Hollywood films, much of what he says for his film could be said of them: a great many Hollywood films with movie stars also treat love, jealousy, murder, forgiveness, and so on—and, like it or not, these subjects are also dealt with in a style "authentic" to an American cultural-dominant at a particular point in time. This is to say that although these films are also thoroughly culture-specific and "authentic," they, too, could be considered "universal." It is common knowledge that Hollywood films (along with U.S. television dramas) have been very popular all around the world—in Europe, Africa, South Asia, and the Far East—"the same for everybody everywhere," "for anybody who goes to the movies." Nevertheless, I find it hard to imagine that any children who saw *Atanarjuat* outside of Nunavut (I doubt whether many southern children would sit through this long film!) would be playing Atanarjuat in the streets.

My account thus far has meant to say the following: Zacharias Kunuk and his coworkers are first and foremost committed to Inuit film for the Inuit. Kunuk takes validation of his work by his community as the most important testimony to his success. He works from what he understands as an Inuit perspective, and he reminds his people, in the phrase I have taken from Silko, of the way the world always was and still is to Inuit people. But he also, as I mentioned above, complicates the contemporary meaning of indigenousness and the traditional, dramatizing what it might mean to be Inuit in the contemporary world. To take a phrase from Julie

Cruikshank (1997), in *Atanarjuat* Kunuk and his Isuma colleagues "negotiate with narrative"—film narrative, to be sure. This is to say—shifting now to a fine discussion by Elaine Jahner—that because "legal questions about sovereignty are all, to some degree, questions about the boundaries of communities" (2003, 270), a community can use the transmission and reception of certain narratives as a way of defining their distinctive, bounded identity, indeed, their sovereignty. We will later examine the film's particular redaction of the Atanarjuat story, most particularly its attention to shamanism.[33]

Kunuk and his coworkers at Isuma Productions are also committed—as Hilden, Huhndorf, and Bessire, among others, have persuasively argued—to moving the center, to provoking southern viewers to see and experience the world differently and so perhaps to act differently. Kunuk has made a film that contests the South's representations of the world. For any southerner to understand what it is that they have imagined presents, as I have said, a substantial and difficult challenge, yet one that is most exciting and potentially great in its rewards. So far as the film reaches toward a southern audience willing to accept its challenge, it enacts a cosmopolitan commitment to Inuit sovereignty.

For all of this, Kunuk and Isuma may well recognize that this second audience is not a very large one. Indicative, I would guess, of perhaps a certain generosity, possibly some confusion, and, indeed, an optimism based on recent events[34]—I'll try to describe those more fully below—they are quite welcoming to an audience in the South whose response to the film is predicated upon a translation of it into universalist, epic, Campbellian, or Shakespearean categories, on the one hand, or into ethnographic/documentary categories, on the other. Although this quite substantial audience may be missing the point—many points!—this just does not seem particularly troubling to Kunuk, Cohn, and Isuma. This, as I have said, is unusual and somewhat surprising, and it needs some explanation. As I've also said, I think the explanation has something to do with the creation of Nunavut in 1999. I'll save this discussion for last.

vi.

I'll comment here as a self-conscious member of the second audience I've described, as a postcolonial critic, someone eager to understand a film as beautiful, complex, and—for me—strange and difficult as *Atanarjuat*. I'll start by admitting that I "got" very little of it when I saw it for the first time in a movie theater in New York. But I've now seen the film four times in its entirety, thanks to videotape and DVD—which have also allowed me to go over many of the scenes a number of times. I've also done a fair amount of reading: interviews with and writing by the filmmakers, history, ethnography, other postcolonial criticism. I hope to do more reading, and of course, I will look at the film again, many times more. But, no matter how hard I continue to work, I simply cannot imagine a time when I could honestly say with Premier Okalik, "Never did I feel a barrier existed between the story and myself." Meanwhile, I'm not in the least tempted to invoke the epic or the ethnographic documentary—to Homerize or Nanook the film—in order to make sense of it; to do that, it seems clear, is surely to establish barriers to understanding that are insurmountable.

These are the issues I hope now to address:

1. Why is shamanism so important to this film when there is no mention of shamanism in any of the older or contemporary versions of the Atanarjuat story (including Saladin d'Anglure's composite)?
2. How do the opening texts and the closing outtakes relate to the film as a whole, and what does this relation have to say about contemporary Inuit identity?
3. Why is it that Kunuk and Isuma are so willing to accommodate, even encourage, responses that surely block any movement of the epistemological and ideological center?

Saladin d'Anglure, a student of Claude Lévi-Strauss, and the ethnographer chosen to offer a considerable body of explanatory material for the official Isuma bilingual screenplay, writes that "the most challenging part in writing the screenplay was undoubtedly the description of shamanism" (2002, 203).[35] But, as I've noted, this "challenge" was not actually posed by either the earlier story versions recorded by ethnographers or by the versions from the 1980s or 1990s collected by Saladin d'Anglure. Shamanism, Saladin d'Anglure states, is "the foundation of the entire system of Inuit beliefs and practices before the coming of the Whites" (203), and there is much to support this claim. As for the absence of any reference to shamans or shamanism in any version of the Atanarjuat stories, Saladin d'Anglure suggests that this "system was so well woven into traditional life that the legend says nothing about it" (203). This is to say that the "legend" wouldn't need to say anything about shamanism because culturally competent hearers would recognize its presence even with no explicit mention.[36]

Perhaps. But while I'm convinced entirely of the centrality of shamanism to the Inuit, it's not clear to me that the Atanarjuat story is a story that is central to Inuit tradition, or that however well-woven shamanism was into traditional life, it is actually somehow woven into the Atanarjuat story. Rasmussen noted that "it is difficult to classify legends on the basis of their substance, for as a rule many subjects come into the tale" (1929, 111).[37] He nonetheless offered a distinction that he believed "the Eskimos themselves make . . . between *oqalugtuat* and *oqalualat*." The first are "the old myths which go so far into the Past that the Eskimos then had their original home in regions lying to the west of the Hudson Bay, possibly right over the Bering Strait." The second are "legends on the subject of people who lived at a time that is still within living memory. They are always local, for which reason they can be placed definitely to the localities where the events took place." Rasmussen also notes that "at first glance," these latter stories "are indistinguishable from the ancient myths" (111).

My sense, from the published versions and from Saladin d'Anglure's composite, is that the Atanarjuat story belongs to the group that Rasmussen called *oqalualat*, the stories that derive from events still within living memory. But, as Rasmussen noted, these stories have important ties to the "ancient myths." I'll venture the guess that the Atanarjuat story that Paul Apak and Zach Kunuk had been attracted to since their youth had the mix, to call it that, of myth and history invoked by Rasmussen. I'll also guess that they both wanted very much to use the film they would make of that story in a decidedly "local" way, for the people of Igloolik foremost, and that they also wanted the film, as I've said above, following Jahner and Cruikshank, to use the transmission and reception of this particular narrative as a way of defining their community's distinctive boundedness, a testimony to its discursive and so also its political sovereignty. As Jahner wrote, the historical "selection process, itself, becomes an exercise in sovereignty" (2003, 272). The kind of stories people tell and appreciate define who they are.[38] As the response of the audience at Igloolik demonstrated, the film succeeded in affirming an Inuit identity for the contemporary Inuit community as that of a people who tell and appreciate the Atanarjuat legend as it is represented in this film; they find in it, to cite Jahner once more, "a specific symbolic economy with verifiable social consequences" (271). I'll look at other identity issues a bit later on.

Assume that Kunuk was attracted to the Atanarjuat story and wanted to tell it as a foundational narrative for the people of Igloolik—a story that confirms for this community who they are, their bounded identity affirmed by means of a representation of its usable past. Assume that he knows that "shamanism is the foundation of the entire system of Inuit beliefs before the coming of the Whites" (Saladin d'Anglure 2002, 203). Then, if the versions of the story he knows don't have any explicit mention of shamanism—even if shamanism is perhaps implicit in the story for some community members—it would therefore seem important to make shamanism prominent, "foundational" in some regard in the film. In an autobiographical piece reprinted among the materials surrounding the screenplay, Kunuk, lamenting the fact that "four thousand years of oral history [were] silenced by fifty years of priests, schools and cable TV," asks, "How were shamans tied? Where do suicides go? What will I answer when I'm an elder and don't know anything about it? Will I have anything to say?" (Angilirq 2002, 13). While this film will not answer the question of where suicides go, its opening sequences most certainly show us how shamans were tied. It is also interesting to learn from a sidebar of the screenplay that the last shamanic "leader at Igloolik was Ittuksarjuat, the grandfather of Paul Apak Angilirq. He died in 1945" (169). (And the new film, as I've noted, focuses intensely on the shaman, Aua.) Some of Kunuk's earlier work included material about shamanism, and in the screenplay of *Atanarjuat* (as I've said, the screenplay is not the shooting script for the U.S. version I've seen), shamanism is important throughout. Many of the scenes involving shamans are in the film as well, although there is little to alert most viewers that shamanistic activity is specifically being represented. The film opens with a contest between shamans, and Paul Apak's screenplay, although not the film itself, has the evil shaman return later in the film. It is also a ceremony performed by the brother and sister, Quilitalik and Panikpak, both of whom are shamans, which prepares for driving out the evil, with Panikpak finally ordering the "bad" characters to leave the community.

The particular shaman who brings trouble is a foreigner, not someone from the local community, and his visit changes the lives of the people of Igloolik. "As a story about a community ravaged by outside influences," Shari Huhndorf has observed, "the film functions as a colonial allegory as well as a narrative about identity reconstruction in the wake of this catastrophe" (2003, 824). This is a powerful insight. In the screenplay, although not in the film, Tuungarjuaq is asked where he comes from, and he answers,

"Up that way... near the walrus" (Angilirq 2002, 37). The place he is referring to is Aivalik, "place of the walrus." But Aivalik is near Repulse Bay, and Repulse Bay is just on the Arctic Circle, to the *south* of Igloolik; thus, the mysterious shaman from the North is actually from *down* that way, not *up* that way.[39] Colonialism did come to the Inuit from the South, specifically, from England and the voyages of Middleton in the mid-eighteenth century, followed by those of Commander William Parry in the 1820s, and the later incursions of Captain George Comer late in the nineteenth and early in the twentieth century. In the 1920s Rasmussen worked with Inuit shamans, but I don't think Danes could represent northern intruders. Further, the new film does not portray Rasmussen and his two associates as life-changing intruders—although the missionaries who did change the lives of the Inuit came from the South. I must leave this matter with no satisfactory explanation of why the mysterious shaman from the North seems actually to come from the South—unless, to repeat, this invokes the direction of colonial incursion—and perhaps points as well to the deceitfulness of invaders who bring trouble.

vii.

The brief summary of the film I offered earlier doesn't literally describe what the viewer encounters. What an American viewer first sees on the screen is the logo of Lot 47 Films.[40] Then there are a few moments showing a lone man with dogs, in twilight, on the snow. Further text is superimposed upon these images as the words "Igloolik Isuma Productions Presents" and "A National Film Board of Canada Co-production" appear. When the film proper is over, nearly three hours later, the credits run alongside outtakes that depict members of the cast in contemporary clothing, while also revealing the cameras and some of the equipment that were involved in the actual production of the film.

I want to suggest that the first few minutes of the film and these concluding outtakes make an important statement. They confirm the fact that the film's subject matter, traditional Inuit life, is here being represented by means of contemporary technology—no sign of which had otherwise appeared in the film.[41] The film's representation of an Inuit sense of the way the world always was and still is is thus only possible in relation to the southern world.[42] Indeed, we are engaging the Inuit world as it always was, thanks to the support of the National Film Board of Canada, which is credited in a text superimposed on the images of the man and dogs. The National Film Board of Canada has been a supporter of indigenous cinema, and Kunuk, to be sure, is required to present the Lot 47 logo and to credit the National Film Board of Canada. But the way in which he does this—framing the shots of the man and his dogs with these texts—insists upon the fact that although this film may *seem* to represent a world separate and apart from the dominant culture, no such representation is possible separate and apart from the complicated nexus of the southern world—Toronto, New York, Cannes, and elsewhere.

Unless one understands this—and I don't think it's possible to understand it until *after* one has seen the outtakes at the end—it would indeed be tempting to accuse Kunuk of either a disreputable essentialism, or perhaps an equally or more disreputable inauthenticity.[43] Essentialism, because, as I've said, he seems to represent a world in which no one and nothing but traditional Inuit people exist in their eternal Inuit-ness. Inauthenticity because his film does fully acknowledge its relation to the National Film Board of Canada, and to Lot 47 Films, and, with the outtakes, subverts any sense of an Inuit life untouched by the West. The first accusation is familiar enough; the second accusation derives from what I will call a *projective essentialism* usually but not exclusively indulged by the dominant culture.[44]

Projective essentialism assumes that once indigenous people have incorporated any aspect of Western thought or culture, they are no longer authentic nor can they truly be themselves. Projective essentialism refuses to recognize the ways in which the selective appropriation of aspects of the dominant culture, at least up to a point, does not so much make indigenous people the same as persons in the dominant culture but, to the contrary, provides them with expanded options for being different, for being themselves. Any accusations of essentialism—you claim to be always and only you, and that can't really be the case—or accusations of inauthenticity—you have incorporated aspects of us, so that you also can't really be you anymore—would both derive from a partial reading of the film, one that ignores the opening texts and the concluding outtakes or one that leans too heavily on the opening texts and the concluding outtakes. *Atanarjuat* offers an Inuit view of the world as it always was while acknowledging the fact that it can offer such a view only by a careful and selective engagement with the West. But contradictions of this sort, as we shall see further, are well-known consequences of colonialism.

The outtakes and the opening texts stake out a distinctive position in relation to these matters. On one hand, as I have said, they break the illusion, reminding us that this representation of the world as it always was occurs in the world as it is now, a world that most certainly does include the West. The outtakes also begin by telling the audience that the film is dedicated to Amelia and Paul Angilirq, and that these people have specific dates of birth and death (Amelia, 1957–2000; Paul, 1954–1998). And they jar us with images of the crew filming Atanarjuat's run for his life, and of Oki—or, rather, Peter-Henry Arnatsiaq—in a motorcycle jacket. Finally, viewers see the film crew headed off in their boat, clad not in skins but in nylon parkas. Does this ironically undercut the authenticity and/or Inuitness of the film? I think it does not; rather, it complicates these issues in positive ways. Insofar as Kunuk and his many coworkers at Isuma Productions have tried to give us a sense of the way the Inuit see the world as it always was, we are reminded here, as I've said now several times, that they are doing this with technological means available in and from a very different world. But this doesn't mean that Kunuk and the Inuit of Igloolik and Nunavut have in any way broken with the traditional world they have represented.[45] Rather, what they do is not so different from what the oral storytellers do, notwithstanding that the technology of transmission is certainly different.

In the first chapter of this book, my discussion of trickster tales made the case that the primary conceptual modality in traditional oral cultures involved *both/and* rather than *either/or* constructions. In *Atanarjuat*, whether as a consequence of a residual orality or persistent traditionality, *both/and* rather than *either/or* perspectives also seem to operate. It's certainly not that Kunuk is somehow "Homer with a video camera"; rather, one might refer to him, as I've just done above, as a traditional Inuit armed with digital technology—not in the least a contradiction in terms. In the preceding chapter, I quoted the Cherokee scholars Jack and Anna Kilpatrick who wrote of "the amazing ability of the Cherokees to maintain an equilibrium between two opposing worlds of thought" (1964, v). Although, as indicated, I think it is more accurate to say two *different* rather than two *opposing* worlds of thought, the Kilpatricks' observation seems apt, and not only for the Cherokees. If it is the case, to cite again an example I've given from the Kilpatricks, that "a Cherokee businessman on the way to his country club" can also "be wrapped in deep speculation as to the exact height of the slant-eyed giant, Tsuhl'gul" (v), then it is also the case that Kunuk might be wondering about how shamans were tied while filling out the application forms for funding by the Film Board of Canada, or arranging for the purchase of digital video equipment.

The coexistence of cultural worlds that are neither in opposition nor entirely complementary is represented even as the outtakes roll along with the credits. For one thing, the song that the spirit of Kumaglak had directed his wife to sing continues uninterrupted as the outtakes appear; there isn't a shift to some form of contemporary pop or rock or what have you as the southern world is acknowledged. That would be thoroughly to shift registers, to operate in the key of modernity exclusively, a gesture that would, I suspect, very nearly make a mockery of what came before. But, then, not all of the outtakes break the illusion either. Yes, there is Oki in his motorcycle jacket, and there is the camera and the microphone boom recording him knocking Quilitalik down as he searches for Atanarjuat; there is Atanarjuat—Natar Ungalaaq—jumping up and down to keep warm while wrapped in a blanket. But there are also two frames showing a woman—I can't identify her—pulling a large fish out of the water and presenting it to another woman. Both remain in costume; the camera taking their picture is no more visible than cameras were throughout the film. These unsubverted images may well be missed by the viewer; nonetheless, I read them as supporting the both/and perspective on Inuit identity. For all that the outtakes complicate the representation offered in the film itself, that representation—its status as Inuit-imagined past, rhetorical agency, narrative sovereignty—is not undone by the outtakes.

Saladin d'Anglure observes that among the indigenous peoples of the world today, "Inuit probably stand alone in having peacefully achieved so many political, economic, and social gains through negotiations with the government they live under" (2002, 227).[46]

He adds the important point that "the creation of Nunavut on April 1, 1999, coincided with the start of Atanarjuat's six-month location shooting," and that "the two events are not unrelated" (Saladin d'Anglure 2002, 227). In 1999 Nunavut—the name means "our land" in Inuktitut—became a self-governing territory within Canada's confederation. The Nunavut Land Claims Agreement granted title to Inuit for lands comprising some 350,000 square kilometers (Nunavut is about a fifth of all of Canada, 1.9 million square kilometers) and established equal representation of Inuit within the Canadian government on a number of important issues.[47] By the year 2007, Can $1.2 billion will have passed from the Canadian government to the Nunavut Trust. Inuit, who comprise approximately 85 percent of the population of Nunavut, will have a major say in land usage, mineral rights, and development of every kind. Inuktitut is the official language of the territory.[48] The 1999 signing of the agreement in Iqaluit, the capital of Nunavut, represented the culmination of some thirty years of delicate and complex negotiations. Although much, of course, remains to be done, the Inuit of Nunavut have achieved a very great deal in their negotiations with the Canadian government.

I think there is probably no way to know with any certainty whether or to what degree non-indigenous Canadians negotiated these changes with the Inuit because they somehow came to see the world differently over those thirty years. My guess, as an outsider, is that it's entirely possible that they did so strictly on the basis of an adherence to certain idealized Western values—fairness, honesty, equality, and the like.[49] If that is the case, then a filmmaker who wants to use his art for the benefit of his people can, on the one hand, produce something quite uncompromisingly Inuit: a film in Inuktitut that, as I've said, affirms by means of narrative who his people were and are, a film that, in Saladin d'Anglure's words, serves as an "affirmation of cultural identity" (2002, 227) and is received as exactly that by the people of Nunavut. Such a film uncompromisingly challenges the southern audience to think *differently*, and thus perhaps to move the colonial center. And yet—this is an imagined narrative on my part—perhaps Zach Kunuk, secure in the knowledge that he has produced a film fully validated by his own people and likely to be appreciated on its own terms by some few outsiders, and, too, occupying a promising sociopolitical position in Nunavut—perhaps he can feel perfectly comfortable about inviting the good will and approbation of all those many viewers who might flock to the film only if they are granted permission or encouraged to translate it into their own comfort zones. Why not, after all? Let them go on clueless. (And, as indicated above, why not use the money to benefit

Igloolik and the Inuit?) If they find something to like, that's just fine. After all, Canada didn't have to adopt an "Inuit perspective" before negotiating the self-government of Nunavut. This is, as I have said, the way I imagine the third of *Atanarjuat*'s three audiences to have come into being.

Quoting *Nanook*

Of course, it isn't possible to quote Nanook himself; Flaherty's film is a silent film released just five years before the first talkie (or semi-talkie, *The Jazz Singer* [1927]), and no one of the title cards ascribes speech to him. Nanook as he is represented doesn't have language or a voice—although he is once set to playing the fool in his curiosity about sound. In an early section of the film, at the white man's trading post, Nanook is shown trying to chew a gramophone record, perhaps better to discern (by means of taste?) its ability to reproduce sound. As Vilhjalmur Stefansson pointed out almost immediately (1927), the gramophone had been known up North for many years; the staged scene, as Monika Siebert has noted, "establishes another staple of ethnographic representation and the Western thinking about the indigenous: their fundamental state of authentic separateness . . . combined with a natural curiosity about and openness to the wonders of Western technology" (2006, 539).

This is what Ann Fienup-Riordan calls "Eskimo Orientalism," and, as she makes clear, "representations of Eskimos provide another window into the history of the *West*" (1995, xi, emphasis added) far more than they mirror actual Inupiaq and Yup'ik men and women. In Flaherty's film, Nanook and his family are consistently presented as in a fierce struggle with harsh nature. But, as Fienup-Riordan writes, "The reality of Nanook's world was that it was being threatened most by the larger society" (52). Shari Huhndorf has pointed to the way in which "the European presence and the effects of colonialism are virtually (although not completely [there are, to be sure, the early trading post scenes]) erased" in *Nanook* (2001, 101). But they are completely erased in *Atanarjuat*—although the film does, as I've argued, make a strong political statement. A very modest part of that statement involves quoting *Nanook*.

Here it's important to remember Huhndorf's reminder that Kunuk and the Inuit of Nunavut are likely to respond to *Nanook* in a manner quite different from southern postcolonial critics. If *we* criticize it for its demeaning and dismissive view of Eskimos (in spite of a certain admiration for their courage in a difficult environment) and its untroubled conviction that these people will soon be no more, the thriving Inuit today need hardly be troubled by what is, as their contemporary situation makes clear, an absurd notion hardly worth bothering about. This might mean that the Inuit can manage to do what academic critics find difficult to do—what I'm sure many of our nonacademic friends have urged us to do—to just take it for what it is. The problem for academic critics is that our training is such that "what it is" inevitably includes all sorts of things that don't actually meet the eye; "what it is" includes what it *implies* beyond what it *shows*. These vocational habits lead to both our insights and our blindnesses.

Atanarjuat quotes *Nanook of the North* both critically and appreciatively. On the one hand, the film engages in what a few years back might have been called siting by citing: quoting, that is, in such a way as not only to invoke but to comment upon the original by situating it in a different context, performing a sort of critical intertextualism—and I'll mention at least one instance of this. But, on the other hand, Kunuk, who knows *Nanook* well, also quotes it on occasion simply, it would seem, for pleasure—and, as I've said, with reference to Huhndorf's insight, why not? His people's history has refuted Flaherty's ideological premise, so Zach Kunuk can just take it for what it is. Thus, he redoes some of its scenes with color, with sound, with more visual clarity, and maybe, in some degree, with more accuracy.

As an instance of critical citation, I want to consider the last frames of *Nanook* and the first frames of *Atanarjuat*. The similarities, like the differences—regardless of whether the filmmakers were consciously quoting *Nanook* or not—are very striking. *Nanook* ends with images of dogs howling (silently, of course) in the blowing snow; the title card reads, "The Melancholy North." The very first frames of *Atanarjuat* also show dogs howling in the snow—and of course now we can hear them—although there is a lone man among them (but he is silent). It would be difficult to characterize this scene in a couple of words, but I think "melancholy" would not especially come to mind. I am suggesting that Kunuk's *Atanarjuat* thus begins exactly where Flaherty's film left off, and it is a new beginning indeed. For example, the scene that immediately follows the opening shots in *Atanarjuat* offers what *Nanook* never does, a fairly large, multifamily community engaged in matters other than subsistence. There are songs, there are shamans, there is laughter, and there is conflict as well. None of this appears in *Nanook*, where the fight to survive is all.

To quote Monika Siebert once more, "The visual allusions pile up: dogs get kicked, raw meat gets eaten, knives and sled runners get licked, igloos go up" (2006, 538–39). And none of this citing involves much in the way of siting. These things are interesting to the Inuit, and even had they not appeared in *Nanook*, they might well have appeared in a film set among the Inuit before the invasion of Europe. It seems also possible that Atanarjuat's extraordinary run across the ice might be a dramatic expansion of a scene in which Flaherty has Nanook tiptoeing among the ice floes. After all, in the traditional stories on which Atanarjuat is based, Atanarjuat's escape doesn't necessarily involve a run across the ice. So, too, with such things as the close-ups of the oil lamps. Siebert says that "while reproducing these documentary conventions," *Atanarjuat* "also offers a subtle critique of same" (539). That is probably accurate, although my sense is that *revision* is a better word than *critique*. I think that Kunuk and Isuma really do like *Nanook*, such that their quotation isn't always critique; sometimes the revision is more nearly in the nature of an update and an improvement upon it. The references to *Nanook* seem to say, Here are things the South thinks about "Eskimos," and some of these things aren't so far off. With our new sense of autonomy—not to mention our new technological capacities—we don't have to try to alter the whole picture, so let's just work with it in our own way.

Acknowledgments

I'd like here to thank the many individuals who have helped me with this book over the years I've been working on it, and also to say something about its history.

I am grateful to my colleague and friend Patricia Penn Hilden for talk about a great many matters, and in particular, for her comments on a draft of the *Atanarjuat* chapter. Shari Huhndorf also read a draft of that chapter and provided insights and raised questions that enormously aided my understanding. I thank Virginia Kennedy as well for her comments on *Atanarjuat*, and also for her thoughts on a great many matters. And thanks to Monika Siebert for sending me her work on *Atanarjuat*, and for commenting on my own. Special thanks go to Scott Richard Lyons, whose comments and suggestions about all sorts of things have been of enormous value to me. Scott's own work-in-progress promises to advance a variety of critical conversations. Late in my work, it was my good fortune to receive the sound advice of Jace Weaver, for which I am grateful. My Sarah Lawrence colleague and dear friend, Bella Brodzki, although not a specialist in Native Studies, also provided thoughtful support in many ways.

Thanks are due as well to Chadwick Allen, Nina Baym, Maurice Charney, Eric Cheyfitz, Michael Elliott, Daniel Heath Justice, Jan Gabler-Hovel, Michael Hittman, W. J. T. Mitchell, Malea Powell, Robert Dale Parker, LaVonne Brown Ruoff, Brian Swann, and Sean Teuton for their help. My European friends and colleagues, Harald Gaski in Tromsø, and Fedora Giordano in Turin, along with

Eloina Prati dos Santos of Brazil, invited me to speak at their universities and contributed a variety of comments and kindnesses. My research assistants Devennie Wauneka and Jaime Warburton contributed to making work just a bit easier; I am grateful to both of them. Last but decidedly not least, I have yet again to thank the librarians of Sarah Lawrence College: Judith Kicinski, now retired, has for many years been a great help and support, as has Janet Alexander. I am, in addition, much indebted to Geoff Danisher. Thanks are also due to two anonymous reviewers of the original manuscript of this book and to my editors at the University of Nebraska Press, Gary Dunham and Elisabeth Chretien.

Although each of the chapters in their present form appears in this book for the first time, most have appeared elsewhere in earlier and less developed form. Some of the ideas developed in chapter 1 on the trickster were first offered in a talk at Washington State University in 2002, and then as the Stephen Crane Memorial Lecture at Syracuse University (thanks to Monika Siebert for the invitation); at an international conference in Belo Horizonte, Brazil (my invitation came from Eloina Prati dos Santos); and at the Indian Studies Workshop of the European Association for American Studies in Turin, Italy, in 2003 (thanks, for this, to Fedora Giordano). A Portuguese translation of my presentation in Brazil was published in 2003, and the proceedings of the Turin Conference in 2004 printed my talk in English. A longer, but very different, version of this material appeared in *Comedy: A Geographical and Historical Guide* (2005), edited by Maurice Charney.

Chapter 2, "Representing Indians in American Literature, 1820–1870," was first prepared for a series of volumes called *American History through Literature, 1820–1870*, in which a much briefer account appeared. A small portion of the list of works with Indian subjects that comprises the final section of chapter 2 also appeared in that volume. Chapter 3, "Resisting Racism: William Apess as Public Intellectual," began as a short talk called "William

Apess as Indigenous Public Intellectual" at the Native American Literary Symposium in 2004, for a panel chaired by Scott Lyons. This expanded version appears here in print for the first time. A much earlier (French) version of chapter 4 appeared in *Recherches Amérindiennes au Québec* as "Répresenter la dépossession des Cherokees," and an English version of the French translation (but with no endnotes!) appeared in SAIL (*Studies in American Indian Literature*) in 2005. A very early and very different version of the fifth and final chapter was initially presented as a talk at the Institute for Sami Studies at the University of Tromsø, Norway, in 2005 (thanks for the invitation go to Harald Gaski), and a slightly briefer version of the chapter appeared in *Critical Inquiry* in 2007. Chapter 5's final section, on *Nanook of the North*, is published here for the first time. I am grateful to all for permission to use parts of previously published materials.

Notes

Preface

1. Only chapter 2, "Representing Indians," largely restricts itself to the sociopolitical or ideological function of the representation of Indians in a range of works of American literature in the nineteenth century.

2. See White, "Introduction," in *Metahistory* (1973). Also important for these matters is Northrop Frye's *Anatomy of Criticism* (1957).

3. Traditional Native oral stories have different structural patterns than those in Western narratives, but these have not been established very well as yet. The oral stories critics know are based on narratives that likely precede the European invasion, so resistance to colonialism cannot have been part of the cultural work they sought to perform—although there is no question that the earliest stories can be and have been adapted for this purpose.

1. Trickster Tales Revisited

1. Jacobs was one of the earliest collectors of oral narratives to take up the issue of how narrators and their audiences themselves referred to stories (1959, 25–65). He noted that "most folkloristic publications contain story titles which Euramerican authors devised and which therefore *reflect non-native criteria for selection of significant content*" (250, my emphasis). He remarks that the particular Coyote who "made everything good" in this story may have been unique among characters called Coyote, and points out that some Chinookan groups ascribed this positive transformation to Salmon (255).

2. Although Tomson Highway speaks of trickster as "that little guy, man or woman—it doesn't matter because the Cree language doesn't have any gender" (in Ryan 1999, 3), it nonetheless seems reasonable to say that when we find a trickster with a penis, avid to have sex with women, the likelihood of his being male is substantial.

3. Rice offers a detailed account of the Lakota trickster in chapters 3 and 4 of his *Before the Great Spirit* (1998). His view of trickster is largely in accord with the earlier observers, Stephen Riggs and J. O. Dorsey, who, in the words of the anthropologist Robert Lowie, both describe "the Dakota Unktomi [Dakota variant of the Lakota Iktomi] . . . as the incarnation of knavery" (1909, 432). Rice also says that Iktomi "is an adolescent potentiality in each person for creation or destruction" (1998, 55), although Iktomi usually tends toward the latter. Ella Cara Deloria's *Dakota Texts* of 1932 begins, however, with a story called "Ikto [Iktomi] Conquers Iya the Eater," in which Ikto—atypically, as Deloria points out—performs a deed that is beneficial to the people, a deed that in other stories is attributed to the Lakota culture hero Stone Boy.

4. Ballinger's earlier study (2000) appears as the fourth chapter of his book (2004).

5. Compare to Hyde: "trickster is a boundary-crosser," and there are "also cases in which trickster *creates* a boundary" (1998, 7).

6. In 1868 Brinton said of the trickster he calls Michabo that "he seems half a wizard, half a simpleton," a paradox he solves by noting that "this is a low, modern, and corrupt version of the character . . . bearing no . . . resemblance to his *real and ancient*" character (in Hultkrantz 1997, 4, my emphasis).

7. This was a matter that attracted a good deal of attention. In a brief note, the eminent anthropologist Robert Lowie essentially agrees with Boas. Lowie: "Granting the absence of a figure looming as a distinct culture-bringer [in the tales of some Native nations] and the overshadowing literary importance of the trickster, granting further the tendency to ascribe origins to definitely named and conceived personages, it seems to me the path of least resistance to attribute to the trickster the origins of whatever cultural possessions incite primitive curiosity" (1909, 432).

Lowie continues that "the trickster may be an older type of character in a given mythology rather than a properly so-called culture-hero" (433), thus taking a position on another aspect of the discussion. See just below. Edward Piper's dissertation, "A Dialogical Study of the North American Trickster Figure and the Phenomenon of Play" (1975), gives quite a full account and summary of these debates.

8. But Radin almost immediately complicates this view, writing that trickster "embodies the vague memories of an archaic and primordial past, where there as yet existed *no clearcut differentiation between the divine and the non-divine*" (1956, 168, my emphasis). Radin's assumption that the *mature* mind works by

differentiation into binomial, *oppositional* pairs (e.g., divine/non-divine) is an important matter for this essay, and one to which we shall return. Ballinger offers some insightful comments on this subject as well (2004).

9. Ballinger offers a brief critique of the psychological evolutionism of Radin and also that of Melville Jacobs (2004, 14–15, 29). We'll take a further look at Jacobs below.

10. Although, as we shall see, it continued in the 1950s in the highly influential work of Claude Lévi-Strauss and later, so far as trickster is concerned, in the work of Laura Makarius (see note 19, below).

11. For a fascinating study of a trickster figure (Bugs Bunny) in the development of children, see Abrams and Sutton-Smith, whom I discuss more fully in the version of this chapter published in *Comedy* (2005). The authors are admirably aware of the problems of cross-cultural generalizations, and more or less aware that their exclusive focus on Bugs Bunny as trickster has its problems. But they know a good deal about tricksters around the world, and their inventories of such items as trickster's "Appearance," "Behavior," "Clumsiness," and "Playfulness dimensions" (32–34) are richly suggestive. Piper's account of "the phenomenon of play" also touches on some of these issues.

12. Melville Jacobs, skeptical of Lévi-Strauss's "Hegelian oppositions" (in Seaburg and Amoss 2000, 96), nonetheless also believed that myth tales frequently treated particular points of stress or anxiety in a culture that were inadequately resolved in social practice.

13. Carroll sets trickster to mediating between the desire to have unlimited sex ("uncontrolled sexuality") and the desire to live socially ("culture"). The opposition here resides in the problem that "the first would lead to the destruction of the second" (1981, 301).

14. There is also important work by Mac Linscott Ricketts (1966), Barbara Babcock-Abrahams (1975), and Andrew Wiget (1987, and, in particular, 1991). William Hynes and William Doty's edited collection, *Mythical Trickster Figures* (1993) gives a substantial history of scholarship on trickster, along with recent commentaries and reconsiderations. Lawrence Sullivan calls Edward Piper's 1975 dissertation, "A Dialogical Study of the North American Trickster," cited above, the "best summary of scholarship on the North American Trickster" (1982, 242n12). I agree that Piper's study is detailed and extremely useful, although I have not seen it cited elsewhere. Lewis Hyde's 1998 volume is extremely lucid and learned, although in places excessively ingenious. And Ballinger's book-length study (2004) is valuable. I will make specific reference to Babcock and Wiget (1991) below.

15. Rhetoric seems formally to have been "invented" in fifth-century BCE Sicily by Corax and Tisias, probably under the patronage of the tyrant Hiero I. Corax is said to have produced the first treatise on rhetoric; Tisias is said to have been the first paid teacher of rhetoric. Irony was one of the rhetorical tropes described by Corax and Tisias. The invention of rhetoric, a technique for persuading in *speech*, comes about only as a development of *writing*, for it was just around this time that Greek alphabetic writing was strongly challenging the oral transmission of knowledge in the Athens of Socrates and Plato. I will soon offer some thoughts regarding the different habits of mind encouraged by orality and literacy. In some of the chapters that follow, I will consider irony as a narrative *structure* as well as a rhetorical *trope*. Irony is thus different from the other structures of Western narrative—the tragic, comic, and romantic—in that it exists on both the structural and stylistic levels. (One can't, for example, refer to a tragic or comic *statement*.)

16. Lewis Hyde writes that "trickster is the mythic embodiment of ambiguity and ambivalence, doubleness, and duplicity, contradiction and paradox" (1998, 7), but he does not take this as ironic. Indeed, he notes that trickster "embodies and enacts that large portion of our experience where good and evil are hopelessly intertwined" (10). This perception, as we shall see, has not been typical of the dominant, dualistic paradigm of Western thought, although I think it pretty well expresses insights typical of Native American thought. Ballinger usefully suggests that "it may be that the dramatization of the equivocal and paradoxical is a distinguishing trait of American Indian mythologies" (2004, 112).

17. This is not at all to suggest that ironies of both a "propositional" and a "presentational" kind are absent in traditional oral narrative. These ironies, however, are not engaged in the epistemological work of binding "widely separated contraries into a single figure," as Sullivan has claimed.

18. By no means do I go against all scholarship. Thus, Kimberley Blaeser cites Jarold Ramsey's sense that trickster tales constitute "a dynamic interposing of the mind between polar opposites, allowing us to hold onto both opposites, as if affirming either/and" (1993, 51), but not either/or. Trickster, Blaeser herself comments, "mediates between supposed contradictory forces or elements by retaining aspects of both, by revealing them to be coexisting parts of one whole, interconnected, often indistinguishable elements of the one" (51).

This is very different from Lévi-Straussian mediation—although, inasmuch as the "contradictory forces or elements" are, indeed, only "*supposed,*" I don't think there is actually any need for "mediation." Neither Ramsey nor Blaeser finds any of this ironic. Ballinger, as I will be indicating further, is also very good on this matter, insightfully remarking that it is the Western commitment to dualistic thinking that creates "problems" in Native materials not thus committed (e.g., 27–30).

19. Allan Ryan's *Trickster Shift* (1999) provides a full accounting of the ironic trickster as he appears in the work of Native Canadian (First Nations) visual artists, with reference to some writers as well. Gerald Vizenor has been foremost among Native writers of the United States in championing a postmodern, ironic version of trickster as consistent with traditional oral tricksters. This view has been criticized by Andrew Wiget (1991) in a review to which Vizenor has responded sharply (1994). Julian Rice's work on tricksters (1998), cited above, is also skeptical of the postmodern view of the traditional trickster.

20. Compare to Ballinger: "We make nodding recognition at [Jarold] Ramsey's description of Indian societies as 'sternly normative' . . . and then return to our delight in the comically rebellious Trickster, glorying in him as a release from social repression" (2004, 26).

21. Whiteley does say that trickster displays "an *ironic,* ambivalent sense of the human condition" (1998, 668, my emphasis). In the context of his discussion, however, I think it reasonable to understand this as meaning that trickster is always both/and, or, in Whiteley's own words, that trickster may represent "an indeterminacy principle" signaling "the provisionality of all established forms" (668). This seems exactly right, although I argue below that, rather than ironic, this aspect of trickster may be read as a gesture in the interest of dramatizing possibilities beyond what convention allows.

22. See, for example, Goody and Watt (1969), "The Consequences of Literacy."

23. An *ironic* method in the very strict etymological sense of the Greek term *eiron,* meaning one who pretends to know less than he does and, by extension, one whose words have a meaning different from their apparent sense.

24. The hero or villain here does indeed appear to be alphabetic writing. As it developed in the West, early alphabetic letters on the page seem to have retained some visual connection to a material referent, although the shape of the letters changes very quickly, turning them into arbitrary signifiers. On the alphabet's role in distancing us from the "sensuous surround," see David

Abram (1997). Ballinger very shrewdly notes, "Quite possibly, dualistic Western consciousness has created the scholarly quandary over the apparent indeterminacy of American Indian tricksters" (2004, 28), a conclusion each of us came to independently.

25. The connotations of *ethnos* have changed since the time of the ancient Greeks. *Then*, what *we* had was an *ethos* and the ethnic was foreign, indeed un-Greek or barbarian, not in the least admirable or attractive. *Now* the ethnic is still foreign, but it is taken as admirably rich in authentic culture, with a very powerful *ethos* of its own.

26. In the same way persons of color are not whoever they might be but, rather, *not-white*; non-Western cultures, Native American cultures among them, are not whatever they might be but, rather, *not-civilized*.

27. An alternative mode, what can be called the dialectic, is instantiated by Hegel, Marx, and others. But it is not until the Derridaean or poststructuralist attack on the logos and phallogos that either/or exclusivity has been seriously challenged. Ballinger also questions the either/or of the West (2004, 36 and 56).

28. Compare to: "[It] is only as language is written down that it becomes possible to think about it" (Havelock 1986, 112).

29. There are undoubtedly exceptions to my generalization. Thus, for example, in Michael Running Wolf and Patricia Clark Smith's recent retellings of Glous'gap stories, the authors write, in their introduction, that Glous'gap "is our spiritual teacher, the ultimate warrior, medicine-person, and *occasional trickster*" (2000, ix, my emphasis). But no one of the sixteen stories they retell actually represents him as trickster—nor do they indicate what they surely know, that Glous'gap's name means "liar." Nor does Glous'gap appear as "Liar, or the Cunning One" (165) in the two Glous'gap stories Whitehead provides.

30. Ballinger is quite attentive to Babcock's work, although he is primarily interested in arguing against Babcock's discussion of trickster's "marginality" (Ballinger 2004, see 26 and 78). In his conclusion, he makes good use of Babcock's title, a quotation from Aldous Huxley, although this could use supplementation from Hyde's work, which, surprisingly, he does not cite.

31. Compare to Ballinger: "Unfortunately, there have been few extended commentaries on tricksters and their role in their cultures by American Indians themselves" (2004, 6). This is true, but "few" is not the same as "none." I try to work with what Native commentaries there are below.

32. William Seaburg and Pamela Amoss, for example, write that Melville Jacobs, like Boas, did not systematically "interrogate his consultants in the field about the meaning of the folklore he collected" (2000, 25), although he did question consultants about cultural worldview (64).

33. Toelken tells the fascinating story of how he took George Wasson to visit Hugh Yellowman, thinking that Mr. Yellowman would be interested in hearing Mr. Wasson's rich account of "Coyote and Strawberries." But Yellowman seemed increasingly uncomfortable as Wasson narrated, finally whispering to Toelken his amazement that Wasson's Coyote eats fish! Did Wasson, Yellowman asks, learn that from the missionaries? Because everyone, every Navajo, at any rate, knows that Coyote would never eat fish! "Of course, here," writes Toelken, "we are speaking not of what a character like Coyote can or cannot do, but about *those culturally constructed concepts in which people will or will not think*" (Wasson and Toelken 2001, 191–92, my emphasis).

34. Shortly after I had completed this portion of the paper, Professor James Ruppert kindly sent me a comment made by Belle Deacon (Deg Hit'an) (it now can be found in Ruppert's *Our Voices: Native Stories from Alaska and the Yukon*). Mrs. Deacon says, "One called Old Jackson told this story to four of us girls. And he told us to listen to it good, because if you don't get the stories [now], even if you never think about it [again], you don't ever get the story. He told us to really think about it. It comes from way [back] generation[s], from the story beginning. They pass it on to one another. That's what he told us" (personal Communication, 5/12/02).

In the final chapter of this book, we will see how oral storytelling forms the basis of a contemporary Inuit film that serves to confirm Inuit culture and affirm to the people an ongoing Inuit identity.

35. Melville Jacobs notes that among the Northwest Coast people he worked with, "Actors who were given animal, fish, bird, or insect names sometimes differed in behavior, not in significant features of body structure, from actors who were avowedly human in temperament. From the Indians' viewpoint a Myth Era actor who was named Skunk was really a human-like being possessed of a supernatural which was both a skunk and human-like. At a later pre-cultural time he metamorphosed into a skunk, to remain a skunk for all eras to come" (1959, 6).

But, as Seaburg and Amoss note, Jacobs tended not to take these animal characters as actually representing those found in the natural world (2000, 28). Paiute Coyote stories, for example, begin, *Sumu onosu numeka nan quane ynas*, "Once long ago when we were all the same." Tommy McGinty's sense of the matter regarding Crow is "crow was both *human being* and *bird*, either way, back and forth" (Legros 1999, 33), a formulation I find helpful.

36. David M. Abrams and Brian Sutton-Smith speak of nonsense elements in the play of children as providing "adaptive potentiation" (1977, 46), a way of introducing flexibility into understanding as it develops (45). Abrams and Sutton-Smith state that this also seems to work culturally, in social not only psychological terms—although they forthrightly admit that insofar as this may be the case, as of the time of their paper (1977) there was no clear account of just *how* this might work. They refer to a paper by Laura Makarius on ritual clowns (1970) in which clowning is said to serve as an "exploration of alternative forms of behavior" (46). Similarities and differences between tricksters in narratives and clowns in ritual or ceremonial performance have often been noted. See also Piper (1975).

37. Compare to Mattina's reference above (1985, 16) to "the *lay members*" of tribal communities. I take this to imply Mattina's sense of the existence in these communities of what Molina and Evers have called "community-based intellectuals" (2001, 21), with a rather more complex sense of the possible meanings and functions of the stories.

38. Curiously, Sullivan quotes Irving Goldman's 1975 comment that "*we have an oppositional vocabulary to separate religious from nonreligious, natural from supernatural; they do not*" (in Sullivan 1982, 226), only to ignore this non-oppositionality so that he may go on to solve it by instantiating the ironic. Goldman, a senior colleague whose Introduction to Anthropology class I audited when I was a very young teacher, died while I was formulating this essay (2002). This endnote mention is a small gesture toward honoring him and his work.

39. We have noted Whiteley's sense that an "indeterminacy principle" in myths "is instantiated by Trickster" (1998, 668). Speaking about Hopi clowns as "dialectically deconstruct[ing] the human condition" in ritual performance, Whiteley concludes his essay, stating, "Trickster, in a word, is the philosopher" (669). It has been my claim that those who *tell* trickster tales are the philosophers and pedagogues whose re-presentations of trickster serve the purpose of *both* dialectical deconstruction *and* normative instruction.

2. Representing Indians in American Literature

1. Samuel Morton, for example, made a very great many exact cranial measurements, but the extrapolation from these measurements of moral and

intellectual capacity was almost entirely subjective. Even less exact were the "data" of phrenologists who sometimes were and sometimes were not taken seriously. See Horsman (1975).

2. Four or five distinct "races" were usually posited: Caucasian, Mongolian, Indian, and African, or Caucasian, Mongolian, Ethiopian, American, and Malay, with Indians, according to Morton, being "divided into two families—the American and the Toltecan" (Horsman 1975, 156).

3. Consistent with Reginald Horsman's terminology, I will use "racialism" and "racialist" to speak of what today would be called "racist," believing, with Horsman, that although some of the meanings of "racism" and "racist" today do overlap with beliefs and practices of the nineteenth century, there are enough differences between that time and this to warrant a slightly variant terminology.

4. I take my sense of tragedy and comedy primarily from Northrop Frye's *Anatomy of Criticism* (1957) and from Hayden White's magisterial *Metahistory* (1973). There are some differences between the two, but their accounts, I believe, are largely consistent. The literature on the four Western modes of "emplotment"—White's term—tragedy, comedy, romance, and irony or satire is voluminous.

5. This ironic narrative also appeared in the Cherokees' "memorials" to Congress in 1830, seeking to forestall passage of the Indian Removal Bill, although these were not published to a wide audience. The Cherokee memorials, as I tried to show in an earlier study, sought to recast the Removal Bill's implicit narrative of American comedy/Indian tragedy in the ironic mode. As an ironic story, Cherokee Removal would not tell of the sad-but-just vanishing of eastern Indians; rather, it would tell "a story of . . . victimization . . . the merely pathetic story of people in the wrong place at the wrong time who, despite all their efforts to save themselves, were nonetheless crushed not by right but by might alone . . . the force of American imperial power" (Krupat 1992, 161).

6. My hope is to extend a line perhaps begun by Albert Keiser in 1933 (*The Indian in American Literature*), which is followed by the work of Roy Harvey Pearce (1953) and Robert Berkhofer (1979). Fine studies of the Indian in specific forms of representation, such as in drama, cinema, textbooks, and the news, have also appeared.

7. As I'll have occasion to note further below, this comes as a call for American writers to use the Indians as Sir Walter Scott had used the Scottish past to

create a specifically American epic genre in poetry or prose. One of the earliest of these calls comes in John Gorham Palfrey's 1820 review of Eastburn and Sands's *Yamoyden* (see below), and the issue is clearly expressed in the title of Rufus Choate's essay, "The Importance of Illustrating New-England History by a Series of Romances like the Waverly Novels" (1833).

8. Bergland (2000) notes that Hawthorne and Apess both lived in Essex County, Massachusetts, for a time, before Apess moved to Mashpee in 1833. There is no evidence that the two met or that either knew of the other's work. Nor have I found any specific evidence that Melville actually knew of Apess.

9. See, in particular, Vine Deloria's *Red Earth, White Lies* (1995).

10. My commentary is influenced by recent studies of the homoerotic aspects of some of Melville's work. But in James Fenimore Cooper's *Wept of Wish-ton-wish* (1829), which I will consider briefly below, the Narragansett chief Conanchet is described as having "limbs [that are] full, round, faultlessly straight, and distinguished by an appearance of extreme activity, without however being equally remarkable for muscle," and with a "full though slightly *effeminate* chest" (in Gould 1996, 167, my emphasis). As Philip Gould remarks, "Conanchet's physique itself symbolizes the cultural logic of androgyny," a "logic" instantiated by several women writers of the period and fiercely contested by Cooper (167). I'll also look further at this matter. Melville's description of Tashtego's body, however, comes later, and I do think it is best read psychologically.

11. The phrase is meant to refer to Philip Deloria's *Playing Indian* (1998). See also Shari Huhndorf, *Going Native* (2001).

12. In 1862, crowded by white settlement, upset by the delay in payments agreed to by the U.S. government, and with many of their people starving, a large number of Santee, along with some Wahpeton and Sisseton Sioux, attacked settlements in Minnesota under the leadership of this same Little Crow.

13. Sayre notes that Thoreau spoke with her on June 26, 1856 (1977, 226n).

14. And yet, as Sandra Gustafson has written, in a powerful essay to which we will return, from his first significant publication, the "Historical Discourse" of 1835, forward, Emerson felt "discomfort with the Puritans' heritage of racial violence," something that will occupy us in the next chapter (1994, 32).

15. Mark Twain's generally negative views of Indians occur in publications after the half century of our concern, that is, his *Roughing It*, with its

utter disgust with the Gosiutes, first appeared in Connecticut in 1872, and of course, his major work comes later than that. We should, however, note his essay, "The Noble Red Man," which appeared in 1870 and quite thoroughly disparaged Indians.

16. In its original 1814 publication, the essay had some substantial criticism of the American military in its recent war against the Creeks. This is dropped in the essay's republication. See Laura Murray (1996, 216 and 228n9).

17. See Carr (1996), chapter 3, "The Myth of Hiawatha," for a fine account of the sources and contexts of Longfellow's poem.

18. Carr notes that Longfellow did, however, write "a speech for King Philip in terms of most melancholy compassion" (1996, 120) while still at school.

19. Compare to Carr: "What is most striking about the . . . verse form of *Hiawatha* is its insistent naiveté, its refusal to make possible any complexities or subtleties, its efficiency in conveying the picture of the childlike Indian" (1996, 128).

20. But Palfrey, as Jill Lepore quotes him, was hardly a partisan of the Indians. Palfrey had also said in his review that "we doubt whether poetically, and we do not doubt whether historically speaking, it was best to represent the settlers as entirely in the wrong, and the Indians as wholly in the right" (in Lepore 1998, 202). This will be the point of view taken by Edward Everett in his 1835 address commemorating the English fallen in King Philip's War.

21. See Gould's *Covenant and Republic* (1996).

22. Kerber quotes Child's contribution to the *Boston Standard*, which includes the remark, "It vexes me to see them [Native people] so constantly alluded to as a 'race destined to pass away.' What need is there of their passing away?" (in Kerber 1975, 287n). This clearly opposes appeals to natural law in favor of free moral choice.

23. The title is bound to seem strange. Wish-ton-wish is a settlement in Connecticut. Ruth Heathcote, one of the settlers, is captured by Indians in the period of King Philip's War. She is given the name Narra-mattah, and she marries an Indian man named Conanchet. Her father, devastated, calls her "the wept of my household." Ruth and her husband die, and her tombstone is engraved with no name for her other than "The Wept of Wish-ton-Wish." See Bergland (2000).

24. Thus Fuller sets herself at odds with Lydia Maria Child, her one-time friend, in regard to the necessity of the Indians vanishing. She also disagrees with Child in regard to Cherokee Removal, writing that the Cherokees in

Georgia were "frustrated by . . . barbarous selfishness" (in Maddox 1991, 144). Similarly, she dismisses the possibilities of intermarriage that were interesting to Child and Sedgwick, claiming that "Amalgamation" would produce loss of "what is best in either type" (in Maddox 1991, 145).

25. Fuller herself preserves at least one Indian story that she claims has never before been in print. She offers the story of "Muckwa the Bear" (1991, 125–26), which she interprets in rather bizarre fashion—as she interprets other bits and pieces of cultural information, for example, about dogs, with more energy than information. She does not give a source for the story of the bear.

26. Typical of the continued invisibility of Indians in scholarly and critical discourse about America is the fact that this review does not appear in Jeffrey Steele's substantial volume called *The Essential Margaret Fuller* (1992). Fuller's journalism is collected in Myerson and Bean.

27. Compare to Larzer Ziff: "as political policy acknowledged the Indians' legal existence only after they surrendered their sovereignty . . . so literary representation acknowledged the Indians' culture only after they surrendered their history" (in L. Murray 1996, 216).

28. See "Works with Indian Subjects" at the end of this chapter for tribal names and affiliations.

3. Resisting Racism

1. For example, Kim McQuaid's very helpful, "William Apes, Pequot" (1977). Donald Nielsen discusses Apess in "The Mashpee Indian Revolt of 1833" (1985). I have a chapter on Apess in *The Voice in the Margin* (1989), and another in my *Ethnocriticism* (1992). LaVonne Ruoff includes Apess in her "Three Nineteenth-Century Indian Autobiographers" (1990); David Murray's chapter on Apess, in his *Forked Tongues* (1991), also appeared before O'Connell's edition of the complete works. Since then, there has been a substantial body of work on Apess.

2. See, for example, Sandra Gustafson's very interesting account, "Nations of Israelites " (1994), Laura J. Murray's "The Aesthetic of Dispossession" (1996), Cheryl Walker's *Indian Nation* (1997), Laura Donaldson's "Son of the Forest, Child of God" (2000), and Renée Bergland's *National Uncanny* (2000). Irene Vernon briefly discusses Apess in her "Claiming of Christ" (1999), and Carolyn Haynes takes him up in her "A Mark for Them All to . . . Hiss At" (1996), an essay that contains what I take as a misreading of my own work on Apess.

A far better essay, although it both misreads and attacks my work, is Maureen Konkle's "Indian Literacy, U.S. Colonialism, and Literary Criticism" (1997). Konkle has removed her attack in the chapters on Apess in her book, *Writing Indian Nations* (2004), which offers a good deal of new historical detail. See also, Scott Manning Stevens's "William Apess's Historical Self" (1997), and Robert Warrior's "Eulogy on William Apess" (2005).

3. O'Connell's early conjecture was indeed that the death resulted from complications of alcoholism, although he later revised that opinion. Maureen Konkle makes a great to-do about critics she castigates for their evil determination to have Apess die a drunk. But we all—myself included—relied on what had seemed careful research on O'Connell's part; consequently, we simply, if erroneously, accepted his earliest guesses. Robert Warrior has offered useful conjecture about the cause of Apess's death, as has Konkle herself.

4. The author's name here, as elsewhere in his work, was Apes, spelled with one "s" not two. Barry O'Connell has made the case for spelling the name Apess, and, with some few objections, Apess has now become standard.

I have called such texts "autobiographies by Indians," reserving the term "Indian autobiography" for the many life stories of Native people that were mostly written by non-Natives. See *For Those Who Come After* (1985) and the introduction to *Native American Autobiography* (1994).

5. Although Apess does not use Pequot words or phrases in his writing (he does provide a translation of the Lord's Prayer into what he calls Philip's language), some of those whom he interviewed for *The Experiences* . . . would surely have spoken to him in Pequot not English.

6. In Philip Deloria's words, they use "'Indians' in critical relation to the cultural and ideological production of *American* identities" (2003, 677, emphasis added), an issue that Deloria had engaged in detail earlier (1998), and that Jill Lepore likewise engages in the subtitle to her 1998 book *The Name of War: King Philip's War and the Origins of American Identity*. Deloria and Lepore (and many other contemporary critics) are elaborating a line of reasoning initiated by Roy Harvey Pearce in 1953.

7. See the "Memorials" of the Cherokee people to Congress in 1830, arguing against the Indian Removal Act. They are reprinted in Krupat, "Figures and the Law: Rhetorical Readings of Congressional and Cherokee texts." Apess was almost surely the author of several Mashpee memorials to Massachusetts officials. See Nielsen (1985).

8. In "Indian Nullification," for example, Apess quotes Ebenezer Attaquin,

president of the Mashpee Tribal Council, who wrote, "Perhaps you have heard of the oppression of the Cherokees and lamented over them much, and thought the Georgians were hard and cruel creatures; but did you ever hear of the poor, oppressed and degraded Marshpee Indians in Massachusetts and lament over them?" (1992, 177).

He also later quotes "An Indian's Appeal to the White Men of Massachusetts," of which he may well be the author. The "Appeal" includes such observations as: "How will the white man of Massachusetts ask favor for the red men of the South, while the poor Marshpee red men, his near neighbors, sigh in bondage? Will not your white brothers of Georgia tell you look at home, and clear your own borders of oppression, before you trouble them?" (205).

Compare to Konkle: "Apess tells the story of how one gets from the Puritans to New Echota," the treaty signed by the Ridge party agreeing to Cherokee removal (2004, 133). Scott Manning Stevens, in a very fine study I came upon only belatedly, pointed to "Apess' growing interest in historiography and its uses" subsequent to his autobiographical work (1997, 76).

9. A growing body of recent commentary has elaborated the degree to which Black Hawk's 1833 autobiography can be read as a resistance text. See, in particular, Neil Schmitz and the new edition of the autobiography edited by Gerald Kennedy. Black Hawk, however, did not write his book; rather, he narrated his story to an interpreter, the part-Potawatomi Antoine LeClaire, and the final text was produced by a young journalist, John B. Patterson, as noted in the previous chapter.

10. I first referred to Apess as a public intellectual in a paper presented in April 2004, at the Native American Literary Symposium, at Mystic Lake, Minnesota. Since then, I have discovered Robert Warrior's mention of Apess's "career as a public intellectual" (2005, 4), and also seen that the subtitle of Konkle's book is "Native Intellectuals and the Politics of Historiography" (2004). Konkle remarks that Apess "behaved like an intellectual" and "wrote at the moment when it was beginning to be possible to write as a profession" (153), while further noting that the materials in Apess's library in New York "reinforce an understanding of Apess as an intellectual, as someone who thought of himself and other Native people in relation to the rest of the world and in relation to other histories in the wake of European colonialism and imperialism" (156–57). This resonates with Warrior's useful invocation of his former teacher Edward Said. I've referred elsewhere to such a stance as that of the cosmopolitan critic. Sandra Gustafson's "Nation of Israelites" begins with epigraphs from Apess himself, Emerson, and Antonio Gramsci.

11. That Buck and his brother, who became the Confederate general Stand Watie, both took their father's surname is in itself indicative of a progressive shift from the traditional matrilineage of the Cherokees.

12. Konkle offers a fuller discussion of Boudinot and also of his cousin, John Ridge, whose essay of 1826 makes similar points. See Konkle (2004).

13. Her source is an April 29, 1832, letter from Louisa Jane Park to Agnes Major Park. I haven't seen the letter, so I can't tell whether Louisa Jane Park actually does name the "unnamed Native," or whether Konkle guesses from Park's description that it is Apess.

14. Douglass's long career as a public intellectual has been abundantly documented. From his many speeches, newspaper articles, editorials, and other writings, I'd single out, in particular, his participation at the Seneca Falls Convention on behalf of women's rights, and his brief address, "The Rights of Women" (1848), along with his extraordinary public lecture in Rochester, New York, "What to the Slave Is the Fourth of July?" (1852). Had Margaret Fuller survived the wreck of the ship bringing her home, she might possibly have become one of the great public intellectuals of her day—although it is hard to imagine her activity being modeled after such advocates of women's rights as Elizabeth Cady Stanton. I have noted on several occasions Lydia Maria Child's powerful contributions in the interest of justice for the Indians, the slaves, and women.

15. There has been a considerable amount of speculation that Walker was killed by the agents of Southern planters who had every reason to want him dead. But Walker's daughter, Lydia Ann, not quite two years old, died only a week before her father at a time when, as Hinks writes, "pulmonary afflictions were numerous in the city" (1997, 269).

16. Obviously, there are many others who might also contribute to the discussion, in particular W. E. B. DuBois, C. L. R. James, Ngugi wa Thiong'o, Stuart Hall, Raymond Williams, Noam Chomsky, Susan Sontag, Betty Friedan, Grace Paley, and many more.

17. See "Nationalism, Indigenism, Cosmopolitanism: Three Perspectives on Native American Literatures."

18. We have, by now, a variety of terms for this strategy, among them Ngugi wa thiong'o's "decolonizing the mind" and "moving the center," Gloria Bird and Joy Harjo's "reinventing the enemy's language," and Linda Tuhiwai Smith's "reframing," which I will mention further.

19. I noted earlier Konkle's suggestion that Apess's first paragraph has a

certain similarity to the first paragraph of David Walker's *Appeal*. Walker begins, after an address to "My dearly beloved Brethren and Fellow Citizens," by writing, "*Having traveled* over a considerable portion of these United States" (Turner 21, emphasis added). Apess opens by writing, "*Having* a desire to place a few things before my fellow creatures who are *traveling* with me to the grave" (O'Connell 1992, 155, emphases added). The participial openings are parallel, and so, to some degree, is the employment of a form of the verb to travel, but beyond these two striking similarities at the outset, the styles of the two writers differ very considerably.

20. The style here seems to prefigure the mode of Vine Deloria, Jr., most particularly in *We Talk, You Listen* (1970), a phrase that well describes much that is implicit in Apess's manner. This "in your face" stance appears strongly in Thoreau, and, on occasion, in Frederick Douglass as well, along with all of those just named performing the function of oppositional public intellectuals.

21. My account is in sharp contrast to David Carlson's recent reading of Apess's autobiographical work, which claims that it demonstrates his commitment to liberal individualism. Carlson speaks of "Apess' progressive articulation of Indianness as a form of *civil selfhood*, articulated largely in a *public language of rights*" (2006, 112, emphases added). Carlson contends that rights claims "must, by definition, be rooted in an *individualist model of legal identity*" (118, emphasis added). *If* Carlson is correct, then Apess would have moved very far from what seem to be most other Native American political understandings. The political language of "rights," for example, has long been cited as one of the most unfortunate aspects of the Indian Reorganization Act of 1934. Vine Deloria, Jr., has for long tried to explain the difference between kin- and relationship-based tribal understandings and the language of rights. Daniel Justice, in his 2006 book, makes these points once more in his various discussions of "peoplehood."

22. There is surely no question of "influence" here, but I would note that Apess's horrifying image of the inscription of crime on the *skin* is elaborated and developed in Franz Kafka's story, "In the Penal Colony" (1948).

23. Konkle (1997, 2004) demonstrates Apess's insistence on the national/*political* status of Native peoples. Dannenberg had earlier asserted that "Apess' aims are always political, and to wage politics in Apess' day was to struggle with racist ideologies" (69). Near the end of her essay, Dannenberg claims that "the complexity of [Apess's] political project has not yet been fully appreciated" (79). Konkle's book takes many steps in the direction of such appreciation, and this chapter hopes to add to it.

24. Kerber quotes Gerrit Smith and David Lee Child among others of the period who link the American treatment of Indian and black people, and I think their words are worth remembering. Smith said to an antislavery meeting in Albany, New York, in 1838 that the government "instead of throwing its special protection around the two feeblest elements of our population—our aborigines and our colored brethren—its policy has been to peel and crush and exterminate the one, and to reduce the other, and keep it thus reduced, to mere beasts of burden" (in Kerber 1975, 277).

In the same year, David Lee Child wrote to the Massachusetts Anti-Slavery Society that "the past year has exhibited the American people covering themselves afresh with pollution and blood. . . . If they were answerable for no other crime, their treatment of the Indian tribes would suffice to justly subject them to the direct punishment that offended Heaven has ever bestowed upon any nation" (in Kerber 1975, 278).

The year 1838 was when the eastern Cherokees were forcibly removed to Indian country west of the Mississippi and was the last full year of William Apess's life (he died in 1839). Although he could not have known these words at the time he composed the *Indian's Looking-Glass* and the *Eulogy* for King Philip, it seems certain that he had heard and read words like them. Kerber's essay appeared in 1975, and it does not mention William Apess.

25. Garrison's abolitionist paper, the "Liberator," reported a well-attended speech given by Apess early in 1834 on behalf of the Mashpee. See McQuaid (1977, 620–21). Bergland (2000, 112) also mentions the connection between Apess and Garrison.

26. Orthodox Christian belief of the period specified a single creation, with all men descended from Adam and Eve, through Noah and his three sons. If all humankind descended from the same parents, then all must originally have had more or less equal endowments. Scientific racists either admitted to a single creation, postulating divine intervention at some later date to install inferior races, or, finally, admitted, as did Louis Agassiz, to a belief in polygenesis, multiple creations. See Horsman (1975).

27. Wirt had served as attorney general under President James Monroe, and he had been the Whig Party's candidate for president. Webster had been senator from Massachusetts, and secretary of state under President William Henry Harrison. Everett had been a Harvard professor of Greek and editor of the influential *North American Review*; he became governor of Massachusetts in 1836. Although Everett is, here, in 1833, an ally to be praised on the

basis of his speech to the House of Representatives on May 19, 1830, opposing removal of the Cherokees, his 1835 "Address delivered at Bloody Brook," I believe, played a substantial part in provoking Apess to write his *Eulogy on King Philip.* The quote almost eerily presages the powerful slogan of black activists, "No justice, no peace!"

28. This is interesting speculation, but anyone who has been involved in scheduling anything knows that there are many variables involved in whether one actually gets the date one chooses, or, rather, accepts the only date or dates available. Thus, Apess may or may not have meant to reference Jackson's battle.

29. Cheryl Walker claims that "Apess is offering King Philip as a personification not only of Indian America but of the nation America should aspire to become, a nation of justice for both whites and people of color" (167). I see little evidence in the *Eulogy* to suggest that Philip was a champion of or could be a model for color-blind justice.

30. Konkle (2004) takes Apess's tribal identification of Philip as simply an error, one she conjectures he took from Elias Boudinot's *Star in the West.*

31. The last three letters of Wampanoag apparently were pronounced as a single syllable that rhymed with *log.* Whittier, for example, rhymes Wampanoag with "blackened log" (in Lepore 1998, 210), and Brougham's play would seem to use "pollywog" as a send-up of Wampanoag, pronounced "Wampan*og.*"

32. He does note, however, that Philip's "birthplace was at Mount Hope, Rhode Island, where Massasoit, his father, lived till 1656, and died" (1992, 289).

33. Because Apess, as I will argue, is speaking directly against Edward Everett's "Address . . . at Bloody Brook" (1835), in memory of Puritans who fell in King Philip's War, he may even have in mind Everett's dismissive description of the Pequots as "themselves an invading race," who "had dispossessed the tribes . . . of Connecticut" (9), people who, along with the Wampanoags, "stand [so] low in the scale of humanity" that their "removal from one tract of country to another is comparatively easy" (9). Everett is implying that the situation of the Pequots *then* may have been like that of the Cherokees *now,* in the 1830s.

34. Much work has been done on the politics of *Metamora.* See, for example, Scott C. Martin, "Interpreting *Metamora*" (1999). See also Lepore's chapter, "The Curse of Metamora" (1998) in addition to her copious notes.

35. O'Connell had noted Washington Irving's "Philip of Pokanoket" published in *The Sketch Book* (1819/1820), along with J. W. Eastburn and R. C. Sands's long poem, *Yamoyden* (1820), commenting that "both works' sympathies are entirely with the Indians and critical of the Puritans" (1992, xix, n.9). He also mentions John Augustus Stone's play, *Metamora; or, The Last of the Wampanoags*, first performed in 1830, all three of which titles are referenced by Cheryl Walker (1997) as well. Apess may also have read or known of Lydia Maria Child's *Hobomok* (1824), Catherine Maria Sedgwick's *Hope Leslie* (1827), and James Fenimore Cooper's *Wept of Wish-ton-Wish* (1829), all texts dealing with Indian war in the seventeenth century. Child's *First Settlers of New-England* (1828) also presents Philip sympathetically. Sarah Savage's *Life of Philip the Indian Chief* (1827) makes Philip a tragic hero. Walker suggests that Apess may have known Jedediah Morse and Elijah Parish's *Compendious History of New England* (1804), in which Philip is presented sympathetically and cast "as a tragic hero" (C. Walker 1997, 168). My claim is that Apess is rewriting Philip's "tragic" narrative in the ironic mode.

36. O'Connell references Everett's performance and text but does not develop the possible relations between it and Apess's performance and text. Dannenberg's study of the *Eulogy* does not mention it, asserting that "we do not know specifically what prompted Apess's presentation of the *Eulogy* at a Boston lecture hall, and there is no record of its sponsorship" (1996, 213). Konkle is very clear about the connection between Everett's address and Apess's performance, suggesting that it was "at least in part a response to Everett's own oratorical version of King Philip's war" (2004, 99), although she later seems to weaken this conjecture by writing that it was only "*highly likely* that [Apess] knew Everett's oration" (132–33, emphasis added). I am claiming that Apess is very specifically responding to Everett's address and that he not only knew the text but—I have no evidence of this—could have actually heard the oration delivered.

37. Laura Murray, developing the observation of David Murray (no relation) that, in the nineteenth century, sympathy with wronged Indians was "turned into an aesthetic, rather than a moral, sensation" (D. Murray in L. Murray 1996, 68), which might lead to political insight, calls this the "aesthetic of dispossession." In regard to King Philip, she states clearly that "Apess refuses a tragic emplotment of Philip's life" (223). Again, I am making the case that Apess rejects the tragic mode and emplots Philip's life ironically.

38. This sentence continues with Apess referring to Philip as "the rude

yet all-accomplished son of the forest" (1992, 277), an allusion to the title of Apess's own autobiography. Maureen Konkle (1997) has shrewdly argued that Apess's appeal to the "natural" when referring to Indians not only continues the dominant practice of identifying Indians with nature, but also prepared the ground for Native claims to land title and to sovereignty as having existed in "natural law" prior to the Europeans "positive" law.

39. Compare to Francis Jennings, *The Invasion of America* (1975).

40. I have already noted that we will probably never know for certain the books Apess read and valued over his lifetime; still, it may be worth remarking that Apess's use of the relativizing trope—Who is the real savage, after all?—here, and also in the "Indian's Looking-Glass," can be traced as far back as 1552, when the Spanish priest Bartolomé de las Casas, in his *Devastation of the Indies: A Brief Account*, writes, "This was the first land in the New World to be destroyed and depopulated by the *Christians*. . . . And some of the Indians concealed their foods while others concealed their wives and children . . . to avoid the terrible transactions of the *Christians*. . . . Then they behaved with such temerity and shamelessness that the most powerful ruler of the islands had to see his own wife raped by a *Christian* officer" (1998, 39, my emphases).

Importantly, it next appears in Michel de Montaigne's "On the Cannibals" (1580), in such comments as:

> It does not sadden me that we should note the horrible barbarity in a practice such as theirs [cannibalism]; what does sadden me is that, while judging correctly of their wrong-doings we should be so blind to our own. I think there is more barbarity . . . in lacerating by rack and torture a body still fully able to feel things, in roasting him little by little . . . (as we have not only read about but seen in recent memory . . . among our fellow-citizens and neighbours—and what is worse, in the name of duty and religion) than in roasting and eating him after his death. (1958, 86–87)

Montaigne further notes, "I find . . . that there is nothing savage or barbarous about those peoples [Brazilian Indians] but that every man calls barbarous anything that he is not accustomed to" (82). This is directly echoed in Benjamin Franklin's "Remarks Concerning the Savages of North America" (1784). Franklin: "Savages we call them, because their manners differ from ours, which we think the perfection of civility; they think the same of theirs" (1998, 534). (Franklin was not always so broad-minded when writing about

Indians.) Thomas Jefferson sounds this note as well in parts of his *Notes on the State of Virginia* (1787), for example, his comments on Logan's eloquence. Apess, however he came to it, is a master of this trope—which largely drops out of nineteenth-century writing about Indians, with some few important exceptions, such as that of Lydia Maria Child's *Appeal for the Indians* (1868).

41. Apess is responding to Webster. See O'Connell (1992, 286). Frederick Douglass, who might have known Apess's work, if not the man himself, uses much the same rhetorical strategy in his 1852 address, "What Is the Fourth of July to the Negro?" insisting to his predominantly white audience in Rochester, New York, that "this is *your* day of Independence, not mine."

42. As mentioned just above, O'Connell and others have noted that Apess may also have been responding to Daniel Webster's "Plymouth Oration" of December 22, 1820, celebrating the "mild dignity of CARVER and of BRADFORD; the decisive and soldierlike air and manner of STANDISH, etc.," and others who set foot upon "the Rock, on which New England received the feet of the Pilgrims" (1992, 1). Surely Apess was aware of this and other celebrations of Plymouth Rock that I've noted. But Webster's address was delivered more than fifteen years before Apess's *Eulogy*. Nearer inter-textual possibilities, as I've said, might be David Walker's vehement *Appeal to the Coloured Citizens of the World* of 1830, and Lydia Maria Child's *Appeal in Favor of that Class of Americans Called Africans*, first published in 1833, and with a second edition in 1836, the same year as Apess's eulogy for Philip. The relevance of these texts—which, of course, do not focus on Native peoples—to Apess's reading of American history is their insistence on the injustice of American "progress" and "civilization."

43. This may possibly have to do with an awareness that part of his period's critique of the Puritans involved a critique of martial prowess, as, for example, in *Hope Leslie*'s representation of both Puritan and Indian violence as equivalently "savage."

44. The pun on headmen in relation to the Puritans' monstrous display of Philip's head is quite typical of Apess's style.

45. This condemnation of the Puritans uncannily foreshadows William Carlos Williams's reexamination of American history in his 1925 volume *In the American Grain*. In a chapter called "The Voyage of the Mayflower," in particular, Williams lashes out against the persistence of Puritan narrowness in post–World War I America.

46. Everett rather blandly imagines that this forced removal of the New

England tribes merely "united [them] with their brethren farther west and north, supplying the waste [!] of their continual wars, and [so they were] *easily incorporated among them*" (1835, 10, emphasis added). This either ignores or utterly falsifies the complexity of relations between New England peoples and Indian nations to their west and north. Much the same ignorance or avoidance of the facts, it should be said, appeared in the debate over Cherokee removal.

47. Once more, Apess may have found the inspiration for such a rhetorical move in Everett, for late in his address—and Apess's ventriloquization of the president also comes late in his own address—Everett had invented a florid but violent speech for King Philip (1835, 30–31).

48. On this matter, Konkle quotes Charles Bright: "The entire process of acquiring, surveying, parceling, and disposing of Western territories was taken over by the federal government and tied to the [national] debt settlement" (in Konkle 1997, 474). Apparently, Apess would seem to have thought that the same linkage between land and national debt obtained for acquisition of the *eastern* lands of the Cherokees by the *state* of Georgia.

49. Kerber provides many quotations from the abolitionists in this vein. For example, here is Nathaniel P. Rogers, writing in an October 1838 issue of the *Herald of Freedom*: "The people of this country have had two objects deeply at heart, ever since the revolution,—the protection of the Indian tribes and the gradual abolition of slavery . . . and they have pursued both steadily, till they have *protected* the Indians nearly all out of the country . . . and they have gradually abolished slavery from about 500,000 up to two million and a half" (in Kerber 1975, 279–80).

4. Representing Cherokee Dispossession

1. This first epigraph provides me with an opportunity to address the issue of what the Cherokees actually did and do call themselves in their own Iroquoian language. Although the *Cherokee Phoenix* used *tsalagi* to refer to the Cherokees, the anthropologist and historian of the Cherokees, James Mooney, concluded that the word "Tsa'lagi or Tsa'ragi" was a word of European provenance that they had accepted (1970, 15). It was Mooney's contention that the Cherokees actually referred to themselves as "*Yun'wiya* or *Ani-Yun'wiya* . . . signifying 'real people' or 'principal people'" (1970, 150). The great Cherokee scholar Jack Kilpatrick notes, however, that he has never "found the Mooney theory acceptable to a single Cherokee of his acquaintance"

(1962, 39). Kilpatrick believes that the Cherokees did in fact call themselves "tsa lagi = he turned aside" (39), as in the term, *Anitsalagi*, "the people who turned aside," or the "'Seceders,' with the implication that the secession took place while in the act of traveling," at some time in "Iroquoian prehistory" (40). Jace Weaver has pointed to the possible origin of the name in a Choctaw word for "people who live in caves," or else from *cheera tahge*, a term for wise ones, meaning possessors of the divine fire (in Justice 2006, 26). Regarding whether the word Cherokee derives from someone's word for cave people, or "people who live in the ground," the eminent Cherokee historian Emmett Starr suggested that it may have been the Senecas, reacting to the sudden and unexpected arrival of the Cherokees, who spoke of them as people who came from the earth (22). In 1995 Joseph Bruchac refers to the Cherokees as "Aniyunwiya/Real Human Beings," as does Daniel Justice in his recent book (2006). So far as I can tell, this seems to be present Cherokee practice, at least in writing.

2. Different historians and writers use different orthographies to represent Cherokee words, some using hyphens, others not, some running together syllables that others separate. I have made no attempt to adhere to a common system of transcription, and have simply followed the form of the authors I cite.

3. A census of Cherokees east of the Mississippi commissioned by the U.S. government in 1835 gave the following figures: a total of 16,542 Cherokees, 201 intermarried whites, and 1592 African slaves (Perdue and Green 1995, 48). Perdue and Green estimate that "by 1835 only about 10 per cent of the [Cherokee] population belonged to a church" (44), although that 10 percent included most of the mixed-blood, educated, and wealthy Cherokees.

4. For a consideration of the Indian Removal Act as narrative, see my "Figures and the Law" (1992).

5. The figure of four thousand dead seems first to have been given by Mooney (1900), based on material in Charles C. Royce (1887), and it becomes more or less established on the basis of Grant Foreman's *Indian Removal* (1932). But even Mooney says, "It is difficult to arrive at any accurate statement of the number of Cherokee who died as the result of the Removal" (1970, 133). Grace Steele Woodward writes that "the exact number of lives lost in the 1838–9 Cherokee emigration is not known," although she accepts Foreman's estimate of four thousand as including those who died "either in stockades prior to removal or on the journey west" (1988, 218). Ehle (1988)

emphasizes the fact that we don't absolutely know for sure in order to suggest that the estimate of four thousand might be a bit high. Russell Thornton's "New Perspective" (1984), as I've noted, gives a "New Estimate" (1964), over a longer period, one that might be double or more. Ehle is among the *yoneg* (white) historians (others include Foreman, Stanley Hoig, and Grace Steele Woodward) whom Daniel Justice finds objectionable from the perspective of a contemporary Cherokee nationalist. I tend to agree with him, overall, although I have nonetheless used these and other historians *selectively*.

6. I mention these more recent incidents of mass dispossession and death only to offer possibilities for contextualizing the particular historical events we are about to consider. Among many other texts, see, for example, Primo Levi on the Holocaust, Peter Balakian on Armenia, and Kim DePaul and Loung Ung on Cambodia. Although much has been published about the killings in Rwanda, I know of no book-length memoir or novel on the subject. The current genocide in Darfur may also one day find representation. I thank Professor Bella Brodzki for help with these matters.

7. Perdue and Green include what they call Rebecca Neugin's *Recollections of Removal*, which they say was printed in Grant Foreman's *Indian Removal* (1932) (1995, 169). That book contains an extended note, on pages 302 and 303, in which Foreman quotes Ms. Neugin as she "recollects" her family's experience of being driven from their homes in the early summer of 1838, almost a century earlier. But I have not been able to find a text of hers called *Recollections of Removal*. Meanwhile, it should certainly be noted that there is relevant written material of a variety of sorts documenting removal in the John Ross Papers, edited by Gary Moulton (1985).

8. This took place at Red Clay, Tennessee, where a reunion of the Cherokee Nation of Oklahoma and the Eastern Band of Cherokees living in North Carolina gathered for the first time since Removal. Wilma Mankiller also discusses this important occasion. In the 1980s Maggie Wachacha was honored by the Eastern Band of Cherokees as a *Ghigan* (Starr, 32) or Beloved Woman, a tradition probably best known as represented in the late eighteenth and early nineteenth century by *Nanije'hi* or Nancy Ward. On this, see also Justice (2006).

9. Nor, I think, have many contemporary Cherokee creative writers. I may well have overlooked some things, but in the work I know by the contemporary Cherokee writers Betty Louise Bell, Marijo Moore, and Ralph Salisbury, for example, there is very little about that period. (This is an observation,

not a criticism.) In Joseph Bruchac's edited collection, *Aniyunwiya/Real Human Beings* (1995), apart from a reprint of Glenn Twist's "The Dispossession" and Marilou Awiakta's account of the 1984 Reunion of the Cherokee Councils of the East and West (Bruchac 1995, 29–41), there is not much about removal. (I know Awiakta's poetry only a little.)

In his novel, *Truth and Bright Water* (1999), Thomas King, a Cherokee author who holds both U.S. and Canadian citizenship, has the narrator, Monroe Swimmer (his last name is that of a renowned, nineteenth-century Cherokee healer) encounter a woman named Rebecca Neugin (see note 7, above) who, with her traveling companions, John Ross and George Guess (Sequoyah), are still on their way to Indian Territory in the late twentieth century. Neugin and her friends are identified as Cherokees only when they appear again briefly later in the novel (148), and nothing more is heard of them. A joke about Neugin's search for her duck refers primarily to the material in Foreman—although Daniel Justice (2006, 173–75) points out that ducks are important more generally in King's work. I thank Professor Michael Elliott for help with King prior to the appearance of Justice's study.

10. The instantiation of a collective "mind" is fairly typical of the period. Indeed, concepts such as "the savage mind" persist at least through the 1950s, perhaps most famously in Claude Lévi-Strauss.

11. Justice also makes clear—I've cited him to this point in the first chapter—the way in which, for Cherokees, dualisms aren't necessarily oppositions (cf. 2006, 27–29).

12. An excellent detailed account of these matters exists in Shari Huhndorf's "Making of an Indian" (2001).

13. Compare to Huhndorf: "In forging a relationship between white Southerners and Indians, Carter drew on the historical ambivalence of white supremacist organizations toward Natives.... It is important to note, however, that these groups more often targeted Native peoples than embraced them" ("Making of an Indian," 2001, 132).

14. This is why David Treuer's recent attempt to rehabilitate *Little Tree* on the basis of its literary qualities (and its putative similarities to Sherman Alexie's *Reservation Blues*) and to reinstall it in the category of Native American fiction is not persuasive. Treuer's insistence that literature doesn't represent reality but, rather, creates it is, ultimately, correct. But one has to be aware of when the created reality runs counter to historical reality. This is why *Little Tree* can be innocently enjoyed for what Treuer would call its "style" by those who

know the difference between historical and created reality, although those who don't know—probably the majority of the book's readers—open themselves to ideological implications that may be obnoxious. (Fictions of virtual reality—like a series of novels based on the assumption that Custer won at the Little Big Horn and went on to become president—can be enjoyed more "safely," as it were, because everyone knows that didn't happen. But most Americans don't know what did or didn't happen in the Removal period.) Treuer refuses to consider the *functionality* of literature. For a fuller account of these matters, see my "Culturalism and Its Discontents" (2008).

15. Lieutenant Henry Timberlake had lived with the Cherokees in the 1760s, and his *Memoirs* (1765) are among the earliest observations of them. Timberlake, thus, is a name that had been known in Cherokee country for some time.

16. Mankiller, who had been associate chief, took over the position of principal chief when Chief Ross Swimmer stepped down in 1985 to head the Bureau of Indian Affairs. She was elected to the position in 1987 and served until 1994, when she declined to run again.

17. Just after these words, Mankiller writes of the 1984 reunion of the Eastern and Oklahoma Cherokee, which Awiakta also attended. This was a much happier occasion.

18. Strictly speaking, Mankiller and her family, as she notes, were not *forced* to relocate. Nonetheless, government pressures, as in the nineteenth century, were quite substantial, notwithstanding that it was possible—however difficult—to refuse relocation.

19. Exactly consistent with this sentiment, of course, is the title of Daniel Justice's book, to which I have several times referred, *Our Fire Survives the Storm* (2006).

20. Glancy has Maritole and her family driven from their homes in October, just *after* the first detachments under Cherokee leadership began their journey west. In fact, the events depicted in the novel's first chapter would more likely have occurred in late May or early June of 1838, not in October. Some few other details in the novel also vary slightly from historical accounts. Otherwise, for the most part, the novel adheres to historical chronology—except that at the very end, in the chapter set in Indian Territory, just after February 27, 1839, Knowbowtee speaks of President Van Buren's rejection of the Cherokees' "Act of Union," drawn up *July 12*, 1839, and someone named Sophia Sawyer tells of returning to Indian Territory to visit in *1840*

(1996, 232). Maritole's final monologue, the conclusion of the novel, is set in the *spring* of 1839.

21. Quaty Lewis's name appears as the heading for several sections, and it may be worth noting that the wife of Cherokee principal chief John Ross was named Quatie. According to Maureen Konkle, she was, "by most accounts a traditional Cherokee woman (she did not speak English)" (2004, 48).

22. I have found only one place in the text where slaves are mentioned. Knowbowtee, thinking about possible "sins" and "wrongdoings" on the part of his people, notes, "The Cherokee held slaves" (Glancy 1996, 140). The list given by Glancy of John Ross's possessions includes four "Negro houses" (79). It is curious to note that by 1860, John Ross, who had fought so long and hard against Cherokee removal, was the principal slaveholder in the Cherokee Nation. It is also curious that the Reverend Evan Jones, in the 1830s strongly opposed to Cherokee slaveholding, was a staunch defender of Ross in 1862, working to allow him to join Union forces in the Civil War (many Cherokees fought on the Confederate side). It was Jones who trained the Reverend Jesse Bushyhead, who is presented in the novel as largely an admirable man. Glancy gives Jones a single monologue (35–36), which, for reasons I can't explain, makes him, to the contrary, stiff and priggish. Justice finds Glancy hostile to Ross and more sympathetic to the Treaty Party, something I had not particularly noticed.

23. So far as I am aware, the first writer to convey not merely a factual but an impressionistic sense of the experience of the Trail is not a novelist but a professional writer of histories. John Ehle, in his *Trail of Tears* (1988), in chapter 20, which deals with the experience of the Trail, includes, along with documents and narrative description, invented passages. One example is from the point of view of the *soldiers*:

> What do we do with that old woman who
> won't leave that there rock?
> She will when she gets hungry.
> Makes our work hard.
> You're being paid. . . . (333)

James Mooney's "The Removal—1838–9," an account in his *Myths of the Cherokee* (1900), also has some impassioned writing (e.g., 1970, 130–34).

24. The Basket Maker is prominent on pages 152 through 158, although not much after. In 2002 Glancy would publish a novel called *The Mask Maker*. Edith,

the title character, is particularly concerned that her masks *not* be associated with words, or thought to speak words: no stories for the Mask Maker, whose sense of these matters is very different from the earlier Basket Maker.

25. In 2004 Glancy published *Stone Heart: A Novel of Sacajawea*, to which she appends a little over a page of bibliography—although the text of the novel does not indicate where details come from or, indeed, which of the details are invented.

26. But, again, she doesn't identify her source. James Mooney began work with A' yun'ini, "he is swimming," "he is a swimmer," or, simply, in English, "Swimmer" (Mooney 1970, 236), a specialist in healing and medicines, in 1888, completing a manuscript that he apparently brought to Washington—where it disappeared! Frans Olbrechts reconstructed it from Mooney's notes and earlier publications, and published it in 1932.

27. It is interesting to note that by the beginning of the 1960s, as Raymond Fogelson has written, among the Eastern Cherokees, "As far as can be ascertained, all of today's conjurers consider themselves to be good Christians and feel that their work is completely consistent with Christian doctrine" (1961, 219). Fogelson adds that "the close rapport between Christianity and conjuring does not seem to be a recent event, since much of Mooney's best material came from persons who combined the profession of native doctor with Sunday school preacher" (220). Perhaps then in Indian Territory, in only a short time, Maritole's determination to believe both Christians and conjurers would not be difficult, the conjurers themselves having become "good Christians" without abandoning their conjuring.

28. Maritole has earlier slept with a sympathetic white soldier, a Sergeant Williams.

29. Thus, the Cherokee conjurers who, by the end of the nineteenth century, were also Christians (see note 27 above), are examples of Jack and Anna Kilpatrick's affirmation of "the amazing ability of the Cherokees to maintain an equilibrium between two opposing [different] worlds of thought" (1964, v), noted in chapter 1. Diane Glancy also subscribes to a both/and view of these matters, although it is her Christian commitment that I find most powerfully expressed.

30. Glancy's acknowledgments thank Conley "for reading the manuscript" (1996, 236). Wilma Mankiller also thanks Conley in her acknowledgments (which come, as is more usual, at the beginning of her book) "for helping [her] conceptualize a book that would include aspects of [her] life as well as Cherokee history" (Mankiller and Wallis 2000, ix).

5. *Atanarjuat, the Fast Runner* and Its Audiences

1. The phrase occurs toward the conclusion of Silko's novel, when the narrator says of its protagonist, Tayo, "He was not crazy; he had never been crazy. He had only seen and heard the world as it always was" (1977, 246). This would constitute what I have called an *indigenist* form of resistance more nearly than a nationalist or cosmopolitan form of resistance to colonialism. (See the first chapter of my *Red Matters*.) I should also register Professor Patricia Penn Hilden's observation, in a wonderfully full and detailed response to an earlier version of this chapter that "there is no such thing as the world as it always was and no Inuit thinks this. No indigenous person considers a world as it always was except in very different terms, at the level of we are here. We have always been here" (personal communication, 3/6/06). My use of the phrase derives from Silko—who seems to me to differ, at least in this novel.

2. The concept comes from an earlier passage of Silko's novel where she writes, "The people had known . . . how everything should be. But the . . . world had become entangled with European names: the names of the rivers, the hills, the names of the animals and plants—all of creation suddenly had two names: an Indian name and a white name" (1977, 70).

3. This is not to suggest that there is some kind of exact equation here, that is, Native people only appreciate what can specifically be shown to have positive worldly effects. But because the West has for long detached esthetic quality from utility of any sort (e.g., the long-held notion that good art promoted good morality and good action), the very different indigenous American notions of the matter need emphasizing.

4. As I have noted earlier, this position runs directly counter to David Treuer's recent emphasis—if not exclusive insistence upon—the literary dimension of "Native American literature."

5. I need to acknowledge my own wariness of the sorts of broad generalizations I've just offered. One knows that being Native today in any of a variety of ways doesn't necessarily equate to familiarity with the traditional epistemological modes and cultural habits of any particular indigenous nation—no more than being French makes you an expert on wine. Nonetheless, people who do identify as Native are more likely than those who do not so identify to have some greater intellectual, and, importantly, experiential familiarity with the thought and culture of one or another Native nation. Meanwhile, at least *some* of the non-Natives who read Native American novels or watch Native American films have already taken steps to familiarize themselves with

a thought and culture that is *other* but, for them (us), intensely interesting at the least.

6. I'm using it here in relation to its invocation by both Patricia Penn Hilden and Shari Huhndorf, whose work I will cite below.

7. It was quite some time after these words were first written that information came from Isuma about its second feature film, *The Journals of Knud Rasmussen*. In an e-mail dated March 8, 2006, Zach Kunuk is quoted as saying, "Our first audience is always Inuit—elders who are still alive and young people looking for a future beyond unemployment, boredom, suicide, and global warming." He continues, "Our film tries to answer two questions that have haunted me my whole life: Who were we? And what happened to us?" I think *Atanarjuat* offers a powerful answer to the first question, while *Journals* speaks to the second. The e-mail announced the screening of the film at Igloolik on Saturday and Sunday, March 11 and 12.

8. See Elaine Jahner, "Traditional Narrative" (2003) and Julie Cruikshank, "Negotiating with Narrative" (1997).

9. Professor Chadwick Allen has pointed out that there is a fourth audience for films like *Atanarjuat*, which is "the growing and increasingly connected international indigenous audience," in particular, as he notes, in Australia and New Zealand, and throughout the Pacific. Thus, "there is increasingly an international indigenous-indigenous audience," one that "does open up possibilities for other kinds of distribution and reception, readings and interpretations" (personal communication, 3/23/06). Although it is not referenced by the Isuma filmmakers, it is nonetheless important to be aware of this fourth audience, which may increasingly need to be factored into any "readings and interpretations" critics offer.

10. A paper on Cherokee readers' habits presented at the Modern Language Association Convention in Washington DC, in 2005 was both theoretically confused and empirically weak. Native American communities in the United States, like non-Native communities in the United States, are more likely to read *TV Guide* and the *Reader's Digest* and to watch a variety of network TV programs than to read or watch the work of Native authors.

11. *Isuma* means "to think" in Inuit, thus "thinking productions," or a production company that is to make us think.

12. *Igloolik* means "place of houses." Modern Igloolik was actually established in the 1950s by the Canadian government, although Iglulik has a history of thousands of years of habitation by the Inuit.

13. Thus, Eva Marie Garroutte suggests the perspective of "radical indigenism" as a perspective that assumes "scholars can take philosophies of knowledge carried by [?] indigenous peoples seriously. They can consider those philosophies and their assumptions, values, and goals not simply as interesting objects of study . . . but as intellectual orientations that map out ways of discovering things about the world," and that "to one degree or another, *reflect* or *engage* the true" (2003, 10). I am sympathetic to this position, although there are problems with it, for example, Garroutte's sensibly modest qualification of "one degree or another." To accept degrees for "the true" would already be to move beyond Western thought where, in many areas, truth is not seen as a matter of degree: it is either/or not both/and. The point is that Western audiences would have to behave, in one *degree* or another, as radical indigenists to make sense of *Atanarjuat* in anything like its own terms.

14. Shari Huhndorf has suggested that inasmuch as Kunuk "used a good portion of the funds [the profits from the film] for economic development in Igloolik," it may be "that what appears to be an unchallenging representation/marketing of Inuit [directed toward maximizing profit] actually has potentially challenging material effects" (personal communication, 7/1/06). This seems to me an important insight. Her current work on Kunuk's films will develop this and other possibilities, and I will cite some other of her observations below.

15. As I have noted, there is actually a text that precedes the first images and another text that is superimposed upon those first images. These are integral to a full comprehension of the film, and, again, they need to be considered in relation to the concluding outtakes.

16. Tungajuak is how the name is spelled in the credits onscreen. The bilingual screenplay spells many of the names differently. But there are a great many differences between the screenplay and the film itself, at least in the American version I have seen. Tuungarjuak, as the name is spelled in the screenplay, is the name that some missionaries used for the devil. Its meaning is more generally "powerful spirit."

17. The screenplay leaves no doubt about this, as it is regularly said of Sauri that he killed his father, apparently by acting as Tungajuaq's helper. When Oki, Sauri's son, stabs his father to death—an unambiguous act of murder—a pattern of killing is continued that must, in the end, be broken.

18. Evans's work began far to the south of Igloolik, in Manitoba. See Perry Shearwood's "The Writing of the Inuit of Canada's Eastern Arctic" (1993).

The language can also be written in Roman characters, but Shearwood points out that "syllabics [by the twentieth century] . . . had come to be regarded as authentically Inuit" and that there was little enthusiasm for "use of the Roman orthography" (180).

19. Bernard Saladin d'Anglure writes that the two brothers are mentioned in Captain George Lyon's journals, published in 1824. Noting that the two brothers were "among the ten helping spirits of Tulimaq, a shaman," he states that "by Lyon's time, the two brothers had become regional heroes" (2002, 197). He gives no page references to Lyon's journal. My own reading of the journal confirms that Lyon spent July of 1822 in Igloolik and, in September, met Toolemak; in November he says he was paid a visit by this "conjuror" (Lyon 1824, 185). Lyon left Igloolik in July of 1823, noting that although he had found the place "tedious and dreary," it was nonetheless "a very important settlement to the Esquimaux" (284). I could not, however, find any mention of the two brothers in Captain Lyon's journal.

20. While the change to a nonviolent ending *may* seem to suggest something of a Christian turn, it has a precedent in the ending of Silko's *Ceremony*, where the very specific choice to avoid violence that the protagonist, Tayo, has to make is not in the least Christian, but rather a way to complete the *ceremony*, the vision, the mythic story offered by the Navajo seer, Betonie. I make no claim whatever that Kunuk was specifically influenced by *Ceremony*.

21. It's possible that one of the versions recorded by Saladin d'Anglure in the 1980s and 1990s mentions shamanism, but it is not likely, inasmuch as the composite version of the story that he gives in his ethnographic commentary contains no reference to shamanism. Kunuk's earlier work, and the new film, are very much interested in shamanism.

22. Premier Okalik was in Australia to attend the "Advancing Reconciliation Conference" at Murdoch University in Perth, and he visited Sidney as well. He had also been there a year earlier for the New South Wales Centenary of Federation celebrations.

Inuk means "a person"; *Inuit*, "people."

All versions of the legend, at least up until 1964, as I've noted, conclude with the death of Atanarjuat's or Amarqjuat's enemies; there is no reference to shamanism. I think the premier is offering a general comment on the feel of the film rather than a judgment of specific details.

23. So, too, was the new film first screened at Igloolik's Ataguttaaluk High School. It then went on a three-month "tour of HD digital projections in 56

remote Inuit communities in Nunavut, Nunavik and Greenland" (e-mail of March 8, 2006, and note 7, above), before opening at the Toronto film festival in September, and playing at the Lincoln Center film festival in New York in early October, with Kunuk and Cohn in attendance.

24. I don't know whether it was counted among the thirty countries Kunuk mentions, but in February 2006 I received notice of six Web sites detailing the film's positive reception in Finland.

25. The negative reviews, although many fewer—and not quoted by the filmmakers or their distribution company, to be sure—also work almost exclusively by relating the film to typical Western assumptions.

26. And this sort of inclusion has repercussions. S. F. Said, reviewing *The Journals of Knud Rasmussen* for *Sight and Sound* in 2006, says of the earlier *Atanarjuat* that "it was as if Homer had laid his hands on a digital video camera" (37). Has he arrived at that conclusion independently? I doubt it—although in any case, as I have indicated, it is a remark that makes no sense.

27. For more on this, see "Quoting *Nanook*" that concludes chapter 5.

28. See, in particular, her chapter "Nanook and His Contemporaries: Traveling with the Eskimos, 1897–1941" (Huhndorf 2001).

29. The sentences I've omitted have Kunuk remembering one of the scenes from *Nanook* with what is surely fondness.

30. Huhndorf makes the important point that "the residents of Igloolik [and perhaps Kunuk himself] interpret *Nanook* entirely differently than does most of the non-Inuit world." If Flaherty represented the Eskimos as a brave but primitive and doomed people, "It would be difficult for the [Inuit] to read that film as a narrative of their own disappearance since . . . they remain a viable, contemporary community" (personal communication, 7/1/06).

31. Can this be the source for so many of the reviewers?!

32. Cohn is sticking to this line. In the e-mail announcing the screening of *The Journals of Knud Rasmussen*, he says that their "first film, *Atanarjuat, the Fast Runner*, was a classic love and revenge story set in the mythic, apolitical past." I have been trying to show that it is not only that.

33. Jahner's essay shows how a version of the Stone Boy story is quite specific to the western Lakota.

34. But also, as Huhndorf has once more pointed out to me, this could be a strategic move rather than a cynical determination to earn as much money as possible because Kunuk "used a good portion of the funds [from the film's earnings] for economic development in Igloolik" (personal communication, 7/1/06).

35. Among the first materials printed in the Isuma screenplay is a letter dated December 28, 2001, from Claude Lévi-Strauss of the *Académie française* to his former student, Saladin d'Anglure, praising aspects of the film and looking forward to the "analysis which [he] will write," and that "will greatly help in understanding the film" (9). This letter, "translated from the French," also appears translated into the Inuktitut syllabary!

That there is so much ethnographic and explanatory material included with the screenplay is in some measure surprising. Kunuk has been quoted as saying, "For 175 years, since the Parry expedition of 1822–3, Igloolik Inuit have been observed, examined, measured, and studied by other cultures. To our knowledge, this practice of anthropology/ethnography has been a one-way street. Qallunaat [non-Inuit] study Inuit, but Inuit do not study Qallunaat. This uneven exchange influences all levels of relations between the two cultures: political, economic, social, and so forth, with Qallunaat values and assumptions defining both cultures" (in Ginsburg 2003, 829).

I thank Shari Huhndorf for reminding me of this quote.

36. Compare to this Maria Chona's comment to Ruth Benedict, quoted by Louis Owens, that "the song is very short because we understand so much" (1992, 13). To be sure, a culturally informed audience would bring to mind all sorts of material that isn't explicitly referenced, but that is not to say that everything important to the culture is automatically implicit in every song or story.

37. Kunuk had early on announced his next project as one involving shamanism, and *The Journals of Knud Rasmussen* treats the coming of Christianity to Igloolik and the poignant and painful farewell to shamanism on the part of Aua (Avva in the subtitles), a renowned shaman, in the 1920s. Aua is played by his descendant, Pakak Innuksut.

38. In Scott Lyons's terms, it is an act of "rhetorical sovereignty," to which Monika Siebert (see below) has made useful reference. My discussion here is based on my introduction to Jahner's "Traditional Narrative" in Elliott and Stokes (2003), and in my *Red Matters* (2002).

39. The name Repulse Bay derives from the disappointment of Captain Christopher Middleton, who, in 1742, discovered that he had entered not the "northwest passage," the sea route from the Atlantic to the Pacific he had sought, but, rather, a body of water that was a bay not a thoroughfare. This, wrote Middleton, "was the Bay of Repulse, the bay where I was pushed away." Nunavut has retained the name, although the local people call it Najuat. So

far as I have been able to discover, Aivalik, "place of the walrus," from where the shaman in the screenplay comes, is also adjacent to Repulse Bay.

40. Lot 47 is the independent film company that distributes *Atanarjuat* in the United States. Founded in 1999 by Scott and Jeff Lipsky and based in New York City, the company's name derives from an obscure anecdote in film history. I think it is sufficiently interesting to take the space to tell it here. In 1939 the great Charlie Chaplin was planning to stay with his mistress, Heidi Freund, at an elegant hotel in Atlanta, Georgia, where he'd taken her to see the premiere of *Gone with the Wind*. But when the couple arrived, Chaplin belatedly realized that many people there knew him and that it would not do to be seen with his mistress, a German mistress at that—this was 1939, and Chaplin had just made a masterpiece of his own, *The Great Dictator*. So Chaplin had his driver leave the city to try to find a remote place for the couple to stay. The place he found was the Camelot Motel, just off Georgia State Road 47. The Camelot Motel had a neon sign displaying its name, but the first four letters of the motel's name—*C-a-m-e*—had gone dark; hence, we have Chaplin and his mistress in the . . . *lot* motel off Road *47*. When the brothers Lipsky, passionate about film history, formed their distribution company, they called it Lot 47 Films.

41. Monika Siebert has elaborated the gesture toward "modernity" that the outtakes offer in relation to the "traditionality" of the film and has explored the politics of indigenousness in an officially multicultural nation, Canada.

42. Paraphrasing Bill Readings, Siebert writes, "to live in Nunavut means *to have been Inuit once*" (2006, 545, my emphasis). My reading is different. I think what the film says is that to live in Nunavut is to be Inuit in a manner consistent with the past ("tradition" as a name for culturally consistent change) under very different conditions than those that prevailed in the past.

43. Noting the way in which the "outtakes do work to interrupt the illusion of the autonomous pre-contact world," Siebert also sensibly notes that they risk "being missed altogether by impatient viewers who leave the screening rooms as soon as the final credits begin to roll" (2006, 532). Or they may be taken as just amusing gestures on the part of the filmmakers and of no particular importance. I think they are much more than that.

44. What I am calling projective essentialism is consistent with what Ann Fienup-Riordan refers to as "Eskimo orientalism" (1995, xi).

45. This puts me at odds with Norman Cohn's recent statements (see note 34 above) where he reiterates that *Atanarjuat* "was a classic love and revenge

story [that again!] set in the mythic, apolitical past." Surely *Atanarjuat* is set in the past, and it is based on "myth"—although myth that almost surely has strong historical reference—but that hardly makes it apolitical. I've been arguing that its "beauty" is very much a function of its practical social power.

46. My Sami colleague and friend, Professor Harald Gaski, writes, "I tend to agree with the French Canadian anthropologist, but would've added a line about the Sami as another people who've done the same. Still, I think Canada has taken over the leadership internationally when it comes to granting rights and responsibilities to the indigenous groups themselves, like Nunavut" (personal communication, 2/1/06).

Professor Chadwick Allen thought Saladin d'Anglure's "statement... understandable, given its context, but a bit of an overstatement." He noted that "Maori in Aotearoa/New Zealand have managed to achieve an awful lot of success in land and resources rights... through nonviolent protests, through working with Parliament and the Waitangi Tribunal" (personal communication, 2/6/06).

47. But as Shari Huhndorf has again pointed out to me, the agreement establishing Nunavut "was premised on Inuit cultural difference"—although the Inuit were willing and able "to assume a territorial-style government, and the incommensurability of these ideas has generated all kinds of problems" (personal communication, 7/1/06).

48. It is also recognized as an official language in the Northwest Territories of Canada, in Nunavik (a part of Quebec) and in Greenland. Although only some three thousand Alaskan Inuit, out of an Inuit population of perhaps thirteen thousand, speak Inuktitut, the language is taught in Inuit areas. A rough estimate of Inuktitut speakers all told is something like ninety thousand.

49. And Siebert has elaborated the way in which embracing the indigenes works toward Canada's self-definition as a multicultural nation.

Bibliography

Abram, David. *The Spell of the Sensuous: Perception and Language in a More-Than-Human World.* New York: Vintage, 1997.

Abrams, David, and Brian Sutton-Smith. "The Development of the Trickster in Children's Narrative." *Journal of American Folklore* 90 (1977): 29–47.

Andrews, William, ed. *The Oxford Frederick Douglass Reader.* New York: Oxford University Press, 1996.

Angilirq, Paul Apak. *Atanarjuat, the Fast Runner.* Toronto: Coach House Books, 2002.

———. "Interview with Paul Apak Angilirq." By Nancy Wachowich. In Angilirq, *Atanarjuat, the Fast Runner*, 16–23.

Apess, William. "Eulogy on King Philip." In O'Connell, *On Our Own Ground*, 277–310.

———. "The Experiences of Five Christian Indians of the Pequ'd Tribe." In O'Connell, *On Our Own Ground*, 119–62.

———. "An Indian's Looking-Glass for the White Man." In O'Connell, *On Our Own Ground*, 155–61.

———. "Indian Nullification of the Unconstitutional Laws of Massachusetts Relative to the Marshpee Tribe; or, The Pretended Riot Explained." In O'Connell, *On Our Own Ground*, 166–274.

———. "A Son of the Forest: The Experience of William Apess, a Native of the Forest." In O'Connell, *On Our Own Ground*, 3–97.

"*Atanarjuat*: Production Diary," http://www.atanarjuat.com/production_diary/index.html.

The Atlas of Canada, atlas.gc/sit/English/learningresources/fact/Nunavut_communities/repuls.html, s.v. "Repulse Bay, Nunavut."

Awiakta, Marilou. "Red Clay." In Bruchac, *Aniyunwiya/Real Human Beings*, 29–41.

Babcock, Barbara. "'A Tolerated Margin of Mess': The Trickster and His Tales Reconsidered." In *Critical Essays on Native American Literature*, edited by Andrew Wiget, 153–84. Boston: G. K. Hall, 1985 [1975].

Balakian, Peter. *Black Dog of Fate.* New York: Broadway Books, 1997.

Ballinger, Franchot. "Coyote, He/She Was Going There: Sex and Gender in Native American Trickster Stories." *SAIL/Studies in American Indian Literatures* 12 (2000):15–43.

———. *Living Sideways: Tricksters in American Indian Oral Traditions.* Norman: University of Oklahoma Press, 2004.

Baym, Nina. "Reinventing Lydia Sigourney." *American Literature* 62 (September 1990): 385–404.

Berg, Liisa. "Song of Hiawatha: Kalevala's Cousin?" http://www.kaikucom/kalevalainhiawatha.html. Accessed July 20, 2003. Pp. 1–12.

Bergland, Renée. *The National Uncanny: Indian Ghosts and American Subjects.* Hanover NH: University Press of New England, 2000.

Berkhofer, Robert. *The White Man's Indian: Images of the American Indian from Columbus to the Present.* New York: Knopf, 1979.

Bessire, Lucas. "Talking Back to Primitivism: Divided Audiences, Collective Desires." *American Anthropologist* 105 (December 2003):832–38.

Bevis, William. "Native American Novels: Homing In." In Swann and Krupat, *Recovering the Word*, 580–620.

Bird, Louis. "The Legend of Wissaakechaahk, and Cannibal Exterminators." Edited by Paul DePasquale. In *Algonquian Spirit: Contemporary Translations of the Algonquian Literatures of North America*, edited by Brian Swann, 247—91. Lincoln: University of Nebraska Press, 2005.

Black Hawk. *Black Hawk: An Autobiography.* Edited by Donald Jackson. Urbana: University of Illinois Press, 1964 [1955].

———. *Black Hawk's Autobiography.* Edited by Roger Nichols. Ames: Iowa State University Press, 1999.

———. *Life of Black Hawk.* Edited by J. Gerald Kennedy. New York: Penguin, 2008.

Blaeser, Kimberly. "Trickster: A Compendium." In *Buried Roots and Indestructible Seeds: The Survival of American Indian Life in Story, History, and Spirit*, edited by Mark Lindquist and Martin Zanger, 47–66. Madison: University of Wisconsin Press, 1993.

Blodgett, Jean, ed. *North Baffin Drawings: Collected by Terry Ryan on North Baffin Island in 1964.* Toronto: Art Gallery of Ontario, 1986.

Boas, Franz. "The Eskimo of Baffin Land and Hudson Bay from Notes Collected by Captain George Comer, James S. Mutch, and Reverend E. J. Peck." *Bulletin of the American Museum of Natural History* 15 (1901): hdl.handle.net/2246/1251.

———. Introduction to *Traditions of the Thompson River Indians of British Columbia*, collected and annotated by James Teit. Vol. 6, *Memoirs of the American Folk-Lore Society*. Boston: Houghton, Mifflin, 1898.

Boudinot, Elias [Buck Watie]. "An Address to the Whites, Delivered in the First Presbyterian Church on the 26th of May, 1826." Philadelphia, 1826.

Bright, William, ed. *A Coyote Reader*. Berkeley and Los Angeles: University of California Press, 1993.

Brightman, Robert. ACAOOHKIWINA *and* ACIMOWINA*: Traditional Narratives of the Rock Cree Indians*. Canadian Ethnology Service, Mercury Series Paper 113. Quebec: Canadian Museum of Civilization, 1989.

Brinton, Daniel G. *Myths of the New World*. Westport CT: Greenwood, 1969 [1868].

Bruchac, Joseph, ed. *Aniyunwiya/Real Human Beings: An Anthology of Contemporary Cherokee Prose*. Greenfield Center NY: Greenfield Review Press, 1995.

Camhi, Leslie. "For Your Ice Only: Inuit Director Wins Camera d'Or." *Village Voice*, May 30, 2001, http://www.villagevoice.com/film/0122,camhi,25256,20html.

Carlson, David. *Sovereign Selves: American Indian Autobiography and the Law*. Urbana: University of Illinois Press, 2006.

Carr, Helen. *Inventing the American Primitive: Politics, Gender, and the Representation of Native American Literary Traditions, 1789–1936*. New York: New York University Press, 1996.

Carroll, Michael. "Lévi-Strauss, Freud, and the Trickster: A New Perspective upon an Old Problem." *American Ethnologist* 8, no. 2 (1981): 301–13.

Carter, Forrest. *The Education of Little Tree: A True Story*. Albuquerque: University of New Mexico Press, 1986 [1976].

Cheyfitz, Eric, ed. "The (Post)Colonial Construction of Indian Country: U.S. American Indian Literatures and Federal Indian Law." In *The Columbia Guide to American Indian Literatures of the United States*, 1–124. New York: Columbia University Press, 2006.

Child, Lydia Maria. "An Appeal for the Indians." In Karcher, *Hobomok*, 1–150, 216–32.

———. *The First Settlers of New-England; or, Conquest of the Pequods, the Naragansets,* and Pokanokets, as Related by a Mother to Her Children, and Designed for the Instruction of Youth. Boston, 1828.

———. *Hobomok, and Other Writings on Indians.* Edited by Carolyn Karcher. New Brunswick NJ: Rutgers University Press, 1986 [1824].

Conley, Robert J. *Mountain Windsong: A Novel of the Trail of Tears.* Norman: University of Oklahoma Press, 1992.

Cooper, James Fenimore. *The Wept of Wish-ton Wish.* Philadelphia, 1829.

Cruikshank, Julie. "Negotiating with Narrative: Establishing Cultural Identity at the Yukon International Storytelling Festival." *American Anthropologist* 99 (1997):59–69.

Danker, Kathleen. "Because of This I Am Called the Foolish One: Felix White, Sr.'s, Interpretations of the Winnebago Trickster." In Krupat, *New Voices*, 505–28.

Dannenberg, Anne Marie. "'Where, Then, Shall We Place the Hero of the Wilderness?': William Apess' Eulogy on King Philip and the Doctrines of Racial Destiny." In Jaskoski, *Early Native American Writing*, 66–82.

de las Casas, Bartolomé. "From the Very Brief Relation of the Devastation of the Indies." In *The Norton Anthology of American Literature*, edited by Nina Baym et al. 5th ed. Vol. 1, 16–17. New York: W. W. Norton, 1998.

Deloria, Ella Cara. *Dakota Texts.* New York: AMS, 1974 [1932].

Deloria, Philip. "American Indians, American Studies, and the ASA." *American Quarterly* 55 (2003): 669–80.

———. *Playing Indian.* New Haven CT: Yale University Press, 1998.

Deloria, Vine, Jr. *Red Earth, White Lies: Native Americans and the Myth of Scientific Fact.* New York: Scribner's, 1995.

———. *We Talk, You Listen.* New York: Dell, 1970.

Denis, Claude. *We Are Not You: First Nations and Canadian Modernity.* Peterborough, Canada: Broadview, 1997.

DePaul, Kim, ed. *Children of Cambodia's Killing Fields: Memoirs by Survivors.* New Haven CT: Yale University Press, 1997.

Dippie, Brian. *The Vanishing American: White Attitudes and United States Relations.* Middletown CT: Wesleyan University Press, 1982.

Donaldson, Laura. "Son of the Forest, Child of God: William Apess and the Scene of Postcolonial Nativity." In King, *Postcolonial America*, 201–22.

Douglass, Frederick. "The Rights of Women." In Andrews, *Oxford Frederick Douglass Reader*, 98–100.

———. "What to the Slave Is the Fourth of July?" In Andrews, *Oxford Frederick Douglass Reader*, 108–30.

Eastburn, James Wallis, and Robert C. Sands. *Yamoyden, A Tale of the Wars of King Philip: In Six Cantos.* New York, 1820.

Ehle, John. *Trail of Tears: The Rise and Fall of the Cherokee Nation.* New York: Doubleday, 1988.

Elliott, Michael, and Claudia Stokes, eds. *American Literary Studies: A Methodological Reader.* New York: New York University Press, 2003.

Emerson, Ralph Waldo. "The Adirondacs." In *Poems by Ralph Waldo Emerson.* Vol. 9, 182–95. New York: William H. Wise, 1929 [1867].

———. "The American Scholar." In *The Norton Anthology of American Literature*, edited by Nina Baym et al. 6th ed. Vol. B, 1235–47. New York: W. W. Norton, 2003.

———. "The Divinity School Address." In *Norton Anthology of American Literature*, edited by Nina Baym et al. 6th ed. Pp. 1148–59. New York: W. W. Norton, 2003.

———. *The Journals of Ralph Waldo Emerson.* Abridged and edited with an introduction by Robert Linscott. New York: Modern Library, 1960.

———. "Letter to President James Van Buren." In *The Norton Anthology of American Literature*, edited by Nina Baym et al. 7th ed. Vol. B, 1269–71. New York: W. W. Norton, 2007.

Ettuk, Jimmy. "Atanaaqjuat's Revenge." In Blodgett, *North Baffin Drawings*, 1986.

Everett, Edward. "Address Delivered at Bloody Brook, in South Deerfield, September 30, 1835." Boston, 1835.

Evers, Larry, and Barre Toelken, eds. *Native American Oral Traditions: Collaboration and Interpretation.* Logan: Utah State University Press, 2001.

Fenton, William M., and John Gulick, eds. *Symposium on Cherokee and Iroquois Culture.* Smithsonian Institution Bureau of American Ethnology, *Bulletin 180.* Washington DC: U.S. Government Printing Office, 1961.

Fienup-Riordan, Ann. *Freeze Frame: Alaska Eskimos in the Movies.* Seattle: University of Washington Press, 1995.

Fogelson, Raymond. "Change, Persistence, and Accommodation in Cherokee Medico-Magical Beliefs." In Fenton and Gulick, *Symposium on Cherokee and Iroquois Culture*, 205–12.

Foreman, Grant. *The Five Civilized Tribes: Cherokee, Chickasaw, Choctaw, Creek, Seminole.* Norman: University of Oklahoma Press, 1989 [1934].

———. *Indian Removal.* Norman: University of Oklahoma Press, 1976 [1932].

Franklin, Benjamin. "Remarks Concerning the Savages of North America." In *The Norton Anthology of American Literature*, edited by Nina Baym et al. 5th ed. Vol. 1, 516–19. New York: W. W. Norton, 1998.

Fuller, Margaret. *Summer on the Lakes in 1843*. Urbana: University of Illinois Press, 1991 [1844].

Frye, Northrop. *Anatomy of Criticism*. New York: Atheneum, 1967 [1957].

Ganter, Granville, ed. *The Collected Speeches of Sagoyewatha, or Red Jacket*. Syracuse NY: Syracuse University Press, 2006.

Garroutte, Eva Marie. *Real Indians: Identity and the Survival of Native America*. Berkeley and Los Angeles: University of California Press, 2003.

Ginsburg, Faye. "*Atanarjuat* Off-Screen: From Media Reservations to the World Stage." *American Anthropologist* 105 (2003):827–31.

Glancy, Diane. *The Mask Maker*. Norman: University of Oklahoma Press, 2002.

———. *Pushing the Bear: A Novel of the Trail of Tears*. New York: Harcourt Brace, 1996.

———. *Stone Heart: A Novel of Sacajawea*. Woodstock NY: Overlook, 2004.

Goody, Jack, and Ian Watt. "The Consequences of Literacy." In *Literacy in Traditional Societies*, edited by Jack Goody, 27–68. Cambridge: Cambridge University Press, 1969.

Gould, Philip. *Covenant and Republic: Historical Romance and the Politics of Puritanism*. New York: Cambridge University Press, 1996.

Gustafson, Sandra. "Nation of Israelites: Prophesy and Cultural Autonomy in the Writings of William Apess." *Religion and Literature* 26 (1994):31–54.

Harjo, Joy, and Gloria Bird, eds. *Reinventing the Enemy's Language: Contemporary Native Women's Writing of North America*. New York: W. W. Norton, 1997.

Havelock, Eric. *The Muse Learns to Write: Reflections on Orality and Literacy from Antiquity to the Present*. New Haven CT: Yale University Press, 1986.

Hawthorne, Nathaniel. *The Scarlet Letter*. New York: Knopf, 1992 [1850].

Haynes, Carolyn. "'A Mark for Them All to ... Hiss At': The Formation of Methodist and Pequot Identity in the Conversion Narrative of William Apess." *Early American Literature* 31 (1996): 25–44.

Hilden, Patricia Penn. *From a Red Zone: Critical Perspectives on Race, Politics, and Culture*. Trenton: Red Sea, 2006.

Hinks, Peter. *To Awaken My Afflicted Brethren: David Walker and the Problem of Antebellum Slave Resistance*. University Park: Pennsylvania State University Press, 1997.

Hoig, Stanley. *The Cherokees and Their Chiefs: In the Wake of Empire*. Fayetteville: University of Arkansas Press, 1998.

Hollinger, David. *Postethnic America: Beyond Multiculturalism*. New York: Basic Books, 1995.

Horsman, Reginald. "Scientific Racism and the American Indian in the Mid-Nineteenth Century." *American Quarterly* 27 (1975):152–68.

Huhndorf, Shari M. "*Atanarjuat, The Fast Runner*: Culture, History, and Politics in Inuit Media." *American Anthropologist* 105 (December 2003):822–26.

———. "Nanook and His Contemporaries: Traveling with the Eskimos, 1897–1941." In *Going Native: Indians in the American Cultural Imagination*, 79–128. Ithaca NY: Cornell University Press, 2001.

———. "The Making of an Indian: 'Forrest' Carter's Literary Inventions." In *Going Native*, 129–61.

Hultkrantz, Ake. "Theories on the North American Trickster." *Acta Americana* 5 (1997):5–18.

Hyde, Lewis. *Trickster Makes This World: Mischief, Myth, and Art*. New York: Farrar, Straus and Giroux, 1998.

Hymes, Dell. "Coyote, the Thinking (Wo)man's Trickster." In *"Now I Know Only So Far": Essays in Ethnopoetics*. Lincoln: University of Nebraska Press, 2003.

———. "A Theory of Verbal Irony and a Chinookan Pattern of Verbal Exchange." In *The Pragmatic Perspective: Selected Papers from the 1985 International Pragmatics Conference*, edited by Jef Verschueren and Marcella Papi, 293–338. Amsterdam: John Benjamins, 1985.

Hynes, William, and William Doty, eds. *Mythical Trickster Figures: Contours, Contexts, and Criticisms*. Tuscaloosa: University of Alabama Press, 1993.

Irving, Washington. "Philip of Pokanoket." In *The Sketch Book of Geoffrey Crayon, Gent.*, edited by Susan Manning, 250–64. New York: Oxford University Press, 1996 [1819–20].

Jacobs, Melville. *The Content and Style of an Oral Literature: Clackamas Chinook Myths and Tales*. Chicago: University of Chicago Press, 1959.

———. *The People Are Coming Soon: Analysis of Clackamas Chinook Myths and Tales*. Seattle: University of Washington Press, 1960.

Jahner, Elaine. "Traditional Narrative: Contemporary Uses, Historical Perspectives." In Elliott and Stokes, *American Literary Studies*, 266–89.

Jaskoski, Helen, ed. *Early Native American Writing: New Critical Essays*. New York: Cambridge University Press, 1996.

Jennings, Francis. *The Founders of America: From the Earliest Migrations to the Present*. New York: W. W. Norton, 1993.
——. *The Invasion of America: Indians, Colonialism, and the Cant of Conquest*. Chapel Hill: University of North Carolina Press, 1975.
Justice, Daniel Heath. *Our Fire Survives the Storm: A Cherokee Literary History*. Minneapolis: University of Minnesota Press, 2006.
Kafka, Franz. "In the Penal Colony." In *In the Penal Colony: Stories, and Short Pieces*. New York: Schocken, 1948.
Karcher, Carolyn, ed. *Hobomok, and Other Writings on Indians*. New Brunswick NJ: Rutgers University Press, 1986 [1868].
Keiser, Albert. *The Indian in American Literature*. New York: Octagon, 1975 [1933].
Kennedy, Virginia. "Margaret Fuller and Nineteenth-Century Indian Removal." Master's thesis, Montclair State University (NJ), 2001.
——. "Ralph Waldo Emerson, William Apess, and Native American Identity." Unpublished paper, May 2000.
Kerber, Linda. "The Abolitionist Perception of the Indian." *Journal of American History* 62 (1975):271–95.
Kilpatrick, Jack F. "An Etymological Note on the Tribal Name of the Cherokees and Certain Place and Proper Names Derived from Cherokee." *Journal of the Graduate Research Center, Southern Methodist University* 30 (1962):37–43.
——, and Anna G. Kilpatrick, eds. *Friends of Thunder: Folktales of the Oklahoma Cherokees*. Dallas: Southern Methodist University Press, 1964.
King, C. Richard, ed. *Postcolonial America*. Urbana: University of Illinois Press, 2000.
King, Thomas. *Truth and Bright Water: A Novel*. Toronto: HarperCollins, 1999.
Konkle, Maureen. "Indian Literacy, U.S. Colonialism, and Literary Criticism." *American Literature* 69 (1997):457–86.
——. *Writing Indian Nations: Native Intellectuals and the Politics of Historiography, 1827–1863*. Chapel Hill: University of North Carolina Press, 2004.
Koestler, Arthur. *The Act of Creation*. New York: Dell, 1964.
Kroeber, Karl, ed. *Traditional American Indian Literatures: Texts and Interpretations*. Lincoln: University of Nebraska Press, 1981.
Krupat, Arnold. "Culturalism and Its Discontents: A Review of David Treuer's *Native American Fiction: A User's Manual*." *American Indian Quarterly* 33 (2008).

———. "Figures and the Law: A Rhetorical Reading of the Indian Removal Act." In *Ethnocriticism: Ethnography, History, Literature*, 129–72. Berkeley and Los Angeles: University of California Press, 1992.

———. *For Those Who Come After: A Study of Native American Autobiography*. Berkeley and Los Angeles: University of California Press, 1985.

———. "Monologue and Dialogue in Native American Autobiography." In *The Voice in the Margin: Native American Literature and the Canon*, 132–201. Berkeley and Los Angeles: University of California Press, 1989.

———, ed. *Native American Autobiography: An Anthology*. Madison: University of Wisconsin Press, 1994.

———. "Nationalism, Indigenism, Cosmopolitanism: Three Perspectives on Native American Literatures." In *Mirror Writing: (Re-)Constructions of Native American Identity*, edited by Thomas Claviez and Maria Moss, 213–36. Berlin: Galda and Wilch, 2000.

———. "Native American Trickster Tales." In *Comedy: A Geographical and Historical Guide*, edited by Maurice Charney, vol. 2, 447–61. Westport CT: Praeger, 2005.

———, ed. *New Voices in Native American Literary Criticism*. Washington DC: Smithsonian Institution Press, 1993.

———. *Red Matters: Native American Studies*. Philadelphia: University of Pennsylvania Press, 2002.

Kunuk, Zacharias. "I First Heard the Story of Atanarjuat from My Mother." In Angilirq, *Atanarjuat, the Fast Runner*, 12–15.

———. "The Public Art of Inuit Storytelling." Transcript of Spry Memorial Lecture and question-and-answer session, Vancouver, November 25, 2002. http://www.com.umontreal.ca/spry/spry-kz-lec.html.

Legros, Dominique, ed. *Tommy McGinty's Story of Crow: A First Nation Elder Recounts the Creation of the World*. Canadian Ethnology Service Paper 133. Hull, Quebec: Canadian Museum of Civilization, 1999.

Lepore, Jill. *The Name of War: King Philip's War and the Origins of American Identity*. New York: Knopf, 1998.

Levi, Primo. *Survival in Auschwitz*. New York: Simon and Schuster, 1958.

Lévi-Strauss, Claude. "The Structural Study of Myth." In *The Structuralists: From Marx to Lévi-Strauss*, edited by Richard and Fernande de George, 169–94. New York: Anchor, 1993 [1955].

"Lot 47 Reviews," www.lot47.com/thefastrunner/reviews.html. Accessed April 23, 2004.

Lowie, Robert. "The Hero-Trickster Discussion." *Journal of American Folklore* 22 (1909):431–33.

Lyon, Captain G. F. *The Private Journal of Captain G. F. Lyon, of HMS* Hecla, *during the Recent Voyage of Discovery under Captain Parry, 1821–3. With a Map and Plates.* London: John Murray, 1824.

Lyons, Scott R. "Rhetorical Sovereignty: What Do American Indians Want from Writing?" *College Composition and Communication* 51 (2000):447–68.

Maddox, Lucy. *Removals: Nineteenth-Century American Literature and the Politics of Indian Affairs.* New York: Oxford University Press, 1991.

Makarius, Laura. "The Crime of Manabozho." *American Anthropologist* 75 (1973):663–75.

Mankiller, Wilma, and Michael Wallis. *Mankiller: A Chief and Her People.* New York: Saint Martin's, 2000 [1993].

Martin, Scott. "Interpreting Metamora: Nationalism, Theater, and Jacksonian Indian Policy." *Journal of the Early Republic* 19 (1999):73–102.

Mattina, Anthony. *The Golden Woman: The Colville Narrative of Peter Seymour.* Tucson: University of Arizona Press, 1985.

McQuaid, Kim. "William Apess, Pequot: An Indian Reformer in the Jackson Era." *New England Quarterly* 50 (1977): 605–25.

Melville, Herman. *The Confidence Man: His Masquerade.* New York: W. W. Norton, 1971 [1857].

———. *Moby Dick; or, The Whale.* New York: W. W. Norton, 1967 [1851].

Misterbaby. "*Fast Runner (Atanarjuat): Reader's Reviews,*" http://movies2.nytimes.com/gst/movies/movie.html?v_id=246171. Accessed June 3, 2003.

Molina, Felipe, and Larry Evers. "'Like This It Stays in Your Hands': Collaboration and Ethnopoetics." In Evers and Toelken, *Native American Oral Traditions,* 15–57.

Montaigne, Michel de. *Complete Essays.* Translated by Donald M. Frame. Stanford: Stanford University Press, 1958.

Mooney, James. *Myths of the Cherokee.* New York: Johnson Reprint Corporation, 1970 [1900].

———. *The Swimmer Manuscript: Cherokee Sacred Formulas and Medicinal Prescriptions.* Revised, completed, and edited by Frans Olbrechts. Smithsonian Institution Bureau of American Ethnology *Bulletin 99.* Washington DC: U.S. Government Printing Office, 1932.

Morse, Jedediah, and Elijah Parish. *A Compendious History of New England Designed for Schools and Private Families.* Charlestown MD, 1804.

Moulton, Gary E., ed. *The Papers of Chief John Ross*. 2 vols. Norman: University of Oklahoma Press, 1985.

Murray, David. "Christian Indians: Samson Occom and William Apes." In *Forked Tongues: Speech, Writing, and Representation in North American Indian Texts*, 49–64. Bloomington: University of Indiana Press, 1991.

Murray, Laura. "The Aesthetic of Dispossession: Washington Irving and Ideologies of (De)Colonization in the Early Republic." *American Literary History* 8 (1996): 205–31.

Myerson, Joel, and Judith Bean, eds. *Margaret Fuller, Critic: Writings from the New York Tribune, 1844–1846*. New York: Columbia University Press, 2000.

Nielsen, Donald. "The Mashpee Indian Revolt of 1833." *New England Quarterly* 58 (1985):400–420.

Ngugi wa Thiong'o, *Moving the Center: The Struggle for Cultural Freedom*. London: Heinemann, 1993.

Obituary of William Apess. *New Bedford Gazette and Mercury*, May 7, 1839.

O'Connell, Barry, ed. *On Our Own Ground: The Complete Writings of William Apess, A Pequot*. Amherst: University of Massachusetts Press, 1992.

Okalik, Paul. Speaking notes at a screening of *Atanarjuat, the Fast Runner*, August 9, 2001, Sydney, Australia. www.gov.nu.ca/Nunavut/English/premier/press/afr.shtml.

Ong, Walter. *Orality and Literacy: The Technologizing of the Word*. New York: Methuen, 1982.

Ortiz, Simon. "Towards a National Indian Literature: Cultural Authenticity in Nationalism." In Weaver, Womack, and Warrior, *American Indian Literary Nationalism*, 253–60.

Osterman, H., ed. *Knud Rasmussen's Posthumous Notes on East Greenland Legends and Myths*. Copenhagen: C. A. Reitzels Forlag, 1939.

Owens, Louis. *Other Destinies: Understanding the American Indian Novel*. Norman: University of Oklahoma Press, 1992.

Parins, James. *Elias Cornelius Boudinot: A Life on the Cherokee Border*. Lincoln: University of Nebraska Press, 2006.

———. *John Rollin Ridge: His Life and Works*. Lincoln: University of Nebraska Press, 1991.

Parker, Robert Dale. *The Invention of Native American Literature*. Ithaca NY: Cornell University Press, 2003.

———, ed. *The Sound the Stars Make Rushing through the Sky: The Writings of Jane Johnston Schoolcraft*. Philadelphia: University of Pennsylvania Press, 2007.

Pearce, Roy Harvey. *Savagism and Civilization: A Study of the Indian and the*

American Mind. Berkeley and Los Angeles: University of California Press, 1988 [1953].
Perdue, Theda, ed. *Cherokee Editor: The Writings of Elias Boudinot.* Athens: University of Georgia Press, 1996.
———, and Michael Green, eds. *The Cherokee Removal: A Brief History with Documents.* Boston: Bedford, 1995.
Piper, Edward. "A Dialogical Study of the North American Trickster Figure and the Phenomenon of Play." PhD diss., University of Chicago, 1975.
Radin, Paul. *The Trickster: A Study in American Indian Mythology.* New York: Schocken, 1956.
Rasmussen, Knud. "Intellectual Culture of the Iglulik Eskimos." *Report of the Fifth Thule Expedition, 1921–1924,* no. 1 (1929).
Rickets, Mac Linscott. "The North American Indian Trickster." *History of Religions* 5 (1966): 327–50.
———. "North American Tricksters." In *Encyclopedia of Religion,* edited by Lindsay Jones, vol. 15, 48–51. New York: MacMillan, 1987.
———. "The Shaman and the Trickster." In Hynes and Doty, *Mythical Trickster Figures,* 87–105.
Rice, Julian. *Before the Great Spirit: The Many Faces of Sioux Spirituality.* Albuquerque: University of New Mexico Press, 1998.
———. *Lakota Storytelling: Black Elk, Ella Deloria, and Frank Fools Crow.* New York: Peter Lang, 1988.
Robinson, Harry. *Write It on Your Heart: The Epic World of an Okanagan Storyteller.* Compiled and edited by Wendy Wickwire. Vancouver: Talonbooks, 1989.
Royce, Charles C. *The Cherokee Nation of Indians.* Chicago: Aldine, 1975 [1887].
Running Wolf, Michael, and Patricia Clark Smith. *On the Trail of Elder Brother: Glous'gap Stories of the Micmac Indians.* New York: Persea Books, 2000.
Ruoff, A. LaVonne Brown. "Three Nineteenth-Century Indian Autobiographers." In *Re-Defining American Literary History,* edited by Ruoff and Jerry Ward, Jr., 250–69. New York: Modern Language Association, 1990.
Ryan, Allan. *The Trickster Shift: Humour and Irony in Contemporary Native Art.* Vancouver: University of British Columbia Press, 1999.
Said, Edward. "Identity, Negation, and Violence." *New Left Review* 171 (1988): 46–60.
———. *Representations of the Intellectual: The 1993 Reith Lectures.* New York: Vintage, 1996.
Said, S. F. "Everyday White," *Sight and Sound* 9 (2006):36–38.

Saladin d'Anglure, Bernard. "An Ethnographic Commentary: The Legend of Atanarjuat, Inuit and Shamanism." In Angilirq, *Atanarjuat, the Fast Runner*, 196—229.

Sartre, Jean-Paul. Preface to *Wretched of the Earth*, by Frantz Fanon, 7–31. New York: Grove, 1979.

Savage, Sarah. *Life of Philip the Indian Chief*. Salem MA: 1827.

Sayre, Robert. *Thoreau and the American Indians*. Princeton NJ: Princeton University Press, 1977.

Schmitz, Neil. *White Robe's Dilemma: Tribal History in American Literature*. Amherst: University of Massachusetts Press, 2001.

Scott, A. O. "A Far-off Inuit World, in a Dozen Shades of White." March 30, 2002, http://movies2.nytimes.com/mem/movies/review.html?res=9D04E7DC163AF933A05750C0A9649C8B63.

Seaburg, William, and Pamela Amoss, eds. *Badger and Coyote Were Neighbors: Melville Jacobs on Northwest Indian Myths and Tales*. Corvallis: Oregon State University Press, 2000.

Sedgwick, Catherine Maria. *Hope Leslie*. New York: Garrett, 1969 [1827].

Shearwood, Perry. "The Writing of the Inuit of Canada's Eastern Arctic." In Krupat, *New Voices*, 174–85.

Siebert, Monika. "*Atanarjuat* and the Ideological Work of Contemporary Indigenous Filmmaking." *Public Culture* 18 (Fall 2006):531–50.

Silko, Leslie Marmon. *Ceremony*. New York: Viking, 1977.

Smith, Linda Tuhiwai. *Decolonizing Methodologies: Research and Indigenous Peoples*. New York: St. Martin's, 1999.

Smith, William Jay. *The Cherokee Lottery: A Sequence of Poems*. Willimantic CT: Curbstone, 2000.

Starr, Emmett. *History of the Cherokee Indians and their Legends and Folk Lore*. Milwood NY: Kraus Reprint Company, 1977 [1921].

Steele, Jeffrey, ed. *The Essential Margaret Fuller*. New Brunswick NJ: Rutgers University Press, 1992.

Stefansson, Vilhjalmur. *The Standardization of Error*. New York: W. W. Norton, 1927.

Stevens, Scott Manning. "William Apess's Historical Self." *Northwest Review* 35 (1997):67–84.

Stone, John Augustus. "Metamora; or, The Last of the Wampanoags." In *Favorite American Plays of the Nineteenth Century*, edited by N. Barrett Clark. Princeton NJ: Princeton University Press, 1943 [1829].

Sullivan, Lawrence. "Multiple Levels of Religious Meanings in Culture: A

New Look at Winnebago Sacred Texts." *Canadian Journal of Native Studies* 2 (1982):221–47.

Swann, Brian, and Arnold Krupat, eds. *Recovering the Word: Essays on Native American Literature.* Berkeley and Los Angeles: University of California Press, 1987.

Timberlake, Henry. *Memoirs: 1756–1765.* Salem NH: Ayer, 1971 [1765].

Thornton, Russell. "Cherokee Population Losses during the Trail of Tears: A New Perspective and a New Estimate." *Ethnohistory* 31 (1984): 289–300.

Toelken, Barre, and Tacheeni Scott. "Poetic Retranslation and the 'Pretty Languages' of Yellowman." In Kroeber, *Traditional American Indian Literatures,* 65–116.

Treuer, David. *American Indian Fiction: A User's Manual.* Saint Paul MN: Graywolf, 2006.

Turner, James. Introduction to *David Walker's Appeal to the Coloured Citizens of the World,* by David Walker, 9–19. Baltimore: Black Classic Press, 1993 [1830].

Twain, Mark. "The Noble Red Man." In *Mark Twain: Life as I Find It,* edited by Charles Neider, 100–108. Garden City NY: 1961.

Twist, Glenn J. *Boston Mountain Tales: Stories from a Cherokee Family.* Greenfield Center NY: Greenfield Review Press, 1997.

Ung, Loung. *First They Killed My Father: A Daughter of Cambodia Remembers.* New York: Harper Collins, 2000.

Vernon, Irene. "The Claiming of Christ: Native American Postcolonial Discourses." *MELUS* 24 (1999):75–88.

Vizenor, Gerald. "Shadow Survivance." In *Manifest Manners: Postindian Warriors of Survivance,* 63–106. Hanover NH: University Press of New England, 1994.

Wahnenauhi (Mrs. Lucy L. Keys). "The Wahnenauhi Manuscript: Historical Sketches of the Cherokees, Together with Some of their Customs, Traditions, and Superstitions." In Jack Kilpatrick, ed. *Anthropological Papers,* Numbers 75–80, Smithsonian Institution Bureau of American Ethnology *Bulletin 196,* Washington DC: U.S. Government Printing Office, 1966, 175–214.

Walker, Cheryl. *Indian Nation: Native American Literature and Nineteenth-Century Nationalisms.* Durham NC: Duke University Press, 1997.

Walker, James. *Lakota Belief and Ritual.* Edited by Raymond DeMallie and Elaine Jahner. Lincoln: University of Nebraska Press, 1980.

———. *Lakota Myth*. Edited by Elaine Jahner. Lincoln: University of Nebraska Press, 1983.

Warrior, Robert. "Eulogy on William Apess: His Writerly Life and His New York Death." In *The People and the Word: Reading Native Nonfiction*, 1–48. Minneapolis: University of Minnesota Press, 2005.

Wasson, George, and Barre Toelken. "Coyote and the Strawberries: Cultural Drama and Cultural Collaboration." In *Native American Oral Traditions: Collaboration and Interpretation*, edited by Larry Evers and Barre Toelken, 176–99. Logan: Utah State University Press, 2001.

Weaver, Jace. *That the People Might Live: Native American Literatures and Native American Community*. New York: Oxford University Press, 1997.

———. "Trickster: The Sacred Fool." In *Other Words: American Indian Literature, Law, and Culture*, 246–57. Norman: University of Oklahoma Press, 2001.

Weaver, Jace, Craig Womack, and Robert Warrior. *American Indian Literary Nationalism*. Albuquerque: University of New Mexico Press, 2006.

White, Hayden. *Metahistory: The Historical Imagination in Nineteenth-Century Europe*. Baltimore: Johns Hopkins University Press, 1973.

Whiteley, Peter. "Native American Philosophy." In *Routledge Encyclopedia of Philosophy*, edited by Edward Craig, vol. 6, 662–72. London: Routledge, 1998.

Wiget, Andrew. "Review of *Narrative Chance: Postmodern Discourse on Native American Indian Literatures*." *Modern Philology* (May 1991):476–99.

———. "Telling the Tale: A Performance Analysis of a Hopi Coyote Story." In Brian Swann and Arnold Krupat, *Recovering the Word*, 287–338.

Wilkins, Thurman. *Cherokee Tragedy: The Ridge Family and the Decimation of a People*. 2nd ed. Norman: University of Oklahoma Press, 1988.

Williams, William Carlos. "The Voyage of the Mayflower." In *In the American Grain*. New York: New Directions, 1956 [1925].

Womack, Craig. *Red on Red: Native American Literary Separatism*. Minneapolis: University of Minnesota Press, 1999.

Woodward, Grace Steele. *The Cherokees*. Norman: University of Oklahoma Press, 1988 [1963].

Index

Ableegumooch, 5
Abnaki Indians, 38
abolitionism, 80, 88, 188n49
Abrams, David, 18
Adams, John Quincy, 88
adaptive potentiation, 18
Address Delivered at Bloody Brook in South Deerfield, An, September 30, 1835, in Commemoration of the Fall of 'Flower of Essex' at that Spot in King Philip's War, September 18, 1675 (Everett), 61, 93–94, 96, 185n36
"Adirondacs, The" (Emerson), 40–41
African Americans, 47, 48, 119
Agassiz, Louis, 41
"Alaskan Fragments" (Rose), v
Algeria, 82
Algonquian peoples, 5, 44
alphabetic literacy, 15, 16, 171–72n24
American Indian Literary Nationalism (Weaver, Womack, and Warrior), ix
American national mythology, 30–31, 33
American Revolution, 105
"American Scholar, The" (Emerson), 76
Anansi, 3
Anderson, Rufus B., 61
Angilirq, Amelia, 155
Angilirq, Paul (Paul Apak), 155
Anishinaabe, 5
Apak, Paul, as *Atanarjuat* scriptwriter, 137, 139, 140, 145, 146, 151, 152

Apes, William. *See* Apess, William
Apess, William: in the Army, 73; birth and childhood of, 73; on Cherokee removal, xiv, 105; on color of skin, 85–86, 182n22; contemporaries of, 75–79, 176n8; death of, 74, 79, 178–79n3; Free and United Church founded by, 73; ironic discourse of, 31, 48, 85–86, 88, 90, 100; on King Philip, 89–99; marriages of, 74; on national/political status of Native peoples, 83, 87, 181n18, 182n23; as Pequot writer, 34, 52, 60, 61, 62, 97–98; as public intellectual, 75–101; religious beliefs of, 73; resistance writing of, xiii, 34, 60, 61, 62, 74–101; rhetoric in writing, 96, 99–100, 187n41, 188n47; works of: *Eulogy on King Philip*, 62, 74, 75, 90–99; *Experiences of Five Christian Indians of the Pequ'd Tribe, The*, 61, 74; *Indian Nullification of the Unconstitutional Laws of Massachusetts Relative to the Marshpee Tribe; or, The Pretended Riot Explained*, 61, 74; "An Indian's Looking-Glass for the White Man," 74, 76, 81, 83, 84–85, 89, 181–82nn19–20; *Son of the Forest, A: The Experience of William Apess, a Native of the Forest*, 60, 74
Appeal for the Indians, An (Child), 47, 70, 78
Ararat, 76, 86

Arctic Circle, xiv
Aristotle, 16
Arnatsiaq, Peter-Henry, 155
Assiniboine, 5
Astor, John Jacob, 43
Astoria (Irving), 43
Atanarjuat, the Fast Runner (2001): audiences of, 132–33, 140–42, 196n7, 196n9, 198–99n23; confirming Inuit identity, 131–62; ending of, 139, 198n20; Lot 47 distribution of, 142–43, 144, 153–54, 201n40; outtakes of, 153–57, 201n43; recognition and criticism of, 142–49; role of shamanism in legends, 136, 137, 139, 148, 149–53, 198nn21–22, 200n36, 200n38; second audiences of, 149–53; traditional Inuit story of, xii, xiv–xv, 137, 138–40, 198n19
Atwood, Margaret, 144
Aupaumat, Hendrick, 59
autogenously dialectical, 25, 26
Awiakta, Marilou, 109

Babcock, Barbara, 17, 18
"Badger and Coyote Were Neighbors," 7
Ballinger, Franchot, 3
Basket Maker, 121, 193–94n24
Baym, Nina, 48, 56
Beecher, Lyman, 80, 94
Benjamin, Walter, 21
Berger, Arion, 144
Bergland, Renée, 33, 47
Bering Strait, 35
Bessire, Lucas, 134, 142, 148
Bevis, William, 26
Bird, Louis, 20, 21, 22–23, 25
bisociation, 17
Blackfeet, 5
Black Hawk, 52, 53, 61, 180n9
Black Hawk War of 1831, 50, 53
Blas, Gil, 3
Boas, Franz, 3, 6, 16, 138, 139, 168n7

Borderers, The (Cooper), 49
Boston Mountain Tales: Stories from a Cherokee Family (Twist), 104, 113–15, 123, 127
both/and concept, xii, 156
Boudinot, Elias: as Buck Watie, 58, 59, 78; Christian progressive views of, 54, 59, 76; as public intellectual, xiv, 52, 58, 77–80
Boudinot, Elias (elder), 78
Bradford, William, 29
Brinton, Daniel, 2–3, 6, 16, 168n6
Brougham, John, 65, 68, 91
Brown, John, 38
Buffalohead, Roger, x
burlesques, 56
Bushyhead, Jesse, 120, 124, 126, 193n22
Butrick, Daniel, 108–9

Camhi, Leslie, 146
Campbell, Joseph, 143
Canada: First Nations, 53; Native history and literature, 53; Nunavut, 135, 140–41, 149, 157–58, 201n42
Cannon, B. B., 113
Carr, Helen, 43
Carroll, Michael, 9, 169n13
Carter, Forrest, xiv, 103, 108, 112–13
casinos, 115
Cass, Lewis, 58
Catlin, George, 40, 51, 63
Ceremony (Silko), 131, 132, 135, 195n1
Chees-quat-a-lau-ny/Yellow Bird, 68, 70
Cherokee Council, 79
Cherokee Editor, 54
Cherokee Lottery, The: A Sequence of Poems (William J. Smith), 104, 114, 115–16
Cherokee Nation of Indians (Royce), 110
Cherokee Phoenix, 54, 78, 103, 106, 118–19
Cherokee Removal, xiii, xiv, 39, 47, 75, 77, 175n5
Cherokees: in American literature, 1820–1870, 50; civilization of, 52; conjuring practices, 125–26, 128, 193nn26–27,

193n29; contemporary writers, xiv, 107–8; death toll from Trail of Tears, 107, 189–90n5; dualism in oral traditions, 13; first encounter with Europeans, 105; forced relocation of, xiii, xiv, 31, 39, 47, 75, 77, 103–29, 175n5; Keetoowah fire, 118, 126; Memorials to Congress, 75, 78, 95, 179n7; planter class of, 79, 108; populations east of Mississippi, 105, 189n3; practice of adopting/changing names, 78; reunion of Oklahoma and Eastern bands, 117, 190n8, 192n17; signing Treaty of New Echota, 79, 89, 106, 111; as slaveholders, 39, 47, 106, 120, 193n22; sovereignty in Georgia, xiv, 31, 54, 86, 106; surviving Trail of Tears, 79; syllabary of, 31, 78, 106, 108, 121, 122, 127; as Tsa'lagi or Tsa'ragi, 103, 188–89n1

Cheyenne, 5

Cheyfitz, Eric, 131

Child, Lydia Maria: on assimilation of Indians, 52, 75, 88; works of: *Appeal for the Indians, An*, 47, 70, 78; *The First Settlers of New-England; or, Conquest of the Pequods, Naragansets, and Pokanokets, as Related by a Mother to her Children, and Designed for the Instruction of a Youth*, 47, 60; *Hobomok*, 46, 47–49, 58, 90

Chippewas, 5, 50, 54

Churchill, Mary, 13

Clackamas Chinook, 7

Cohn, Norman: as *Atanarjuat* videographer, 137, 145; on classic features of *Atanarjuat*, 146–47, 201–2n45; English version of *Atanarjuat*, 134, 135, 145, 146, 199n32

colonialism: consequences of, 155; indigenous resistance of, xiii, xiv, 81, 82, 83, 131–62, 195n1, 195n3; internal, xi, xii

Colville Indians, 19, 22

Comer, George, 138, 139, 153

comic structures, 30

communitism, x

complementary constructs, 13

Confidence Man, The (Melville), 36–37

conjunctural constructs, 13

Conley, Robert J.: as Cherokee writer, xiv, 107, 110–13, 119, 194n30; on Trail of Tears and eternal return, 129; works of: *Mountain Windsong: A Novel of the Trail of Tears*, 103, 110–13, 127

Content and Style of an Oral Literature, The (Melville Jacobs), 7

continuance, x

Cook-Lynn, Elizabeth, x

Cooper, James Fenimore: contemporaries of, 43; Leatherstocking novels, 45–46; works of: *The Borderers*, 49; *The Deerslayer; Or, The First Warpath: A Tale*, 63; *The Last of the Mohicans; Or, A Narrative*, 59; *Notions of the Americans*, 46; *The Pathfinder; Or, The Inland Sea*, 63; *The Pioneers; Or, the Sources of the Susquehanna: A Descriptive Tale*, 58; *The Prairie. A Tale*, 59; *The Wept of Wish-ton-Wish*, 45, 49, 60, 90, 177n23; *Wyandotte*, 45

Copper Joe, 21

Copway, George, 52, 53, 65, 66

Cotton, John, 29

Coyote: cultural constructs of, 173n33; postmodern, 115–16; trickster tales of, 4, 8, 20

"Coyote Made Everything Good," 1, 167n1

Crania Americana; or, A Comparative View of the Skulls of Various Aboriginal Nations of North and South America: To Which Is PreFixed an Essay on the Varieties of the Human Species (Morton), 63

cranial measurements, 40, 63, 174–75n1

Cree, 2, 5, 167n2

Creek Indians, 106

Creek War, 106, 110

Crow, 4, 173–74n35

Index 221

Cruikshank, Julie, 132, 147–48, 151
cultural authenticity, x
culture, sociopolitical functions of, xi
Culture and Imperialism (Said), 83
Cusick, David, 52, 54, 55, 59
Danker, Kathleen, 19, 20, 21, 23
David Walker's Appeal to the Coloured Citizens of the World, but in Particular, and Very Expressly, to Those of the United States of America (David Walker), 80–81
Dawes Allotment Act, 31
Deerslayer, The; Or, The First Warpath: A Tale (Cooper), 63
Deloria, Philip, 82
Deloria, Vine, Jr., 182nn20–21
Denerstein, Robert, 143
DePasquale, Paul, 20, 22
dialectic mode, 172n27
difference, 14
"Dispossession, The" (Twist), 113–14
"Divinity School Address, The" (Emerson), 76–77
Douglass, Frederick, xiv, 76, 77, 80, 181n14
Drake, Benjamin, 62, 64
Drake, Samuel, 61, 62–63, 64

Eastburn, James, 31, 42, 46, 57
Education of Little Tree, The (Carter), 103, 112
either/or concept, 156
Emerson, Ralph Waldo: attitude toward Sioux, 40; protesting Cherokee removal, 39, 105, 111; as public intellectual, xiv, 75–77; on Puritan identity, 86, 176n14; on Thoreau, 37; works of: "The Adirondacs, 40–41; "The American Scholar," 76; "The Divinity School Address," 76–77
emplotments, xii, xiv, 175n4
Eshu-Elegba, 3
Eskimos, xv, 131–62
essentialism, 154, 201n44

Ettuk, Jimmy, 138, 139
Eulenspiegel, Till, 3
Eulogy on King Philip (Apess), 62, 74, 75, 90–99
Evans, James, 137, 197–98n18
Evarts, Jeremiah, 60
Everett, Edward: Apess address to, 80, 84, 89; commemorating King Philip's War, 61, 80, 93–94, 96, 97, 99, 185n36; as governor of Massachusetts, 50, 61, 89, 183–84n27
Experiences of Five Christian Indians of the Pequ'd Tribe, The (Apess), 61, 74

Fanon, Frantz, 81, 83
Fienup-Riordan, Ann, 159
Film Board of Canada, 154, 156
Five Civilized Tribes, 52
Flaherty, Robert, xv, 143, 145, 159–61
Foreman, Grant, 107
Foucault, Michel, 82
Fox, 50
Francis, Lydia Maria, 46
Free and United Church, 73
Freud, Sigmund, 16
Friends of Thunder: Folktales of the Oklahoma Cherokees (Kilpatrick and Kilpatrick), 127
Frost, John, 67, 68
Fuchs, Reineke, 3
Fugitive Poses: Native American Indian Scenes of Absence and Presence (Vizenor), x
Fuller, Margaret, 49–51, 64, 177–78nn24–26

Ganter, Granville, 54
Gargantua, 3
Garrison, William Lloyd, 80, 81, 86, 88
Georgia: Cherokee populations, 31, 54, 77, 78, 86, 98, 106; lottery for settlement of native lands, 114, 115
Gitji Manitou, 1
Glancy, Diane: as Cherokee writer, xiv, 110; works of: *Pushing the Bear: A Novel of the*

Trail of Tears, xiv, 104, 108, 116, 119–29, 192–93nn20–22
Glous'gap, 2, 5, 172n29
Gluskabe, 5
Gould, Philip, 47, 49, 90, 93
Gramsci, Antonio, xiv, 81, 82
Green, Michael, 105
Gros Ventre, 5
Gustafson, Sandra, 76, 83, 86

Hall, John, 36
Hare, 4, 5
Harrison, Eric, 143, 144
Havelock, Eric, 15, 16
Hawthorne, Nathaniel, 32–34, 75
Hebraic texts: Western thought related to, 16
Heckewelder, John, 57
Hellenistic texts: Western thought related to, 16
Henry, George/Maungwudaus, 52, 53, 65
Hermes, 3
Hewitt, Chris, 144
Hilbert, Vi, 21
Hilden, Patricia Penn, 134, 142, 148
Hinks, Peter, 80
"Historical Sketches of the Cherokees, Together with Some of Their Customs, Traditions, and Superstitions" (Wahnenauhi, Mrs. Lucy L. Keys), 108
"Historical Sketch of the Cherokee People" (Mooney), 110, 120
Hobomok (Child), 46, 47–49, 58, 90
Hochank, 1, 5
Hoig, Stanley, 103
Hollinger, David, 86
Hope Leslie (Sedgwick), 47, 49, 60, 90
Hopi, 2, 3
Horsman, Reginald, 27, 28, 175n3
House Made of Dawn (Momaday), ix
Houston Chronicle, 143
Howe, Desson, 143
Hoyt, Epaphras, 58

Huhndorf, Shari: critique of Flaherty, 145, 159, 160; on film and identity construction, 152; on viewers relating to *Atanarjuat*, 134, 142, 148, 197n14, 199n34
Hunter, John Dunn, 58
Hyde, Lewis, 2–3, 4, 5, 18, 24

Igloolik, 134, 136, 196n12
Iktomi/Ikto, 2, 5, 168n3
imperialism, domestic, xi
"Indian Hater, The" (John Hall), 36
Indian Nullification of the Unconstitutional Laws of Massachusetts Relative to the Marshpee Tribe; or, The Pretended Riot Explained (Apess), 61, 74
Indian Removal Act, 78, 95, 106
Indian Reorganization Act, 182n21
Indians. *See* Native Americans/Indians
"Indian's Looking-Glass for the White Man, An" (Apess), 74, 76, 81, 83–84, 85, 89, 181–82nn19–20
intellectual sovereignty, x
Inugpasugjuk, 138
Inuit: identity and *Atanarjuat, the Fast Runner*, 131–62; Nunavut territory, xiv, 135, 140–41, 157–58, 202n47, 202n49
Inuktitut, 158, 202n48
Iroquois, 55
Iroquois League of Peace, 44
Irving, Washington: works of: *Astoria*, 43; "Philip of Pokanoket," 41–42, 91, 177n16; *Sketch-Book of Geoffrey Crayon, Gent., The*, 41, 66; *A Tour of the Prairies*, 62; "Traits of Indian Character," 41
Istinike, 5
Isuma Productions, 134, 135, 144, 146, 148, 155
Ittuksarjuat, 152

Jackson, Andrew: Indian removal policies of, 54, 77, 89, 98, 101, 106; native troops fighting with, 89, 106, 110; as president, 49, 106

Index 223

Jackson, Donald, 53
Jacobs, Melville, 1, 7–8, 16, 169n12, 173n35
Jacobs, Peter, 52, 53, 68
Jahner, Elaine, 132, 148, 151
James, William, 17
Jameson, Anna Brownell, 63
Jennings, Francis, 30–31
Jesus, 4
Jewish populations, 76, 86
Jung, Carl, 7
Justice, Daniel Heath, xi, 13, 54, 192n19

Kahgegagahbowh, 66
Kahkewaquonaby/Sacred Feathers/Sacred Waving Feathers, 69
Kalevala, 44
Karcher, Carolyn, 37
Kennedy, J. Gerald, 53
Kennedy, Virginia, 39, 51
Keocuck, 50
Kerber, Linda, 47, 88, 93, 177n22, 183n24
Keys, Mrs. Lucy L./Wahnenauhi, 103, 108
Kilpatrick, Anna, 109–10, 127, 156
Kilpatrick, Jack, 108, 109–10, 127, 156, 188–89n1
King, Dennis, 143
King, Thomas, 190–91n9
King Philip/Metacomet: in American literature, 31, 185n35; Apess eulogy of, 73, 74, 86, 89–99; Puritan defeat of, 42, 43
King Philip's War, 29, 45, 46, 49
Kiowa, 5
Klamath, 5
Kluskap, 5
Koestler, Arthur, 17
Konkle, Maureen: on Native American literature, 53, 54, 55, 78; review of oratories on behalf of Cherokees, 80, 81, 89
Ku Klux Klan, 112
Kunuga, 1

Kunuk, Zacharias: on first screening of *Atanarjuat*, 142; Igloolik childhood, 136; Inuit film for Inuit, 134, 135, 147, 148, 158, 199n34; on Inuit legends in *Atanarjuat*, 139, 140; on *Nanook* references, 160; outtakes of *Atanarjuat*, 155; shamanism implicit in *Atanarjuat*, 151; Spry lecture of, 144, 145–46
Kupaaq, Michel, 138
Kwakiutl, 13, 19

Lakota, 2, 4–5
Last of the Mohicans, The; Or, A Narrative of 1757 (Cooper), 59
Latest Form of Infidelity, The (Norton), 76
LeClair, Antoine, 53
Legros, Dominique, 20, 21
Lepore, Jill, 91, 93
Lévi-Strauss, Claude: students of, 150, 200n35; on trickster tales, 8–9, 10, 14, 16, 26
Liberator, 80
Life and Adventures of Joaquin Murieta, the Celebrated California Bandit (John Rollin Ridge), 54–55, 68
Life and Times of Red-Jacket, or Sa-go-ye-wat-ha; Being the Sequel to the History of the Six Nations (William L. Stone), 64
Life of Ma-Ka-Tai-Me-She-Kia-Kiak or Black Hawk (Black Hawk), 61
Life of Philip the Indian Chief (Savage), 60
Little Crow, 38, 176n12
Loki, 3
Longfellow, Henry Wadsworth, 40, 43–45
Lowell, James Russell, 88
Lowie, Robert, 168n7
Lowrey, George, 108
Lox, 5
Luria, S. I., 14–15
Lushootseed, 21
Lyons, Scott Richard, x

Maddox, Lucy, 33, 34, 37, 50–51
Malcolm, Paul, 143

Manabozho, 5, 44
Mankiller, Wilma, xiv, 107, 117–19, 129, 192n16, 192n19
Mankiller: A Chief and Her People (Mankiller), 117–19
Marshall, John, 105
Mashpee Indians, 73, 74, 86, 91, 179–80n8
Mather, Cotton, 97
Mattina, Anthony, 19, 21–22
Maui-of-a-thousand-tricks, 4
Ma'una, the Earthmaker, 1
Maungwudaus/George Henry, 65, 66
May-Day and Other Pieces (Emerson), 40–41
McGinty, Tommy, 20, 21, 173–74n35
McKenney, Thomas L., 59, 64
McQuaid, Kim, 91
Medicine, Beatrice, x
Melville, Herman, 34–37, 75, 176n8, 176n10
Metacomet. *See* King Philip/Metacomet
Metamora; or, The Last of the Pollywoags (Brougham), 65, 91, 184n33
Metamora; or, The Last of the Wampanoags (John Augustus Stone), 60, 91, 93
Micmac, 1–2
Mink, 5
Minnesota Sioux Indians, 38
Moby Dick (Melville), 34–36
Modoc, 5
Mohawks, 44
Mohegans, 92
Momaday, N. Scott, ix, xi
Monkey/Monkey King, 4
Montaigne, Michel de, 97, 186–87n40
Mooney, James, 109, 110–11, 120, 122, 123, 124, 125, 188–89n1
Moravian Mission, 78, 105–6
Morgan, Lewis Henry, 67
Mormonism, 76, 86
Morton, Samuel, 40, 63
Mountain Windsong: A Novel of the Trail of Tears (Conley), 103, 110–13, 127

Myths of the Cherokee (Mooney), 111, 127
Myths of the New World (Brinton), 2

Name of War, The: King Philip's War and the Origins of American Identity (Lepore), 93
Nanabush, 20
Nanook of the North (1922), xv, 143, 144, 145, 159–61, 199n30
Napi, 5
Narragansett Indians, 36
narrative structures: comic, 30, 175n4; emplotments, xii; four Western types, xii; internal colonialism and, xii; irony, 10, 170n15, 170n17; of traditional Native oral stories, xii, 167n3; tragic, 30, 32, 175n4
National Daily Intelligencer, 77
nationalism, ix, x
National Museum of the American Indian, 51
Native American Fiction: A User's Manual (Treuer), ix
Native American Renaissance, 131
Native Americans/Indians: contemporary perceptions of, 132, 195–96n5; cultural and political discourse in literature of, ix, 55; federal acquisition of lands of, 99–100, 188n48; Jackson's removal policies of, 51–52, 74, 77, 178n27; as living anachronisms/remnants, 52, 78; removal/forced relocations of, x, 51–52, 178n27, 185n37; representing in American literature, xiii, 27–71; as savages, 95–96, 186–87n40; sovereignty of, x, xiv, 31, 54, 86, 106; from Ten Lost Tribes of Israel, 75, 78, 85–86; writers and literature of, ix, 52–56
natural law, 185–86n38
Nature (Virginia Kennedy), 39
Navajo, 2
New England, forced removal of Native tribes in, 99, 187–88n46
New Orleans, Battle of, 89

New York Times, 136, 145
New York Tribune, 50, 51
Nichols, Roger, 53
Nixant, 5
Noah, Mordecai Manuel, 76, 86
"noble savage," 94
North American Review, 46
North Carolina: Cherokee populations in, 31, 104
Norton, Andrews, 76
Notions of the Americans (Cooper), 46
Nunavut: creation of, 135, 149, 157–58; Inuit territory of, xiv, 135, 140–41, 157–58, 201n42, 202n47, 202n49

O'Connell, Barry, xiv, 73, 91, 92
Ojibwe Indians, 43, 66, 69
Okalik, Paul, 140, 149, 198n22
Oklahoma, 31, 79
Ong, Walter, 14, 15
On Our Own Ground: The Complete Writings of William Apess, a Pequot (O'Connell), 73
"On the Psychology of the Trickster Figure" (Jung), 7
Oo'watie. *See* Watie, David
oral traditions: beauty and social function of, x, xii; oratorical power/performance influences of, 84, 182n20; as part of education system, 23, 173n34; philosophy of, 13–17
organic intellectuals, 81, 82
organic oppositional intellectuals, 82
"Origin of the Bear: The Bear Songs" (Mooney), 122, 123
Ortiz, Alfonso, 13–14
Ortiz, Simon, x
Osage, 128
Other Destinies: Understanding the American Indian Novel (Owens), ix
Ottawas, 50
"Our Evening among the Mountains" (Hawthorne), 33

Our Fire Survives the Storm: A Cherokee Literary History (Justice), xi, 54, 192n19
Owens, Louis, ix, xi
Ozha-guscoday-way-quay, 43

Paiute Coyote stories, 173–74n35
Palfrey, John Gorham, 46, 177n20
Pantagruel, 3
Parins, James, 55
Parker, Robert Dale, 54
Parkman, Francis, 66, 67, 70
Pathfinder, The; Or, The Inland Sea (Cooper), 63
Patterson, J. B., 53
Pearce, Roy Harvey, 28, 101
Pequot, 31, 73, 86, 91, 92, 115
Pequot War, 29, 46, 47, 49, 92
Perdue, Theda, 54
"Philip of Pokanoket" (Irving), 41–42, 91, 177n16
Pierce, Maris Bryant, 52, 54, 63
Pinocchio, 3
Pioneers, The; Or, the Sources of the Susquehanna: A Descriptive Tale (Cooper), 58
Plato, 15–16, 170n15
Poems (John Rollin Ridge), 70
Pokanokets, 91
Polis, Joe, 38
polygenesis, 41
Ponca, 5
positive law, 185–86n38
Potawatomis, 50, 53
Prairie, The. A Tale (Cooper), 59
Prison Notebooks (Gramsci), 81
projective essentialism, 154–55, 201n44
"Promised Land, The" (Twist), 104, 113, 114–15
public intellectuals, xiv, 75, 180n10
Purdue, Theda, 105
Puritans: beliefs about Indians, 36; as foundation of America, 47, 75, 89, 90, 92, 97, 187n45; in King Philip's War,

93, 94, 95, 96–97, 184n33, 187n43; in Pequot War, 29, 49; violence of, 96–98, 187n43
Pushing the Bear: A Novel of the Trail of Tears (Glancy), xiv, 104, 108, 116, 119–29, 192–93nn20–22

Queequegunnt, 36

Rabbit, 4, 5, 118, 128
Radin, Paul: on trickster stories, 2, 5, 6–7, 16, 21, 168–69n8
Rasmussen, Knud: Inuit legends recorded by, 138, 139, 150, 151, 153, 200n37
Raven, 4, 9, 25
Red Jacket/Sagoyewatha, 52, 53–54
Red on Red: Native American Literary Separatism (Womack), x
Renard the Fox, 3
Representations of the Intellectual (Said), 81
Repulse Bay, 153, 200–201n39
rhetoric, 10, 170n15
Rice, Julian, 2, 168n3
Ridge, John, 54–55, 79, 80
Ridge, John Rollin, 52–55, 68, 70
Robinson, Harry, 20, 22
Rose, Wendy, v
Rosebud Reservation, 128
Ross, John, 54, 103, 105, 107, 120, 193n22
Royce, C. C., 110
Ruoff, LaVonne Brown, 53, 56, 57
Ruppert, James, 25
Ryan, Allan, 11, 171n19

Sagoyewatha/Red Jacket, 52, 53–54
Sahlins, Marshall, 139
Said, Edward, xiv, 30, 81, 82, 83
Saladin d'Anglure, Bernard: as ethnographer for *Atanarjuat* film, 138–39, 145, 150, 157, 158, 198n19, 198n21, 202n46; on Inuit shamanism, 150, 198n21; as student of Lévi-Strauss, 150, 198n21
Salish, 13

Sartre, Jean-Paul, xiv, 81, 82, 83
Sassamon, John, 96
Sauk, 50
savagism: defining, 29; rhetoric of, 28, 38, 52, 100–101, 186–87n40
Saynday/Sende, 5
Sayre, Robert, 37, 38, 39
Scarlet Letter, The (Hawthorne), 32–34
Schiefner, Anton, 44
Schmitz, Neil, 53
Schoolcraft, Henry Rowe: contemporaries of, 44; as government researcher, 43, 54, 59
Schoolcraft, Jane Johnston, 43, 52, 54
scientific racism, 27, 28, 52, 183n26
Scott, A. O., 136, 145
Scott, Walter, 46
Scott, Winfield, 107
Seaver, James E., 58
Sedgwick, Catharine Maria, 47, 49, 60, 90
Seitz, Matt Zoller, 144
Sende/Saynday, 5
Seneca, 53
Sequoyah: Cherokee syllabary invented by, 31, 78, 106, 108, 121, 122, 127
"Sermon Delivered at Plymouth, on the 22nd of December, 1827" (Beecher), 94
Seymour, Peter, 22
Shanley, Kathryn, v, xv
Sherman, William Tecumseh, 128
Siebert, Monika, 159, 161
Sigourney, Lydia Howard Huntley, 48, 58, 64
Silko, Leslie Marmon, ix, 131, 132, 135, 147, 195nn1–2
Sioux Indians, 2, 4–5, 40, 41, 168n3
Sitconski, 5
Sketch-Book of Geoffrey Crayon, Gent., The (Irving), 41, 66
Sketches of the Ancient History of the Six Nations (Cusick), 59
Skunk, 5, 173n35
slaves/slavery, 80, 88, 97, 183n24

Smith, Donald, 53
Smith, Joseph, 76, 86
Smith, Linda Tuhiwai, 87
Smith, William Jay, xiv, 104, 108, 115–16
Socrates, 15, 170n15
Song of Hiawatha (Longfellow), 40, 43–45
Son of the Forest, A: The Experience of William Apess, a Native of the Forest (Apess), 60, 74
Stefansson, Vilhjalmur, 145, 159
Stevens, Scott, 83
Stone, John Augustus, 42, 60, 91
"Storyteller, The" (Benjamin), 21
storytellers: art of telling traditional narratives, x, 18–26, 138, 139, 172n31; trickster tales conveyed by, 18–26
Strong, Nathaniel, 52, 54, 64
"Structural Study of Myth, The" (Lévi-Strauss), 8
Sullivan, Lawrence, 10, 16–17, 169n14
Summer on the Lakes (Fuller), 49–50, 64
survivance, x, 20
Sutton-Smith, Brian, 18
"Swimmer Manuscript" (Mooney), 124, 125

Tanner, John, 60
Teit, James, 3
terrapin, tales of, 127–28
Tewa, 3, 13
That the People Might Live: Native American Literatures and Native American Community (Weaver), x
Thoreau, Cynthia Dunbar, 39
Thoreau, Henry David, 37, 38, 39
Thoreau and the American Indians (Sayre), 37–38
Thornton, Russell, 107
Timberlake, Henry, 114, 192n15
Toelken, Barre, 19–20, 24, 173n33
Tormes, Lazarillo de, 3
Tour of the Prairies, A (Irving), 62
"Towards a National Indian Literature: Cultural Authenticity in Nationalism" (Simon Ortiz), x

traditional intellectuals, 81–82
Traditions of the Thompson River Indians (Teit), 3
tragic structures, 30
Trail of Tears: Cherokee Removal and, xiii, 31, 79; deaths related to, 105; letters/remembrances of, 108–9, 190–91nn7–9; survivors of, 79, 107
"Traits of Indian Character" (Irving), 41
Treaty of Hopewell, 105
Treaty of New Echota, 79, 89, 106, 111
Treuer, David, ix, xi, 191–92n14, 195n4
Tribal Secrets: Recovering American Indian Intellectual Traditions (Warrior), x
tricksters/trickster tales: affirming cultural norms, xiii; Biblical, 4; both/and feature of, 25; boundary making and breaking, xiii, 5–6, 12, 168n5; contemporary/ironic, 11–12; criticism of oral tales, xiii; duality of, 10–12, 169n14, 170n16, 170–71n18; female tricksters, 3; functions in traditional societies, 12; irony of, 11, 171n18; meanings and functions of, 17–18; myth settings of, 1; as part of education system, 23, 173n34; postmodern, xiii; Rabelaisian behavior, 3; revisiting, 1–26; storytellers and, 18–26; traditional worldview through, xii; Western philosophical thought and, 12–17; worldwide occurrence of, 4
Trois Frères, 3
Tulsa World, 143
Turner, Victor, 17
turtle, tales of, 127–28
Tuscarora Indians, 45
Twain, Mark, 176–77n15
Twist, Glenn J.: as Cherokee writer, xiv, 107, 110; on Trail of Tears and renewal, 114–15, 129; works of: *Boston Mountain Tales: Stories from a Cherokee Family*, 104, 113–15, 123, 127; "The Dispossession," 113–14; "The Promised Land," 104, 113, 114–15

Van Buren, Martin, 39, 77, 111
Veeho, 5
Vizenor, Gerald, ix, x
Wacdjungega, 5
Wachacha, Maggie, 109, 190n8
Wahnenauhi/Mrs. Lucy L. Keys, 103, 108
Wakjankaga, 1, 5, 20, 21, 23
Walker, David, xiv, 76, 77, 80–81, 181n15
Walker, James, 2
Wallace, George, 112
Wampanoags, 73, 86, 91, 92, 184n31
War of 1812, 73
Warrior, Robert, ix, x
Wasson, George, 20, 24, 25, 173n33
Watie, Buck. *See* Boudinot, Elias
Watie, David, 78
Watie, Stand, 181n11
Weasel, 5
Weaver, Jace, ix, x, 4
Webster, Daniel, 84, 89, 94, 183–84n27
Welch, James, ix
Wept of Wish-ton-Wish, The (Cooper), 45, 49, 60, 90, 177n23
Wesucechak/Wisahketchahk, 5
Whiskey Jack, 5
White, Felix, Sr., 20, 21, 23
White, Hayden, xii

Whiteley, Peter, 13–14, 25, 171n21, 174n39
Whitman, Walt, 38
Whittier, John Greenleaf, 88, 91
Whole History of Grandfather's Chair, The (Hawthorne), 33
Wicazo Ša Review, x
Wickwire, Wendy, 20
Wiegand, Chris, 144
Wiget, Andrew, 12, 171n20
Wiissaakechaahk, 21, 22
"Wiissaakechaahk and the Foolish Women," 22
Wilkins, Thurman, 103, 118
Willard, William, x
Winnebago, 1, 2, 5, 21
Wirt, William, 89, 183–84n27
Wisahketchahk/Wesucechak, 5
Wishram, 19
Wolverine, 4
Womack, Craig, ix, x
women's rights, 49–50
Worcester v. Georgia, 106
Wyandotte (Cooper), 45

Yamoyden (Eastburn and Sands), 31, 42, 46, 57, 93
Yellow Bird/Chees-quat-a-lau-ny, 68, 70
Yellowman, Hugh, 20, 23, 25, 173n33